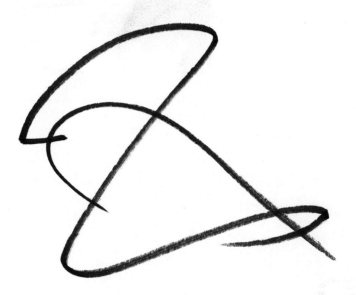

MUGGERIDGE

MUGGERIDGE

THE BIOGRAPHY

Richard Ingrams

HarperCollins*Publishers*

HarperCollins*Publishers*
77–85 Fulham Palace Road,
Hammersmith, London W6 8JB

Published by HarperCollins*Publishers* 1995
1 3 5 7 9 8 6 4 2

Copyright © Richard Ingrams 1995

The Author asserts the moral right to
be identified as the author of this work

A catalogue record for this book is
available from the British Library

ISBN 0 00 255610 3

Photoset in Linotron Bembo by
Rowland Phototypesetting Ltd,
Bury St Edmunds, Suffolk

Printed in Great Britain by
HarperCollinsManufacturing Glasgow

For my partner

CONTENTS

ILLUSTRATIONS

At the Institute of Directors Conference (*Courtesy of the* Daily Mail)
With Alec Vidler
Filming in Rome with Kevin Billington
Filming in Rome with Cardinal Heenan (*Courtesy of the BBC*)
With Cliff Richard (*Courtesy of the Hulton-Deutsch Collection*)
Addressing an anti-abortion rally in Hyde Park (*Courtesy of the Hulton-Deutsch Collection*)
In the pulpit at St Mary-le-Bow (*Courtesy of the* Daily Mail)
Vicky [Victor Weisz] cartoon published in the *New Statesman* (*Courtesy of the Centre for the Study of Cartoons and Caricature, University of Kent, Canterbury*)
Malcolm's reception into the Catholic Church (*Courtesy of the* Observer)
Foyles lunch at the Dorchester, with the author and Lord Longford (*Courtesy of the* Daily Mirror)
Filming at Robertsbridge with Svetlana Stalin (*Courtesy of the BBC*)
With Mother Teresa outside Park Cottage, April 1988
A gathering of the Muggeridge clan in August 1983
Malcolm with his three brothers: Douglas, Jack and Eric
In the study at Park Cottage
Setting off for a walk with Kitty (*Courtesy of Jane Bown*)
Kitty at Malcolm's funeral, supported by her two sons John and Leonard (*Courtesy of the* Evening Argus, *Brighton*)
Malcolm in his study at Robertsbridge (*Courtesy of Patrick Morrisson*)

All photographs are from the Muggeridge collection, unless otherwise stated

INTRODUCTION

I REMEMBER my first meeting with Malcolm Muggeridge very clearly because he gave me an excellent piece of advice. It was at a debate at the Oxford Union in 1961, to which Paul Foot (then the President) had invited Malcolm as his guest of honour. Over drinks after the debate Paul introduced me to Malcolm saying that I had shut myself up in my room and was working desperately for my finals. 'The thing to remember, dear boy,' Malcolm said waving his long cigarette holder, 'is that no one in later life is ever going to be in the least interested in what class of degree you've got.'

I remember that advice so clearly because to a young man in a panic, as I was, the words were very comforting and also because his prediction turned out to be perfectly true. As it happened, I got a Third in Greats – but nobody ever asked about it.

To those of Paul's and my generation Malcolm was a hero because of his iconoclasm. In the stuffy world of the Fifties, he was the man who had dared to attack Sir Winston Churchill in the pages of *Punch* and later been ostracized for mocking what he called 'The Royal soap opera'. I met him again two years later, when his great friend Claud Cockburn was guest editor of *Private Eye* at the height of the Profumo scandal of 1963. It turned out that both of them when working at *Punch* had discussed the possibility of starting a new magazine which would be genuinely satirical and independent of all the commercial pressures they were then working under. Then the *Eye* had come along in answer to their prayers. Claud and Malcolm subsequently acted as Godfathers to the fledgling organ.

To me, who had recently seized control of the magazine from Christopher Booker, Malcolm's interest was an enormous benefit. I had little knowledge of politics, whereas Malcolm knew it all backwards. He had met most of the cabinet – Macmillan, Hailsham, Butler – at one time or another and had little or no respect for any of them. He was, as he remained, a genuine anarchist with no ambitions of his own, who regarded the political world as a comedy and the leading politicians as clowns. To a young man brought up to revere his elders and betters, such a view was intoxicating and even dangerous.

Soon after that first meeting with Claud, Malcolm invited me and my wife Mary to Robertsbridge. It was to be the first of countless visits and, like many of Malcolm's friends, I became familiar with the routine – Malcolm waiting to greet me on Robertsbridge station, his beaming smile and outstretched hand, the ride up the long straight farm track to Park Cottage, Kitty preparing the meagre lunch. Malcolm talked all the time – trudging gumbooted through the Sussex mud, playing patience by the fire, or seated in his study surrounded by books and the pictures of his friends and heroes – Hugh Kingsmill, George Orwell (to be joined later by the Pope and Mother Teresa).

The frustration of any biographer is that unless he is a Boswell he cannot recapture the quality of talk. Most of Malcolm's was gossip, the same favourite figures recurring: Frank Longford and the Pakenham clan, Evelyn Waugh, Graham Greene, Alan Taylor. His tone was generally disparaging, but at the same time affectionate. He seldom bore a grudge and seemed baffled when others took offence. What gave his conversation its special flavour was its gleefully apocalyptic tone. Everything and everyone was going to pot. The Prime Minister – Macmillan, Wilson, Thatcher – was 'pretty well washed up'. The Monarchy would not last my lifetime. The Press was irrevocably doomed. But nothing in this catalogue was a cause for gloom or anxiety. It was all made to seem extraordinarily funny.

Being with Kitty and Malcolm in their serene old age it was hard to accept that until quite recently their life had been turbulent and unhappy, punctuated by separations, rows and upsets of one kind or another. But old friends like Claud Cockburn remembered another Malcolm – a wild, hard-drinking pursuer of women, subject to depressions and hypochondria. When Malcolm grew increasingly religious, such friends found it hard to adjust to his new incarnation but, not having known the old Malcolm, I myself had no such problems. Not, that is, that in private he seemed to change even when he became in his final years an out and out Evangelical. To journalistic friends like me he remained his old satirical self.

The idea that I should write Malcolm's biography was first suggested by Robin Denniston, then head of Oxford University Press, in 1982. It was agreed by the three of us that it would be published after his death. However, as his mental faculties gradually declined, Malcolm found himself unable to write and at the same time dimly aware that his star was on the wane. He began to fret about the book, wanting it to be published while he was still alive. But I resisted, knowing that the longer I waited the easier it would be to see him in his proper perspective.

Malcolm had formulated his own view of his life in his two volumes of memoirs and it was difficult if not impossible to get him to modify any of his views by confronting him with evidence. It transpired, however, that for someone who was so opposed to 'facts' – information, records, etc. – Malcolm had preserved a mass of documentation about his life, notably a voluminous diary starting from his first visit to India in 1922. It was typical of him that he put all this material at my disposal, including a number of intimate letters. His only proviso was that nothing should be published while Kitty was still alive (she died in June 1994).

With the book's long gestation period I have been able to speak to a great many of Malcolm's friends, a number of whom have since died. I would like to thank the following in particular for their help:

A. J. Ayer, Bobby Barclay, P. J. Barnwell, Michael Barsley, Walter F. Bell, Susan Beresford, Sir Isaiah Berlin, Fr Paul Bidone, Kevin Billington, Conrad Black, Christopher Booker, Basil Boothroyd, Andrew Boyle, Desmond Bristow, Prof. W. R. Brock, William Buckley Jr, Hugh Burnett, Mrs Hugo Charteris, Patricia Cockburn, Patrick Cockburn, Lettice Cooper, Anna Coote, Hugh Cudlipp, Michael Cummings, Lord Dacre, Prof. Bryn Davies, Bill Deedes, Nick Dennys, Peter Dickinson, Margaret Douglas, Richard Edis, Nicholas Elliott, Mr and Mrs Henry Fairlie, Catherine Freeman, Fr Gonzalo Gonzales, Graham Greene, Hugh Carleton Greene, Mrs William Hardcastle, Derek Hart, Lord Hartwell, Christopher Hawtree, Anthony Howard, Oliver Hunkin, Ian Hunter, Sir Ian Jacob, Sir John Junor, Mr and Mrs Ludovic Kennedy, Cecil King, Jacqueline Korn, Frank & Elizabeth Longford, Wolf Mankowitz, Mrs René McColl, Leonard Miall, Patrick Morrissey, John Mortimer, J. A. Nasmyth, Richard Nielsen, Michael Peacock, Katerina Porter, Anthony and Violet Powell, Tessa Rothschild, Peter Searby, Prof. Norman Sherry, Jonathan Stedall, Alan and Eva Taylor, Richard Usborne, Alec Vidler, James Vyvyan, Phillip

Warner, Alan Watkins, Auberon Waugh, Colin Welch, John Wells, Sir Dick White, Betty Williams, A. N. Wilson, Peregrine Worsthorne and B. A. Young.

My special thanks are due to Jack Muggeridge (Malcolm's brother) for his tireless support and his assistance in procuring papers and deciphering his brother's handwriting. My thanks are also due to Malcolm's surviving children, especially his son John. Rose Foot and Andrew Lambirth both gave me invaluable help with the research. Finally I would like to thank Deborah Bosley for her help in preparing the manuscript and for all her support and encouragement.

MUGGERIDGE

CHAPTER I

Childhood

MALCOLM'S EARLIEST MEMORY of life was of men – his father and his cronies – talking. They would assemble in the sitting room of the Muggeridge home in South Croydon on Saturday evenings and with the help of small quantities of scotch and water, discuss politics although with literary and philosophical undertones. To avoid being noticed and sent to bed, Malcolm would hide himself in a high-backed damask-covered divan which was called the 'cosy corner', an incongruous piece of furniture which his father had acquired in a second-hand shop. Thus concealed, the boy listened intently to the conversation and when he finally went to bed would go over endlessly in his mind the various schemes that had been proposed, for example the superiority of municipal trams to other forms of transport, all of which he unreservedly accepted would make the world a better place.

Malcolm's father, H. T. Muggeridge, who was to dominate his early life, was a small bearded man with a large frame, a twinkling eye and a rather bulbous nose which he passed on to his son. He was born on 26 June 1864, the eldest son of Henry Ambrose Muggeridge, an undertaker in what was then the Surrey village of Penge (Aspinall's Directory of 1867 lists Henry Muggeridge of Maple Road, Penge under 'Auctioneer' and 'Cabinet Maker and Upholsterer'). When Henry was twelve, his father abandoned his wife and eleven children and Mrs Muggeridge was forced to support them by running a second-hand furniture shop in Penge High Street. Henry left school at the age of thirteen and a half in order to earn a living to help support the family and took a job as office boy in a lawyers' office in the

City. He earned 7 shillings a week which he gave to his mother who gave him a shilling back for travel by early workers' train and 4 pence a day for food.

Every day he bought a glass of milk for a penny and a penny bun and spent the remaining tuppence in the bookshops of Charing Cross Road. He taught himself French and how to play the piano. Later, realizing that he could never become a lawyer, he got a job as office boy at Macintyre, Hogg Marsh and Company, a firm of shirt manufacturers in New Basinghall Street EC2 (later demolished in the Blitz). He remained with the firm until he retired, eventually becoming the company secretary though, to the disappointment of his wife, he turned down a directorship, as he thought it conflicted with his political principles.

From his lunchtime reading, H. T. Muggeridge acquired an absorbing interest in politics and literature. Though later he became a Labour MP, his first commitment was to the Penge Liberal Association and he played an active role in campaigning for a free library in the borough as well as for public baths. By the early Nineties he had become a socialist, joined the Fabian Society in 1892 and later the ILP. He became secretary of the Croydon Socialist Society in 1895 and stood unsuccessfully as a local council candidate in Norwood in 1896 and '97. He was an excellent public speaker though not always allowed a hearing. A lively report in the *Croydon Times* for 5 October 1899 tells of an anti-Boer War demonstration at Duppas Hill where a mob of about 2,000 'patriots' broke up the meeting before it could even begin.

On Mr H. T. Muggeridge mounting the seat with a view to opening the proceedings he was instantly assailed with cries of 'Kruger', 'Put him down', 'traitor', etc. He succeeded in beginning however – 'We only ask for –' he said but had got no further when howls of derision were raised. Somebody called for 'Three cheers for Salisbury' and these were given with a will after which the crowd lustily sang the refrain of 'Rule Britannia'.

Mr Muggeridge: 'We only ask for –' (cries of down with the old Kruger and more of Rule Britannia and yet others calling for cheers for the Queen, Chamberlain, Ronald Grahame and everybody else they could think of – even for the police!).

A rough looking fellow unfurled a dirty and ragged specimen of the Union Jack to the intense delight of the crowd who cheered and cheered again.

Sensing that it was useless to try to proceed with his speech, Mr Muggeridge gave up the attempt – his vacation of the seat being the signal for more cheers.

In spite of the town's predominantly middle-class electorate, socialism had a strong footing in Croydon and by 1903 there were five Labour members out of the thirty-six on the council. Muggeridge was elected in November 1911 and remained a councillor until 1930. His special interest was housing and he was instrumental in getting the first council houses built in Croydon. He also campaigned for Trade Union rates of pay for all municipal employees. He stood for Parliament in South Croydon in four elections unsuccessfully and was finally elected as MP for Romford in May 1929. In December 1930 he was one of a group of MPs from all parties to sign Oswald Mosley's manifesto calling for a planned economy to stimulate exports and plan home consumption. He lost his seat in October 1931 but was re-elected to the Croydon Council in 1933 until he resigned, due to ill health, in 1940, by which time he was 75.

In 1893 at the age of twenty-nine HTM married Annie Booler, whom he met when they were both holidaying in the Isle of Man ('It was a pick-up,' Malcolm used to say). Later he would visit her in Sheffield, though even then, it seemed, politics took precedence over passion and Annie would first hear of her suitor's presence in the town when one of her brothers told her: 'Your Harry is down outside the factory gates spouting.' After their marriage they set up home in Broomhall Road, Sanderstead, a village on the outskirts of Croydon. Annie was a very pretty, fair-haired, working-class girl, the daughter of Ida and William Booler, a foreman of a cutlery factory in Sheffield. She shared none of her husband's political interests, though she did sometimes accompany him to his meetings, sit beside him on the platform and tug on his coat-tails when she thought he had gone on long enough. 'Annie is still living in the world of simple love for those who the great father has given her,' her husband wrote to Alec Vidler in 1926. 'She has no introspection, no doubts, no ambitions – except perhaps still to look beautiful as is, I think, to be envied.'

Annie bore him five sons at three-year intervals – Douglas, Stanley (killed in a motorcycle accident at the age of twenty-three on 19 August, 1922), Malcolm, Eric and Jack. His third son was born on 24 March 1903 and named Thomas Malcolm after one of his father's heroes, Carlyle. He was, according to his own account, a pretty child and at the age of three months won a beautiful baby contest sponsored by Mellins Food. Although Malcolm spoke warmly in later life of his mother's working-class relatives, it would seem that he was never very close to his mother. 'She was extremely pretty,' he wrote, 'with very fair hair and an expression of fathomless innocence . . . only, if you looked deep into it, far from the pellucid surface, you came up with something steely, tough and merciless there.' Kitty Muggeridge always insisted that Malcolm was never really loved by his mother.

Shortly after the birth of the youngest son, Jack, the Muggeridges moved from their three-bedroom semi-detached home in Sanderstead to 17 Birdhurst Gardens, South Croydon, a five-bedroom detached house 'standing in its own grounds' which HTM had built by a co-operative for £1,000 (land and all). Though well constructed, the house was plain inside, the only heating in the large living room being a closed anthracite stove on which Malcolm used to sit when he was at home. This room also contained a pianola – a present from one of HTM's friends. Despite the five bedrooms, three boys (Eric, Jack and Malcolm) had at one stage to share a bed and Jack remembered that Malcolm often had nightmares and sometimes walked in his sleep.

Birdhurst Gardens was a short unmade road, deep in the heart of suburbia. The Muggeridges' neighbours were highly respectable and looked on the socialist visitors at number seventeen with some apprehension. It was not long before Malcolm and his brothers were being spoken of as 'those dreadful Muggeridge boys'.

All the boys doted on their father even though, with his city job and his political meetings in the evenings, he was, more often than not, away from home. He took them for bicycle rides into the country on Sundays and in the evenings read aloud to them from a large illustrated edition of Shakespeare's plays, or sat at the pianola playing Beethoven with a dribbling pipe stuck between his teeth. His wife played little or no part in these activities although she could sometimes be persuaded to sing to his accompaniment. She had no special interest in books and only wrote with difficulty. Envious perhaps of her husband's achievements she kept herself in the background and when, as a young man, Malcolm sailed for India his mother was not at the quayside to see him off (an absence that he did not seem to find remarkable) and seldom wrote to him when he was away.

His father was God. 'From the beginning', he wrote, 'we had some bond, some special intimacy which made me want to share and explore all his thoughts and interests and attitudes.' Malcolm would walk with him to catch the 8.30 train, up a rather steep hill, by the water tower and through the recreation ground to East Croydon Station; at the ticket barrier in the evening, delighted when he recognized the little bowler-hatted figure striding out at the head of the tide of city workers returning home. Often he would go straight to Croydon Town Hall for a meeting of the Borough Council and sometimes, as a special treat, Malcolm was allowed to sit in the public gallery and listen to his father taking part in the debate. But Malcolm's most vivid memories were of his father in the market in Surrey Street on Saturday evenings, erecting his little platform and haranguing passers-by about the need for socialism. He had one particular joke which his son always remembered: 'Now ladies and gentlemen. It's His Majesty's Government, His Majesty's Navy, His Majesty's Stationery Office, His Majesty's this and His Majesty's that. But it's the National Debt. Why isn't that His Majesty's? We'll gladly let His Majesty have that, won't we?'

From the beginning his father had looked on Malcolm as different. 'I now have three young sons', he wrote to his brother Percy in Australia in 1906. 'Little Malcolm, who is two and a half, is the youngest and we think the most promising of all.'

As he grew up, his brothers too came to share their father's view. His youngest brother Jack (the only one he ever really got on with) was always aware of a spiritual element in Malcolm's make-up that was lacking in the others. It was not that he was necessarily cleverer, he was simply more aware. (Jack remembers how Malcolm while still a schoolboy spotted that he was naturally left-handed and helped him to write with his left hand. Predictably, this was immediately corrected when he started school.) He had started piano lessons at a school run by two sisters called Monday just around the corner from the Muggeridges' home and at the age of seven he went to the elementary school. Here began that strange sequence of apparently chance encounters which ran through his life. His teacher was Helen Corke, who at the time she was teaching Malcolm was having an affair with a young teacher at the nearby Davidson Road School whose name was D. H. Lawrence and who was then beginning to write. Helen Corke later told Kitty that Malcolm had been 'very charming but impossible'.

Malcolm was always grateful for the fact that he went to state schools and was thereby spared the various complexes that affected his public school contemporaries. At the age of twelve he won a scholarship to a local grammar school. 'School to us', he wrote, 'was a place to get away from as soon as possible and for as long as possible. Everything exciting, mysterious and adventurous happened outside its confines, not within them.'

As a schoolboy he gave few indications of unusual ability. 'Certainly no one would have accepted that he was exceptional in any way', schoolmate Robert Edgar, later a headmaster, remembered. 'In fact he was inclined to be a bit of a chump . . . the masters' attitude to him was one of amused tolerance.' Another contemporary, Arthur Gibson, recalled: 'We all regarded him as rather an odd fellow. He was an emotional person. Always got very het up and angry over injustices. And frightfully excitable. Excelled at written English and in conversation.' George Ratcliffe, who became head accountant at the London Electricity Board, remembered Malcolm as 'Usually in the bottom half of the form when it came to exams. But always very verbose and self-assured.' (*Women's Mirror*, 19 February 1966)

As far as 'getting het up over injustices' was concerned, Malcolm's brother Jack recalled an incident which bears it out. The headmaster, Mr Hillyer, was a sadistic beater who, after the war years, when discipline in the school was at a low ebb indulged his taste for caning boys in his study or in the library. When one of these sessions was in progress Malcolm entered the library, seized the cane from Hillyer, broke it and walked out without saying a word. He heard nothing subsequently.

As for books and ideas, Malcolm was educated almost entirely by his father. He went through his library – six or seven shelves in a glass-covered case – the books being those which would be found in any progressive Fabian household at that time; Carlyle, Dickens, William Morris, Ruskin, Bernard Shaw, as well as socialist classics by the Webbs and R. H. Tawney. His own most treasured book was *A Pageant of English Poetry* (Clarendon Press) which his father gave him for Christmas in 1914 when he was eleven. It was the first book he possessed and he used to gaze at the frontispiece showing six famous poets (Keats, Tennyson, etc.) and wonder which one he was going to be.

In the Muggeridge home, as elsewhere, idealism and optimism about a new world had been dampened by the outbreak of war in 1914. Like many on the left, HTM, while not a pacifist, had been before the war instinctively pro-German and anti-French. The war unsettled him and Malcolm had a vivid memory of finding his father one morning sitting at the breakfast table staring at the long list of casualties in the morning papers, his face streaming with tears.

To Malcolm, only eleven when the war broke out, the whole thing was exciting and glamorous. His elder brothers joined up, Douglas in the Army, Stanley in the Royal Flying Corps, and he secretly longed for it to continue so that he could wear a uniform and be like the soldiers whom he enviously watched dancing with the pretty girls on Saturday evenings at the Greyhound Hotel. He even went to the local recruiting office when he was thirteen but when he was told to report back with a birth certificate, fled, panic-stricken that his fraudulent application might be reported to the public.

At the age of seventeen, Malcolm fell in love for the first and by no means the last time. Her name was Dora Pitman and they first met on the municipal tennis courts. From then on he spent many hours with her, visiting her home in Thornton Heath. 'Am fearfully in love with a charming little girl Dora,' he wrote; 'she has simply wonderful eyes and writes poetry.'

None of Dora's poems survive, though one of Malcolm's addressed to Dora does because he rather cruelly included it in his play *Three Flats* produced in 1931.

> Come let us sleep beloved and not waste
> Our time in idle passion
> There are a thousand star-lit nights to taste
> Our loins in wild flesh fashion.

No one would wish to be judged by their juvenile efforts, let alone their letters. However, Dora's surviving letters to Alec Vidler suggest that Malcolm had a lucky escape. 'And now I haven't told you how Malcolm is,' she wrote (22 March 1923). 'When we went down there he did not look as well as he should have done, because in a mad rag which they had a few weeks ago he had a jug smashed over his head by accident . . . He is a stupid child . . . I think this has taught him a lesson, however, and I feel sure he will be more careful in the future. In himself he is just the same, dear, lovable boy – a little more serious than he used to be.'

By this time, Malcolm was already a Cambridge undergraduate, having gone up to Selwyn College in October 1920. He spoke disparagingly of the teaching at Selhurst School – many of the masters had joined up in 1914 – but it cannot have been as bad as all that if he was able to gain admission to a Cambridge college.

In 1920 Selwyn was, according to its historian Professor W. R. Brock, 'very small, very poor, very Anglican and academically pretty dim'. There were some 120 undergraduates, about evenly divided between public and grammar school boys. The fees were lower than those of the older colleges and a large number of the students were the sons of clergymen. The college admitted only confirmed members of the Church of England, a restriction which meant that the college was not officially part of the University. As a result, Malcolm had to be confirmed before he could go to Cambridge. This in turn meant that he had also to be baptized. Malcolm always dismissed Cambridge, saying he profited little from his studies. This perhaps was not surprising as he had been compelled to read for a Natural Sciences degree – it being the only subject available at his secondary school for post-matriculation study. Nevertheless the evidence does not altogether support Malcolm's picture of himself as a lonely outsider from a state school pitched into a world of public school snobs and homosexuals and hating every minute of it.

Malcolm joined in the college activities. The Selwyn magazine, *The Calendar*, records that on 18 February 1922 he proposed and carried a motion in the Debating Society that 'The 20th Century shows a general improvement on the 19th'. He joined another debating society, the Friars, and was elected President in 1923. He rowed one of the college boats, played tennis and even soccer but was dropped because he was no good. So far from turning up his nose at the public-school men, he did his best to become like them. (However, one contemporary, C. W. Phillips, later a distinguished archaeologist, remembered him as a very difficult undergraduate – rebellious and unpopular.) His brothers were amazed at the transformation in him after only one term. His accent had become a strange mixture of suburban Croydon and upper-class drawl and his conversation was full of peculiar expressions, hitherto unfamiliar in Birdhurst Gardens. His parents were no longer Mum and Dad but Pater and Mater or 'my people', while things or persons who won his approval were 'awfully good' or 'simply topping' (a description he applied in all seriousness to his girlfriend Dora).

Nothing suggests that H. T. Muggeridge was disconcerted by the change in his son or his apparent defection to the despised bourgeoisie. Like many self-made men he set enormous store by the benefits of education and was determined that his favourite son would have all the advantages that he himself had gone without. All his hopes were pinned on Malcolm and he lavished what money he had to spare on him to the detriment of his other sons. He bought him life-membership to the Cambridge Union and on three occasions bailed him out when he ran up debts at his tailors. Even Malcolm's failure to excel at his studies did little to dampen his pride in his son.

It may have been thanks to his father's connections that Malcolm had obtained a bursary from Croydon Council to help pay the college fees. Thus under the terms of the Board of Education Scheme he was obliged to do four years at Cambridge: three years for the Tripos and a fourth doing a teacher training diploma after which he was expected to teach in a state school for two years. It also involved him in teacher practice in local schools in Croydon during his first two Tripos years. Malcolm gained a teacher's diploma (class 2) in December 1924. The examiner commended his 'splendid control of the class' while at the same time noting: 'Talks too much, hindered by a certain amount of conceit.'

His general summary read as follows: 'After his failure in the Tripos he developed a liking for English. He has a confident opinion of himself. He is most pleasant to deal with. He is frank and pleasing in manner. His interests are wide and varied but he lacks depth. He is friendly and courteous and will make an agreeable colleague. He is somewhat immature and has a child-like outlook. He is devoted to teaching which he prefers above all things . . .'

It was a shrewd assessment of his character which many of those who knew him in later life would recognize. As for the lack of depth and immaturity, it was to be some time before these were to be wholly eradicated.

CHAPTER II

Cambridge and India

IN HIS LATER REMINISCENCES and in his memoirs, Malcolm would describe how he had discovered Christianity in his sixties, after a life of agnosticism or atheism – it is true that the *Chronicles of Wasted Time* contain some fleeting references to a religious period at Cambridge, but no details are provided. The omission is at first sight puzzling because it suited him to portray himself as a believer who had come back into the fold rather than a man who, as many of his critics claimed, had taken up religion in old age almost as a pose of some kind. The prime reason for this strange distortion (conscious or unconscious) was to suppress the enormous influence that Alec Vidler had had on him when he was young and by which he subsequently felt embarrassed. Confirmation of this theory lies in the way Vidler himself, his oldest friend, is treated in his memoirs – only a couple of brief mentions in the course of the long narrative.

They met at Selwyn where Alec was reading Theology. He was four years older than Malcolm, the son of a Rye merchant, an intensely reserved person who from an early age had had a vocation to the priesthood. Alec was a complete contrast to Malcolm. Where Malcolm rushed impetuously from one enthusiasm to the next, he retained a rock-like faith and a quiet inner assurance. Malcolm had been thrown into a completely alien world. He had no friends at Cambridge, no fixed beliefs. Alec Vidler with his air of serenity and conviction represented a source of comfort which, to some extent, he was to remain until Malcolm's death. 'I love you and believe in you more than any man I have ever met', Malcolm wrote (1 October 1921): 'God sent you to answer my prayers, you are so strong.' From this and many other such tributes it is clear that the young Malcolm hero-worshipped Vidler – a passion that in later life he did his best to erase from his mind.

Alec's memory was that it was rowing that first brought them together. He had undertaken to coach the Selwyn 3rd Lent boat in which Malcolm was one of the oarsmen. It was not a successful enterprise. On the first day one of the other rowers, Philip Strong, caught a crab. On the second, the boat failed to get under weigh owing to what Alec called 'catastrophic loss of rudder line by cox at start'. A photograph of the eight shows Alec, tall and dignified at the centre, Malcolm behind him with crossed arms – indistinguishable from hundreds of undergraduates.

Malcolm had no religious upbringing. Neither of his parents were church-goers, although his mother regularly said her prayers kneeling by the bedside every night, while her husband lay in bed reading the *New Statesman*. (Once, according to family tradition, she opened her eyes to say, 'Harry, you owe me half a crown,' before immediately closing them and resuming her prayers.) H. T. Muggeridge was an agnostic who sometimes took Malcolm to meetings with fellow rationalists at the Ethical Church. Like many socialists he placed Jesus Christ in a pantheon of good men who had tried to improve the lot of the poor. Jesus was revered but no more so than Rousseau, Tolstoy or even Marx. At the same time the fact that most official, respectable organizations like the Church of England tended to disapprove of socialists made HTM, with justification, sceptical about organized religion. Malcolm had loyally followed his father's example, but under Vidler's influence he was to experience a dramatic conversion.

In his memoirs Malcolm gives the impression that he was baptized and confirmed into the Church of England purely as a formality to satisfy the Selwyn College regulations. It is clear from Alec Vidler's diary that in fact he was confirmed twice, the second time on 6 March 1921 during his second term. The explanation would seem to be that he attached no importance to the first confirmation but the second was to demonstrate his full commitment to the church. From then on he read the bible and attended Mass regularly both at Cambridge and at home during the holidays. Vidler's diary of 27 November 1922 records: 'Malcolm's eyes bad. He made his confession to Fr. John. *Laus Deo.*'

During the years that followed, the friends frequently visited one another during the Cambridge vacations. Alec Vidler's home was an ancient stone house (a former medieval friary) in Church Square, Rye, at the top of the little hill on which the town is built, with views looking out over Romney Marsh and Rye Harbour towards the sea. Malcolm was enchanted with Rye and nearby Camber Sands (where they went swimming in the nude). In turn Alec made several visits to Croydon to stay with Malcolm. 'Mr Muggeridge', he wrote in his diary, 'I fell in love with right away – in fact I think I had done so before I met him' (i.e. from listening to Malcolm's description of his father). If Alec converted Malcolm to Christianity, the Muggeridges father and son converted Alec to socialism and he remained a Labour Party supporter for the rest of his life. In the young Vidler, H. T. Muggeridge recognized a fellow idealist concerned with helping the poor. No doubt he also welcomed him as a good influence on his wayward son. Malcolm later told his pupils in India: 'When in the vacs I used to get up at six o'clock and go to Mass my father would smile and say nothing. When I said to him that I must give up everything and become a monk he said he wished I would begin my simple life at once so that my expenses at Cambridge would be less.'

In 1922, after leaving Wells Theological College, Alec Vidler spent six months at Oratory House in Cambridge, the headquarters of the Oratory of the Good Shepherd of which he became a member. Vidler arranged for Malcolm to stay there during his final year at Cambridge when he was doing teacher training. The Oratory was a loosely-knit fellowship of celibates and Anglo-Catholics that had been founded ten years earlier in 1912. There was no real community as such, though members, both laymen and priests, kept in touch with one another by correspondence and fixed hours of prayer. It was a typically Anglican organization which, despite the many defections, survives to the present day.

In 1920 the Oratory had acquired a building in Lady Margaret Road, Cambridge which was to be a home for those members of the Oratory who worked in Cambridge, a house for studies and a centre for pastoral work among undergraduates. Father Wilfred Knox, one of those who had sold shares to help buy the building, came to live here in 1921 with a warden and six undergraduates. It was, in the words of his niece Penelope Fitzgerald, 'an unbeautiful, inconvenient, poorly lit, red-brick building with very cold passages and a tangled garden'. Wilfred Knox (1886–1950) was the third of four remarkable brothers – Edmund the comic writer and editor of *Punch*, Dillwyn a classical scholar and member of the team who cracked the Enigma code during the war, and Ronald (known as R. A. Knox) – all of whom Malcolm encountered at one stage or another in his life. Their father was the bishop of Manchester and Wilfred and Ronald were both ordained priests in the Church of England though Ronald later defected to Rome. Wilfred was a shy, utterly unworldly character who regarded poverty as a prerequisite for any priest. 'I cannot find among our Lord's charges to his disciples', he once said, 'that they should live in the style customary to the upper middle classes.' He was, like Alec Vidler, a Labour supporter who believed that the Church's obligations were firstly to the poor. He was also a pacifist. Though easy to mock, his brand of High Church piety had a powerful pull. Malcolm, who never had the slightest interest in possessions or even particularly in physical comfort, liked the austerity of Oratory House. 'The offices were said during the day, periods of silence were enforced in the afternoons, I often walked in the garden with Wilfred Knox.' Sometimes, he remembered, he acted as server when he celebrated Holy Communion.

Both Knox and Alec Vidler were hoping that Malcolm would become ordained and there is no doubt during his time at Oratory House he gave serious thought to the idea. 'Once,' he wrote, 'sweeping up dead leaves with Wilfred, he spoke of the priestly vocation. What use would I be, I asked him. I found his answer curious – that I could persuade people to do things. What things? I asked. But he left the matter there.' Meanwhile he and Alec discussed the formation of an OGS cell, a 'college' in an industrial area.

While Malcolm dithered about his next move he received an

offer from Rev. W. E. S. Holland to teach at a school in India, Alwaye Christian College in Travancore for three years. 'Of course the salary is nothing,' he wrote to Alec,

> but that I feel is to the good. Again he is taking me as a Catholic and the life I shall live will be a community life. Now all this is very attractive. (There is another point too – teaching there counts as Govt Service and as you know I am pledged to that by reason of the grant (Bursarship) I have received). The first objection is that Fr Wilfred is against it. He is very prejudiced against my going abroad . . . The other big objection is my show with you – and my heart is entirely in that: but frankly from my talks with Wilfred, I see little chance of our running a show on our own lines. (I know he is not going to let Gordon come). He has his eye on a man in Birmingham who wants to join the Oratory and I know wants you and me to start an Oratory College with him (don't say anything about this by the way). But you see he would be vicar and I don't see a lot of hope in that. What I thought was that in three years' time you would be ready to take a parish yourself and I could then come to you as a curate and we could run our own show. You see I have come to feel there is not much hope in the Oratory ever orating. It's all at sixes and sevens. Some of the priests in it say they believe in marriage. Some don't, and though I believe you and I could start an oratory college, I don't believe we should be able to remain such.
>
> If there were any prospect of our starting *on our own lines* at Christmas, I shouldn't hesitate. I feel sure you could get a parish in three years. I should have had some valuable experience in that time. We could have drawn up our whole scheme too.
>
> All my love,
> Malcolm

Three weeks later, Malcolm wrote again to say that he had decided to go to India: 'My dear, I feel an awful washout but I must be sure of my ground before I can do anything.' Alec was very disappointed. 'I do not disguise my regret,' he wrote rather pompously. 'Your justification of the action you propose to take seems to me to be an excuse for doing something that has caught your imagination, rather than a rational case for doing your duty.' Not mentioned in their correspondence was the main obstacle to Malcolm's ever joining the Oratory of the Good Shepherd – namely the vow of celibacy that was a prerequisite to membership. In his case it would mean the sacrifice of his girlfriend Dora Pitman – a sacrifice that he was not really prepared to make even for the sake of Alec Vidler.

But already a pattern was established that was to be repeated many times subsequently – Malcolm responding to a difficult situation by 'making off', in this case to India. He described the appeal of escaping many years later in his novel *Affairs of the Heart*:

It is always an alluring prospect to drop anything – a job, a love affair: to creep out in the darkness from a play just before the curtain rises. You walk out through those swing doors never to return: you buy a ticket at the guichet and go elsewhere, you shut a door behind you, leaving forever unpaid bills, unanswered letters, uncompleted projects, dead hopes and dead desires. An illusory vista of release presents itself: on each voyage the sailor has the same sense of relief at seeing land disappear from sight but as soon as he can see it no more, he is eagerly scanning the horizon for something to break the empty monotony.

Malcolm set sail for India in November 1924 on the SS *Moria*. His devoted father came to see him off and together they walked up the quayside talking about politics – Ramsay MacDonald and his newly elected Labour government occupying their thoughts.

Looking back at his life, Malcolm found it hard, and indeed often made little attempt to distinguish his subsequent thoughts and impressions from what he felt at the time. Occasionally he even fought to conceal those feelings when they were on record. For example, before reaching India he spent a few days in Ceylon (now Sri Lanka). At Kandy he went to see Trinity College, the exact replica of an English public school. In the diary he kept for his father he wrote: 'There is a wonderful public school at Kandy. My main purpose in going there was to see this. On the whole it seems good.' Yet when the diary was being prepared for publication (it was in fact never published), Malcolm deleted the last two sentences. He did not wish to stress the fact that he had been over-impressed by this example of the British Empire at work.

Contrary to the world-weary view of the memoirs, Malcolm's early impressions of India were typical of a twenty-one-year-old going out East for the first time. Everything was new and strange and much of what he wrote to his father was touchingly banal:

31 December 1924

After dinner a number of us went to church to see the New Year in. The parson was earnest and full of zeal for 1925. Shame to say I slept like a log through his sermon and only woke up in time to hear the clock strike twelve. Thus, fortunately, I had no time to make my New Year's resolutions . . .

I wonder if you and the Milnes saw the New Year in. England does seem rather charming away from it. One thinks happily of things like the Tower of London and the Bank of England. They are so permanent and English.

(This passage was also deleted from the diaries.)

Malcolm finally arrived in Alwaye after a complicated journey by boat, bus and train: 'Alwaye is a beautiful place', he wrote to his father, 'and the college is set on a hill behind . . . on every side there is a beautiful view. The village itself, like most villages here, is just a cluster of mud huts.' Alwaye was not typical of missionary schools:

'The man whose child it is', he wrote to Alec Vidler

is one Charcko – one of the world's great men. He was a lecturer at Madras Christian College and felt the place to be rather 'tripy' and Europeany, so he and a little band of Syrian Christians decided to start a Syrian Christian Indian college. The CMS [Christian Missionary Society] backed him up so Anglicans came into it as well. This was the Union Christian college. It is an external college of the Madras University.

Our students graduate there. Their ages are the normal undergraduate age – though some are rather older than under-graduates in England. We have about two hundred and fifty students of which all but about thirty are Christians . . . there are fifteen lecturers. I am junior English lecturer.

Its special advantages are 1. That it is Indian. The students wear their national dress. We have a bad name with the Government, thank God, because of our Nationalist tendencies. 2. The students see Europeans working under Indians. A thing, I believe I am right in saying, absolutely unique throughout the whole of India. 3. That the Christianity is Indian in spirit and not imported respectable Anglicanism. 4. That as a member of the staff one is not a missionary and so is free from all societies. 5. That one lives with Indians and so comes to understand their strengths and weaknesses without prejudice.

It lacks: 1. European efficiency. The European is certainly far more efficient than the Easterners so that the college leaves many things to be desired in the drains and sanitation generally. (b) Food and food cooking arrangements. 2. A true educational spirit. Education all over India is utilitarian and examination based.

Malcolm's job was to give lectures in English literature. The lecture room had no walls and looked out over the paddy fields where men were treading round bamboo irrigation wheels. Work was hard because the students had difficulty following English (particularly when spoken in his unusual accent). The topics of the lectures too – Ben Jonson, Dickens, Masques and Pastorals – bore no relation whatsoever to their lives, making the process of communication even more difficult. Apart, however, from natural feelings of homesickness, Malcolm enjoyed himself (looking back in retrospect to 'the delight of those first magical years!'). But as time went on his work came to seem to him more and more irrelevant – to the students, to India and to himself. He described his daily routine to his father:

I shall tell you of a typical day. I get up at five-thirty: there is no staying in bed problem, for as soon as one wakes one's only desire is for one's bath. Bed is not as snug as in England

but sweaty and horrid. Normally I take my bath in the river
. . . Prayers are said at six. Sometimes it is my duty to take
these. Anyway, I go to them. Then at six-thirty my servant
brings me hot water and bananas. This I take for my bowels.
I always spend till seven with verse of some kind as I believe
it is good to start one's day to the tune of poetry. From seven to
nine, I prepare lectures and from nine-fifty to one am generally
doing teaching of some kind or another. (Between nine and
nine-fifty I take breakfast). I have twelve full lectures a week
but quite a lot of supervision as well. In the afternoon up till
three I sleep and from three to five read my own reading. At
five I take tea and then exercise until seven. This exercise is
either tennis or at least some miles of walking. I dine at seven-
thirty or in the evening study Sanskrit, read or take supervision
classes. I am busy now producing *She Stoops to Conquer*.

Of domestic staff I have four servants. One is Kuruvella
who is called the butler. He is a good soul but a perfect fool.
I remember once I was smoking in my bed, and a box of
matches went off in my hand and burnt me. I shouted to
him for ointment and he brought me first Brasso and then
toothpaste. On another occasion he used the Communion wine
in Hooper's room to light the primus stove with.

Malcolm soon became friends with the Indian members of
staff. His especial friend was a Brahmin named Venkataraman
who introduced him to Hinduism and the *Bhagavad-Gita*. It was
with another Indian whom he calls merely Joseph that he had
what was probably his only direct experience as a defending
counsel in a criminal trial. He told the story to his father.

Yesterday was full of adventure. Joseph and I, walking back
to College from Alwaye village, met a crowd of people rushing
along and shouting. Naturally we followed. We found that
they were chasing a wretched Pariah [member of the lowest
caste in India]; and when they caught him they began to ill-use
him and knock him about very badly. So I interfered. They
stopped, not because I appeared terrible but because my skin
was white. I enquired into the matter and found that the
trouble was that he was accused of having stolen forty rupees

and that on being accused he ran away. There being no police and justice of any kind nearer than Alwaye some three miles away, and that being of poor quality, we took him to a nearby school building; made the vice-president of the college judge; chose counsel for the prosecution (I myself defended) and proceeded to conduct a trial. It was a strange business for me in that building. We were almost in darkness and as we proceeded a storm got up, so that our faces were lit occasionally by flashes of lightning. They were rather prone all to shout together but by degrees we got hold of the evidence and I proved, at any rate to their satisfaction, that the fellow was innocent. (God knows if he really was, but he was certainly wretched and his wife and children were there beating their breasts and shrieking to add to the clamour). As Mr Matthew, the judge, pronounced him innocent amid thunderous cheering from the people who, but a little while ago, had nearly killed him, the roof of the building we were in fell in on us. I was quite unhurt but, as you can well imagine, there was chaos indescribable both from those hurt and from those falling over each other in a mad effort to get out.

I have but poorly described all this – you cannot see from this how weird it was – the realization of the wildness of one's surroundings and how, had I not been there, the Pariah would probably have been killed and no one would ever have known or cared except his woman, whom he probably beats regularly (remember these are the lowest people in India – perhaps almost the lowest in the world). And the women, too ugly and distorted from heavy work. All our fault and they are as us and we are to blame.

Malcolm struck up an immediate rapport with his students, many of whom were virtually his contemporaries. Their sense of humour appealed to him and their religious approach to life. He did his best to become one of them, wearing Indian dress made from the homespun cloth recommended by Gandhi. He walked barefoot and tried to teach himself to eat Indian food off a plantain leaf. 'I even managed to simulate certain characteristic Indian gestures', he wrote, 'as spreading my hands with a look of profound disgust to indicate that I did not want another helping or shaking my head from side to side instead of nodding up and down to signify agreement.'

Given his socialist upbringing it was natural that Malcolm should have sympathized with and tried to encourage the nationalist fervour of his pupils. Being almost the same age, in any case, he identified more closely with them than with his fellow sahibs. It was a time of great nationalist ferment. At Amritsar in 1919 a British officer, General Dyer, had ordered his troops to open fire on an unarmed crowd, killing 379 of them. Malcolm told his father: 'General Dyer's public-spirited defence of British interests which caused him to fire into crowds . . . has eaten into the heart of India. So has the action of that equally public-spirited paper the *Morning Post*, presenting him with £10,000 when he got home.' Throughout India there was enormous interest in Gandhi who appealed not only to the political but the religious instincts as well. Malcolm was told about him by a member of the Alwaye staff, a Brahmin.

He spoke of Gandhi with deep emotion . . . how he had given up wealth, position, everything so that now he has only a loin cloth, in order that his country might see from him how to live.

You know it is impossible in England when there is only the Capitalist press to feed one with news, to understand the position of this man Gandhi in India. He is loved and respected through the length and breadth of the continent. One word from him is obeyed by three hundred million people in one day (this is no exaggeration). The salvation is that he preaches constantly against all forms of violence – when his followers break out into any kind of physical force manifestation he does public penance for it.

When he was tried and condemned India wept. England despised her weeping, boasted that by her stern and careful policy she had stopped great trouble, but I feel that the tears were the greater part – that Gandhi with a nation's tears behind him is greater than the Viceroy with an army.

A little later he wrote: 'I love this Gandhi. To all Indians he is the Mahatmaji – this is the sort of loving, respecting nickname.

There is always something to be admired in a man that has a nickname. It means a lot. One can feel this best negatively. No one would call Birkenhead "Birky".'

The excitement was intense when Gandhi paid a visit to Alwaye in the course of a tour to Travancore. Malcolm went down to the station joining a crowd of thousands to see him arrive: 'When Gandhi's train came there was a stir: but mostly students from the college – Gandhi was sitting cross-legged in a third-class compartment, his curious gargoyle face showing no special awareness of the crowd and the notables and the cheers of the students.'

Gandhi alighted and caught sight of a group of untouchables in a special roped-off enclosure. To the obvious distress of those notables who had come to greet him with garlands, Gandhi insisted on joining them and singing a lugubrious hymn. Then he came up to the college to address Malcolm's pupils, speaking to them very quietly in English. 'The effect on the students was terrific,' Malcolm recalled. 'They jumped up and down shouting, "Mahatma Gandhi Ki Jai! Mahatma Gandhi Ki Jai!", their eyes glowing and their dreadful inertia of our excursion through Sesame and the Lilies, our mournful celebration of Dryden finding English brick and leaving it marble, all obliterated and forgotten.'

After Gandhi's visit to Alwaye, Malcolm wrote him a letter telling him that he would do better to promote the industrialization of the Indian economy rather than preach a policy of back to the spinning wheel. He also argued that what the Indian worker needed was better living conditions and contraceptives to keep down the size of his family. If Malcolm's letter to Gandhi raised these political matters, the Mahatma did not choose to comment on them. Instead he made some rather cryptic remarks about the General Strike in England: 'If the mine owners win, they will win not because there are too many miners but because miners do not know how to control themselves. It is difficult to forecast the future of a body of men who not knowing the higher life do not want to restrain themselves and would avoid the responsibilities of citizenship.' The rest of the letter was concerned with advocating abstinence as the best means of birth control.

Apart from political issues, Malcolm found the religious atmosphere of Alwaye greatly to his taste. He became particularly friendly with the Brahmin T. S. Venkataraman and under his influence cultivated asceticism for a time. He gave up smoking and drinking, writing to his father: 'I feel that women have absorbed too much time for me.' To a man of his very powerful sexual drive, asceticism made a strong appeal but it was one that in the end he turned his back on, for the time being at least. The penalty was that sex continued to torment him. He could never be, and never became a happy hedonist. In a passage headed 'A Mystical Experience' he described an unusual incident to his father:

> I went for my usual evening swim. You know my love of the river – the smooth, gentle, clean river, that flows mysteriously to unknown places. Always I am most happy in the water. This night I was especially so until I saw, along the bank, a woman came to bathe . . . she came to the river and took off her clothes and stood naked, her bare body just caught by the sun and I suddenly went mad. There came to me that dryness in the back of the throat; that feeling of cruelty and strength and wild unreasonableness which is called passion. I darted with all the force of swimming I had to where she was and then I nearly fainted, for she was old and hideous and her feet were deformed and turned inwards and her skin was wrinkled and – worst of all – she was a leper . . . this creature grinned at me, showing a toothless mouth, and the next thing I knew was that I was swimming along in my old way in the middle of the stream, yet trembling.
>
> It seems rather absurd to say it but I don't know whether this really happened to me or not. I believe it did, yet I might have dreamed it in my swimming.

Malcolm was contracted to remain at Alwaye for three years. By October 1926 he was beginning to show signs of boredom. Such a development was to become typical of his entire life – of all the jobs and assignments which he undertook. Again and again, we find the same sequence of initial enthusiasm followed at varying intervals by boredom and disillusionment and a tendency to lash out, unthinking, at colleagues and overseers.

'We have a staff meeting,' he wrote to his father (18 October 1926):

> We sit round a table to discuss some big question – say a new plan of tutorial work – the principal is the head – we are all solemn. And suddenly the little devils dance and whisper. 'What does it matter, who cares about your blasted tutorial system, or your equally blasted college or your equally blasted self? Aren't their faces solemn as they deliberate? Aren't their words pompous as they stand up and speak? Would you have believed it possible for a stomach to fold over in quite the way Holland's does unless you'd seen it – would you have thought any man could possibly grow a moustache like Poonen's or have a face as red and shiny as Hooper's,' and so on.

Malcolm had already made a nuisance of himself by preaching what was thought to be a 'heretical' sermon in the chapel. In this, he rejected the notion of Christ's divinity and argued that by making great teachers into gods, human beings only produced wars and fanaticisms. He spoke in praise of his current hero Socrates, in whose words he said 'we find all the great moral truths that there are in the New Testament'. It was a sign that he had, for the time being, abandoned such belief as he had in orthodox Christianity, whilst at the same time biting the hand that fed him. The school's principal, Charcko (a saintly figure by Malcolm's own account) refused to rise to the bait. 'I love you too much even to be angry with you,' he told him, but not long afterwards Malcolm was in trouble again when he published an article about unemployment among university students. In it, he criticized the whole educational system, referring to 'dead' teachers, 'artificial' lessons and 'wax hyacinths and pink paper roses imprinted from the West'. This time he had gone too far and the principal cancelled the farewell party that the school had arranged. Malcolm admitted afterwards that, at the time he wrote it, he gave no thought at all to the possible repercussions of his piece. It was to be the first of a long series of such incidents.

Malcolm left the school by boat accompanied by Venkataraman and Mathail, a Christian sadhu or holy man whom he was especi-

ally fond of, discerning in his gaunt ascetic features 'that indomi-
table, inexorable Christian love: absurd, inane if not insane in its
total refusal to exclude anyone or anything from the range of its
radiance'. These two seemingly felt the need to escort Malcolm
from Alwaye and they sat contentedly in the boat while he marked
his examination papers and then threw them into the water, watching them float away on the current. Arriving in Aleppey they
stayed in a Christian mission, all three sleeping on the floor. Malcolm watched as the two holy men engaged in their devotions,
whilst he himself felt like a Stendhal hero with the world at his
feet, with books to write and women to conquer. Sensing such a
mood perhaps, the Brahmin, usually a deeply reticent individual,
launched into a denunciation of women and the danger they represented to someone of Malcolm's temperament – 'ravening,
destructive, a coarsening and ultimately fatal addiction'. It was not
a warning he was prepared to take to heart. The following day he
took his leave of the two men and set out for Colombo. From here
he set sail for Naples where his father had arranged to meet him.

Malcolm had no idea what to do when he returned to England.
He had done some writing at Alwaye and had a story printed in
the *New Statesman*, greatly to the delight of his father. But it was
obvious that he could not hope to earn a living in this way.
Writing from India in June 1926 he listed three possibilities to
his father: '1. To be secretary to an MP – or almost anything
connected with politics. 2. Journalism – any job on the staff of
a Labour paper. 3. A teacher in any kind of school under the
LCC (London County Council).' He wanted a salary of £3 and
begged his father, 'But my dear Pater, get me a job at anything
in the Labour Party and I'm your man – even if it is to sweep
out the offices in Eccleston Square.' In the end he followed a
suggestion from Alec Vidler, by now a priest in Small Heath,
Birmingham, that he should join him there and become a supply
teacher. This involved teaching in a number of very poor state
schools. Perhaps Alec had been hoping to revive their original
idea of an Oratory 'cell' involving himself, Malcolm and other
celibates. If so, he was again to be disappointed as after only
two terms Malcolm suddenly and unexpectedly announced his
decision to get married to Kitty Dobbs.

CHAPTER III

Marriage and Journalism

DURING THE SUMMER HOLIDAY in 1927, Malcolm had decided to visit the Dobbs family at Knocke, a Belgian coastal resort where he had worked as a courier with Kitty's brother during his Cambridge vacation. He memoirs suggest that this was an irrational impulse but, as Ian Hunter points out in his biography, the likelihood is that Malcolm was partly motivated by the desire to improve his standing in the Socialist Movement – Mrs Dobbs being a sister of Beatrice Webb – not to mention society in general (in his diary for 1936 he wrote 'the family's aristocratic connections obsessed me somewhat. I liked to think about them').

Kitty's mother Rosie was the ninth and youngest daughter of Richard Potter, a wealthy industrialist and director of the Great Western Railway, and his wife Laurencina (once described by John Bright as 'one of the two or three women a man remembers to the end of his life as beautiful in expression and form'). Born in 1865, Rosie had been brought up according to the conventions of the Victorian upper-middle class in a huge house in the Cotswolds with an army of servants, tutors and governesses. In his *Notes on England* (1860–70) the French historian Hippolyte Taine described a visit by a friend to the Potters' house at Standish in Gloucestershire:

> M. being invited to the country discovered that the mistress of the house knew much more Greek than himself, apologized and retired from the field; then out of pleasantry, she wrote down his English sentences in Greek. Note that this female Hellenist is a woman of the world, and even stylish. Moreover she has nine daughters, two nurses, two governesses, servants

in proportion, a large well-appointed house, frequent and numerous visitors: throughout all this, perfect order: never noise or fuss: the machine appears to move of its own accord. There are gatherings of faculties and contrasts which might make us reflect. In France we believe too readily that if a woman ceases to be a doll she ceases to be a woman.

Laurencina Potter died in 1882 when Rosie was only sixteen years old and four years later her father had a stroke from which he never recovered. (He died in 1892.) Rosie now came strongly under the influence of Beatrice her sister, seven years older, who was destined to become the famous Mrs Sidney Webb. They were both highly intelligent, gifted women but Rosie was unworldly and too fond of the opposite sex to follow her sister into public life. Beatrice habitually referred to Rosie with scorn and when she became engaged to a young barrister called Dyson Williams, wrote in her diary, 'Poor fellow, I pity him . . . not up to my other brothers in law . . . in short a nonentity, but then Rosie is the least gifted mentally and physically of the sisterhood.' Williams in fact was by no means a nonentity. He was handsome and witty and had been president of the Oxford Union. Rosie's initial doubts about him were quickly allayed: 'He proved a perfect lover', she wrote, 'and soon succeeded in overcoming my reluctance. Nevertheless during the honeymoon which we spent in the Lake District I felt keenly the want of sympathy on many subjects.'

All the Potter sisters looked down on Williams, but as they also looked down on their little sister they saw nothing wrong with the match. 'He is very much in love and he is a very respectable young man', Beatrice wrote to reassure her sister Mary. But respectable was not the right word for Williams, who had had a number of liaisons with various women, one of which had resulted in his contracting syphilis. He died in 1895, shortly after the birth of their first son Noel, subsequently killed in the First World War. Rosie was now a widow of independent means. She began to travel (at that time a brave and unconventional thing for a woman to do). All her life she was a keen amateur artist. She had lessons from Walter Sickert and her copies of Turner were good enough to deceive Kenneth Clark into thinking they were the real thing. She frequented art galleries and once at a private view at the Royal Academy she was introduced to Oscar Wilde: 'And what, Mrs Williams, have been your soul's experiences?' ('I was so taken aback I did not know what to say,' she wrote).

In Rome in 1897 she met H. G. Wells and George Gissing, who fell in love with her and, when they met again in England, proposed that she should come and live with him (Gissing was by this time separated from his wife, a former prostitute). Rosie wrote: 'He suggested to me some such plan and I was very near acceptance, but one thing and one thing only stood in my way, for I don't think I should have cared much for the world's opinions and my family's disapproval, but I feared that if I defied the conventions openly I should ruin my boy's future.' Later, H. G. Wells invited her to his house to meet Gissing again. He showed Rosie over his house including the bathroom which was painted black, with a huge mirror over the large white bath. She asked him why the room was painted black and Wells said: 'In order to see one's own white self in the midst of darkness.' When Wells took her to the station he spoke to her about his wife and how devoted she was to him, despite his philandering, adding: 'and some woman ought to sacrifice herself to Gissing.' Rosie, however, remained true to her resolve and later that year Gissing met Theresa who lived with him until his death.

Rosie met her second husband George Dobbs (Kitty's father) in Capri in 1897. He was a handsome, mustachioed man who according to Malcolm's greatest friend Hugh Kingsmill always looked ten years less than his age. The son of an Irish land agent in Castleconnor, Co. Kerry, Dobbs took a degree at Trinity College, Dublin and after marrying a second cousin went out to Ceylon as a tea-planter. But his wife died and he returned to Ireland. Rosie was immediately drawn to him. 'Physically,' she wrote, 'GLD attracted me more than any man I had ever met. For the first time in my life I gave myself with joy and experienced in his arms the ecstasy of love when for a few brief moments all is forgotten and we become united body and soul with the loved one.' After this passionate encounter they corresponded and when in 1898 Rosie, again on her travels in Italy, wrote to tell him of her loneliness, Dobbs came over from Ireland to join her. 'We spent a perfect week in Venice', she wrote later, 'visiting churches and picture galleries during the day, and spending the evenings in the lagoons with gondolas listening to the beautiful voices of the Italian boatmen and the sensuous music of their songs, his dear arm around me as in Capri and always I felt the conflict of his presence and the charm of his unselfish nature and of his true and tender love for me. It was then we became lovers indeed.'

George and Rosie travelled back to England as 'Mr and Mrs Dobbs'. A conventional man, he was keen that they should be married as soon as possible but Rosie had her doubts and he returned to Ireland without a definite answer to his proposal. The next thing that happened was that she became infected with scarlet fever. Her friends and relations wrote sympathetic letters but no one liked to visit for fear of infection. George Dobbs, however, showed his worth by coming over from Ireland to be by her side. Rosie recalled: 'The doctor and nurse rigged up a carbolic sheet across my open door behind which George sat and talked to me trying to cheer me up and assuring me of his love . . . it was then that, ill and lonely and longing for his love, I finally decided to marry him. He was the only person who loved me sufficiently to risk infection for my sake.'

Rosie still had reservations about her fiancé, 'because of our want of intellectual sympathy and understanding.' All the same, she decided to give up her other boyfriends. They were married in Chelsea Old Church in February 1899 by a clergyman who had once proposed to Rosie. After their marriage, the Dobbses went to live in Switzerland and it was here on 8 December 1903 at Château d'Oex that Kitty was born during a snowstorm. She was the fourth of five children, all born within seven years. 'Kitty was a fine, strong, little thing', her mother wrote, 'and thrived in the keen mountain air.'

It was about that time that George Dobbs, who had virtually given up work once he married his wealthy bride, became interested in skiing – a sport which until then had been confined to Sweden and Norway. With the help of a young artist, Vivian

Caulfield, he began organizing winter sports. Following the birth of their fifth child Bill, Dobbs, who began to tire of an idle life, took a job working for Sir Henry Lunn, a former Methodist missionary turned businessman (and father of Hugh Kingsmill). Sir Henry, whose name survives today in the travel company Lunn Poly, had established a number of luxurious hotels to which the fanatics of the new sport of skiing were flocking. All Dobbs's children became accomplished skiers and Sir Arnold Lunn's *History of Skiing* (OUP 1927) listed their achievements including Miss Kitty Dobbs (Lady Ski Champion 1924) and her brother Leonard who was considered to be the finest racing skier of his day.

Sir Henry's business was very much a family affair. He employed his brother George as well as his sons Brian, Arnold and Hugh (Kingsmill). But in 1908 he gave Dobbs a permanent job running winter sports at Villars (with responsibility for his Golf Links at Montana in the summer). Dobbs was an ideal appointment. He was sociable, easy-going as well as efficient. 'He knew nearly everyone,' his wife wrote of him with apparent pride.

Kitty was eleven when war broke out in 1914. The Dobbses returned to England and she was sent to school in the West Country and later Bedales, earlier recommended by the parents of a friend of Noel Williams (Rosie's son from her first marriage) as a suitable school for Kitty's brother Leonard – though Hugh Kingsmill remarked subsequently that 'the claim made for co-educational establishments, that they initiate a well-balanced relationship between the sexes, was not substantiated by Leonard's own experience in later years.' This unconventional school, one of the first in England to be co-educational, appealed especially to Mrs Dobbs. She liked the freedom allowed to the pupils, the lack of formal religious education. She noted with approval that the roll call included the sons of a number of well-known artists and poets – William Rothenstein (whose son John was nicknamed Tusky), Muirhead Bone and Sturge Moore. 'Once, I remember,' she wrote, 'Rabindranath Tagore came and chanted in Hindustani. It was rather impressive. The tall white-haired figure in his long robes standing on a platform and chanting in a low voice the more so as a thunderstorm was raging outside and there was a sudden flash of lightning which illuminated the hall and then a clap of thunder.'

Impressive as Tagore may have been, such episodes were not the ideal preparation for a life in the twentieth century. If Kitty was spared the straitjacket of conventional schooling, she left Bedales ill-equipped. Looking back at her early days she said: 'I lived such a frivolous life. I spent most of my time skiing and dancing. I loved amateur theatricals.'

Kitty was generous in spirit and very perceptive about people (a trait she shared with her aunt Beatrice Webb, and, to some extent, her mother). She was guileless and straightforward, never concealing anything. Her weakness, when young, was a prone-ness to violent outbursts and hysterics ('starving herself and indulging in violent tantrums, especially with her mother,' according to Beatrice Webb in her diary). This may explain why Mrs Dobbs at one point took her to see Jung in Zurich – Malcolm liked to remark later in life that he could never have had a less promising patient. The dominant figure in her early life was her mother's sister Beatrice Webb, 'Aunt Bo' as she was known. Brought up under the influence of her father's friend the famous Victorian agnostic Herbert Spencer, Beatrice Webb was a spir-itual woman without a religion who became instead a great pol-itical crusader. As a young girl she had been passionately in love with Joseph Chamberlain but renounced him when she realized that marriage would take away her political independence. Fol-lowing after her sister Kate (later Lady Courtney) into charitable work she developed an interest in co-operatives and trade unions. Through her first-hand investigations into working-class con-ditions she became a convinced socialist. In 1892 she married Sidney Webb, a leading Fabian, and together the two became a formidable 'think-tank', compiling an apparently endless stream of books, reports and white papers. When the Labour Party grew out of the trade union movement the Webbs became its brains, supplying it with all the information it needed to formulate policy on social issues. Sidney Webb (later Lord Passfield) was a Labour minister in Ramsay MacDonald's Government. Regret-tably, this, in many ways, admirable pair became in their old age unthinking and credulous supporters of Soviet Russia, thereby, because of their enormous prestige, exercising a dire influence on Socialist thinking. 'Old people', Mrs Webb wrote, 'often fall in love in extraordinary and ridiculous ways with their chauffeurs for example; we feel it more dignified to have fallen in love with Soviet Communism.'

'For me,' Kitty remembered, 'she [Beatrice Webb] was in a way the first fact of life we learned. She hung over the family like a kind of threat; a constant reminder of the utter futility of our existence . . . in the playgrounds among the idle rich.' Kitty first met her when she was eleven. She and her family had just arrived in England on the outbreak of the First World War in 1914 and were staying in lodgings in Folkestone. Because of what she knew about her aunt, Kitty was determined to show that she was not merely a rich parasite and was anxious to win her approval. The Webbs arrived on a bicycle made for two:

She was a slender, erect woman, black rapacious eyes set wide apart, an aquiline nose with disdainful nostrils, a wide mouth which displayed what seemed an unusually large number of teeth and, at that time, grey hair inclined to hang down in mops. There was something untamed in her which gave her an air of nobility's high breeding. Like all her sisters, she walked with a gypsy's stride and her manner was arrogant. Though beautiful, she gave the impression of some predatory bird, a golden eagle perhaps, soaring in search of prey. Her dress was elegant – a charming bell-like skirt of dove-grey broadcloth, a beautiful silver-buckled belt, a pretty jacket, a large hat tied on with a flimsy grey veil.

What a contrast to her was Sidney! Small, thick, his large head seemed all in one with his neck – only a reddish goatee beard marking the division between the two. His face was red, with a fleshy nose and bulging watery greenish eyes behind thick-lensed pince-nez. One felt rather than saw him to be intelligent. He always wore a very thick heavy serge suit which fitted him like a suit made for a teddy bear with his limbs protruding oddly. He perspired ('Sidney sweats you know' Aunt Bo so often pointed out).

Kitty, who had been so eager to impress her aunt on their first meeting, had little opportunity to do so because their visit was so brief. It was not until she left Bedales and was doing a secretarial course in London that she began to see her more frequently and sometimes stayed in the Webbs' house at 41 Grosvenor Road on the Embankment. Here, she observed Mrs Webb more closely. 'I remember arriving one evening and, when she opened the door, being taken aback because her black eyes glowed red with the sinking of the setting sun in a way I have never seen in a human being, only an animal. The meal would be frugal, but excellently served and cooked, my aunt never partaking of the same dish as her guests – always some separate vegetarian dish, delightfully brown on top.' After dinner, Kitty would sit in the drawing room overlooking the Thames while the Webbs engaged in political dialogue, Mrs Webb puffing on a herbal cigarette. Then they would go to bed early, Kitty being escorted to a room at the top of the house past Sidney's room on the second floor. 'Sidney snores you know,' she would explain.

With no children of her own, Beatrice Webb probably enjoyed these visits more than Kitty did. She also recognized that her niece, in spite of her frivolous background, was intelligent and public-spirited. 'She is decidedly gifted as an actress and linguist,' she wrote, 'physically strong and capable of great endurance.' As for any failings on Kitty's part, like her professed belief in 'free love', Mrs Webb would have made allowance for Rosie's regrettable failings as a mother. At any rate, she decided to take her niece in hand. She had recently conceived the idea of a Parliamentary Labour Club where Labour MPs and their wives, 'unused to London and with small means', could meet and have cheap meals. Kitty was given the job as secretary to help those MPs who visited to handle their correspondence from the club. Unfortunately her shorthand was not up to scratch. 'I got the letters down alright,' she said. 'There were about eight from Hugh Dalton. But not a word could I read back.' Aunt Bo suggested that Kitty should read for a social sciences diploma at the London School of Economics (another of her enterprises). Kitty greatly enjoyed her two years at the LSE but failed the simple exam at the end. To Mrs Webb, who attached such great importance to success, it must have been a disappointment.

Kitty first met Malcolm when he was sharing rooms with her brother Leonard at Cambridge. 'My first impression of Malcolm before I even met him', she said later, 'was what a funny name he had. And also he had the most beautiful handwriting.' Malcolm was fair-haired with bright blue eyes, but with his slightly bulbous nose he could hardly be called good-looking. Like many others since, however, Kitty found his conversation irresistible. Of that first Cambridge meeting, neither retained any memories. The decision to get married, like most of the major decisions in Malcolm's life, would seem to have been made on the spur of the moment. He could not remember proposing. He found Kitty irresistible ('Slim, with dark short hair, features and eyes quick like an animal'), but he also acknowledged that there was an element of snobbery involved because of her relationship with the Webbs. For his part, Mr Dobbs, whose favourite Kitty had always been, seriously opposed him. He disliked intellectuals, although Rosie, like her sister, regarded Malcolm as a genius. The view of Dobbs's colleagues was summed up by one employee of Sir Henry Lunn who exclaimed with horror on hearing of the engagement: 'Dobbs's daughter is going to marry that Red fellow Muggeridge!'

A visit was soon arranged to the Webbs' house at Passfield Corner at Liphook in Hampshire where Beatrice and Sidney lived their rather Spartan existence, looked after by two Scottish maids, Jean and Annie. Beatrice worked continually, meals were frugal and, as Kitty noted on her frequent visits, all the chairs and divans were hard. Although in her seventies, Beatrice Webb remained energetic and liked to go for long walks. She and Malcolm – contrary to his later disparaging comments – took an immediate liking to one another. Obviously she saw eye to eye with him on most political subjects, but more importantly she discerned at once that he was going to make some mark in the world and Mrs Webb admired success above all. She wrote, after the marriage a little later, 'He is the most intellectually stimulating and pleasant mannered of all my "in-laws". An ugly but attractive and expressive face, a clever and sympathetic talker. Ultra modern in his view of sex, theoretically more than practically I think . . . yet I think Malcolm is a mystic and even a puritan in his awareness of loyalties and human relationships. What is attractive about him is the total absence of intellectual arrogance; partly because he has a keen sense of humour and an understanding of his own ignorance, also a knowledge of the world, a sense of proportion.' (Beatrice Webb's diary, 19 January 1931)

The marriage took place at Birmingham registry office in defiance of almost every convention. Neither Kitty nor Malcolm invited their parents, though Mr Dobbs insisted on coming, apparently more with the intention of preventing the marriage than assisting at a happy event. At any rate, during the brief ceremony, just as Kitty was about to give her assent, he interjected, 'You can still get away, Kit!' Kitty, however, was in no mood to listen to her father's advice. After the ceremony in the presence of the clergy at St Aidan's House, she tore up the cheque for £15 that her father's boss Sir Henry Lunn had sent as a wedding present. Alec Vidler, who was not present, was later shocked to be told by Malcolm that he and Kitty had asked the registrar about the procedures for getting divorced while they were about it.

Later Malcolm expressed shame and regret that he had not invited his dear father to the wedding. But as no other relative had been asked it was not so surprising. What he wished later to acknowledge was that in marrying Kitty he had entered into a different social sphere, one in which his parents might prove something of an embarrassment. His parents certainly acknowledged Kitty's superior status by giving up their bedroom to Malcolm and Kitty when they came to stay in Croydon. Mrs Webb looked down on H. T. Muggeridge, describing him to her sister Rosie as 'A Fabian and a very worthy person, though of modest means.'

At any rate, it seems that once he was married, Malcolm transferred his allegiance to his father-in-law George Dobbs, who also had strong ideas about conventions and social hierarchies. He certainly had no wish to have as a son-in-law a man who was merely a supply teacher in Birmingham. Dobbs therefore recommended that Malcolm should apply for a teaching job in Egypt.

He did and was immediately accepted. Malcolm and Kitty set out for Egypt, arriving in November 1927. They went via Cairo to Minia in Upper Egypt to a flat overlooking the Nile. 'Egypt is a funny country', Malcolm wrote to Effie Pitman (the school-girl sister of his first sweetheart Dora), 'because it's all in parallel lines – desert – hills – the river – canals – roads – the railway and then desert again.' His work was undemanding: 'My job here is ideal. I get five hundred a year for doing sixteen hours a week for seven months of the year.' He found the atmosphere similar to that of India, with the same colonial snobberies, and for that reason, uncongenial. He and Kitty relied on one another for company. In the early hours they went riding along the Nile and in the evening played tennis. 'Kitty has bought a mandolin and is practising it now,' he told Effie. 'She is cleverer than I am so I can't bully her which is good. We live a queer, feckless life and I don't know how long we shall stay here. I've just been reading a book by a German on Russia and it has made me want to go there very much and see whether there is anything in it. I think there must be otherwise it would not have persisted.'

After two terms at Minia School teaching English, Malcolm was subsequently given a job at Cairo University. He and Kitty then moved into a house on the edge of the desert near Helmia Zeytoun which they later shared with Bryn Davies, a university colleague of Malcolm's. It was here that their son Leonard (named after Kitty's brother) was born on 11 October 1928. 'Leonard is well,' Malcolm wrote to his father. 'We often wish that mother was here to advise us about him. One knows so little. I have studied two books of babies with some interest and feel entirely qualified to lecture on the subject but not to deal with my own son. For one thing the two books contradict each other . . . Mrs Webb sent us one of hers – very Spartan and no-nonsensey.'

A fascinating picture of the early married life of Kitty and Malcolm is given in Rosie Dobbs's diary for 19 August 1928 when they stayed with her at Knocke en route for Egypt after a brief European holiday:

Malcolm who calls himself a communist and wears a red tie recognizes no class distinction. In fact, the very idea of class is repugnant to him. We had a great argument with him the other day as to the meaning and value of good breeding. He went so far as to say that he disliked in the so-called aristocrat just that quality of good breeding because he nearly always finds it associated with an arrogant attitude towards inferiors and an assumption of superiority . . . Malcolm is full of new ideas on all possible subjects which Kitty fully shares. They are excellent company: she helps him with his work and type-writes his plays. She struck me as having grown and developed intellectually since her marriage but she is one of those women in whom the purely animal maternal instinct is not highly developed and I doubt if she minds much leaving her baby in England provided she feels sure it will be well cared for. As Malcolm says the purely domestic routine duties, even the cause will not satisfy her, she craves for a freer life with more scope for mental development. Many of the modern girls are like her in their attitude toward family life and also towards marriage and all sexual relationships. With freer sexual union between men and women, children will be regarded less as the property of their parents and more as belonging to the state and the latter may in time be entirely responsible for their upbringing. The better this tendency is for the good of the race remains to be seen. Sometimes I feel that women nowadays are deserting the work for which nature has fitted them and are trying to become second-class men. May not this tendency end in degeneration and sterility of the race?

The Dobbses were now joined at Knocke by their son Leonard and Malcolm's colleague Bryn Davies: 'He is a clever handsome Welshman,' wrote Mrs Dobbs, 'very dark and distinctly attrac-tive. He and Kit evidently find much in common and on their return to Egypt he is, I hear, to share their flat at Gizeh. Rather a dangerous experiment to my mind, but Malcolm apparently does not object. He takes the modern view that even if Kit and Davies fall in love with each other he will not interfere. However, it might distress him. The best kind of life he says is not jealous or possessive but only works for the happiness of the beloved. How different from the old-fashioned husband who felt a jealous and almost murderous hatred towards his wife's lover.'

One evening Malcolm gave a reading of his play *Three Flats* which his mother-in-law found clever, 'but rather inconclusive and depressing and in parts perhaps needlessly suggestive'. Even so, she had to admit that he was a 'delightful fellow, full of ideas and enthusiasms, but of a nervous, slightly neurotic temperament.

One day when Kit, as is still her habit, refused to eat there was a terrific row. She got up and left the room. Malcolm followed her and presently we heard strange sounds issuing from their bedroom. George, alarmed, rushed upstairs and found Malcolm on the floor drumming automatically with his feet in a fit of violent hysterics, whilst Kit was sobbing on the bed. She probably said some cruel words to the poor man thus to make him lose self-control. George told him to get up and not make a fool of himself and presently the two came down and finished their supper. Kit having reduced her father and husband almost to tears at length consented to eat her eggs.'

Kitty and Malcolm were regarded by the British community in Egypt as virtual outcasts who went out of their way to defy all the conventions. 'We were all slightly alarmed by the lecturer in English', the British diplomat Sir Laurence Grafftey-Smith recalled. '[He was] then a young man of twenty-four who seemed to be a beatnik ahead of his time and scorned the social trivialities which absorbed us.' (*Bright Levant*, an autobiography by Sir L. Grafftey-Smith)

Kitty, true to her socialist principles, dismissed all the servants who were expecting to look after them in their house at Gizeh; while Malcolm found little to absorb him in teaching English Literature to young Egyptians (many of whom he concluded were 'high' on hashish). Instead he began to take an interest in the political situation and especially the growing nationalist movement, the Wafd, headed by Nahas Pasha. Malcolm's Egyptian students, who in any case found it difficult to follow lectures in English and French, were highly politicized and frequently on strike. Malcolm sympathized. The situation fitted all his socialist theories about imperialism. At the same time writing about it was a possible means of escape. He told his father: 'I am trying to send stories and sketches and articles to every bloody periodical that exists – but naturally with meagre results.' However, one paper did eventually respond – the *Manchester Guardian* (Malcolm had had an introduction to the editor from another of Kitty's aunts, Lady Courtney, whose husband was a stalwart Liberal).

Malcolm was duly thrilled when his first offering was printed in the *Manchester Guardian* (29 October 1929), even more so when he received a letter from E. T. Scott, the editor, asking for more. The climax came when he was told that Arthur Ransome was coming to Cairo to cover the election as the paper's Special Correspondent and was anxious to meet with him. A schoolmasterly figure with pipe and moustache, Ransome (later to be famous for his children's stories) was no mere journalist, he had witnessed in person the events of the Russian Revolution, had known Lenin personally and even played chess with him. His wife, Genia, had been Trotsky's secretary. All this marked him out in Malcolm's eyes as one of the elect. Ransome was equally delighted with Malcolm. From Cairo he wrote to E. T. Scott (a close friend since their days at Rugby together) on 15 December 1929:

He is 26, married to a niece of Lord Courtney, son of a Labour member. Calls himself Labour but considers Labour better served by the MG than by its own representatives. Wants to write, has a congenital interest in politics. Has spent some time teaching in an Indian School or University. Then went back to England, married and came out here to earn a living. Education: Cambridge; nothing much in the way of fancy degrees, because he read science, then history and finally education. I asked him how long it took him to write the sort of articles he had been sending us. He said he never has time to give more than a morning to doing an article. Concealing my respect behind a pompous manner, I did not let him know that I considered him one of the heavenborn. Languages: French, German and a pretty good foundation for Russian (learnt here) plus a certain amount of Arabic. His ambition is to be a special correspondent. I led the conversation to the subject of journalism in general and asked him if he had ever thought of going into a newspaper office. He did not express the revolted horror

that I should have felt at his age at such a suggestion. He
wondered if doing that sort of thing he would be able to earn
400 or 500 a year. He is extrreeeemely [sic] young, but decidedly nice in feel, altogether unlike some other rabbits whose
diseased livers and swollen spleens affect the corridor atmosphere.* I think he is the sort of lad you would find refreshing
to have about and one who, as his articles show, has a natural
instinct for the MG . . . I think you would enjoy having the
creature about.

NB. He washes for one thing and for another, he is
altogether free from conceit.

Both Kitty and Malcolm were thrilled when shortly afterwards E. T. Scott offered Malcolm a job as a leader writer.
Neither of them had liked being in Egypt and Kitty was so
desperate to leave that she even went down on her knees to
Arthur Ransome, imploring him to give her husband a job. Malcolm duly arrived in Manchester in August 1930 and, when he
was joined shortly afterwards by Kitty and the baby Leonard,
they stayed briefly in Kingsley Martin's house in Didsbury –
Martin remembered Kitty hanging her pyjamas out of the
window as an act of defiance – before eventually moving to a
flat in the same house as A. J. P. Taylor (then a young lecturer
at Manchester University) and his wife Margaret.

The *Manchester Guardian* was an extraordinary institution, a
provincial newspaper with a world-wide circulation, respected
in all progressive circles for its constant and considered advocacy
of liberal ideas and causes. (A story was current at the time of a
clergyman who began an impromptu prayer with the words
'Oh God, as thou wilt have read in the *Manchester Guardian* this
morning . . .') In the minds of writers and would-be journalists
it had a special place as the paper of 'good writing', attracting
men of the calibre of C. E. Montague, Neville Cardus, James
Agate and Ransome himself. Its high standing was the achievement of one man, C. P. Scott (1846–1932) who became editor
in 1872 at the age of only twenty-five. In 1905 he bought control

* Probably a reference to Kingsley Martin, recently taken on as a leader writer.

of the paper and from then on acted as a benevolent despot, becoming not only a prestigious editor but an elder statesman, the friend and confidant of political leaders whom he liked to advise and admonish from a position of high-minded principle. Scott thought of himself and his paper more in terms of fulfilling a public service than just providing news. The leader in his view was more important than any mere scoop.

Looking back on his Manchester days, Malcolm remembered the 'screeching trains, the massive blackened public buildings and statues of forgotten worthies and the stagnant Ship Canal', by which he walked interminably. The *Guardian* offices were in Cross Street where a line of pony traps stood during the day waiting to deliver the *Manchester Evening News*, the *Guardian*'s sister paper, to the retailers. He found it new and exciting. 'At once', he wrote, 'I began to catch the fever of journalism, the tray of printers' ink, the yeasty aroma of newsprint; curious aged figures carrying copy on battered trays with dregs of strong tea and the debris of chops and fried fish; the clatter of teleprinters and typewriters and the odd zones of silence somehow existing amidst the noise, like the cloister in a railway station. Paper everywhere, underfoot, clutched, pored over, discarded, even in the lavatories, agency copy available, brooded upon before using.'

In the history of the *Manchester Guardian* the period 1929–32 could not have been more dramatic and from Malcolm's perspective had all the makings of a tragic play. C. P. Scott had finally resigned the editorship in 1929 at the age of eighty-three, handing over to his son Edward (Ted). But to his son's dismay, the old man, tall, bearded and rubicund, could not stay away. He remained as 'Governing Director', kept his old office and continued to cycle three miles from his home to Cross Street in the evening to discuss the leaders for the following day's paper. The tradition was for C. P. Scott to discuss separately with each leader writer his suggestions for the five or six leaders that the paper published ('Got any subjects?' Malcolm reports him asking in his novel *Picture Palace*).

There was one main leader referred to as 'The Long' (1,000–1,100 words) and a number of shorter items, not all of which would be used. Each leader writer had special subjects in which he was supposed to be an expert, Malcolm's being India and Egypt. There were no conferences and according to the *Guardian* historian David Ayerst (*Guardian: Biography of a Newspaper*, 1971): 'A good *Guardian* man was expected to develop such an instinct for the paper's line that he would know without being told what the line should be even on an issue that had arisen that night for the first time.' Malcolm was introduced to this way of working at the beginning of his career when he was detailed to write a short leader (about 150 words) on corporal punishment. Uncertain how to approach it, he ventured to the office of a fellow leader writer, Paddy Monkhouse, to ask what the paper's line on corporal punishment might be. 'Same as capital only more so,' Monkhouse replied without even looking up from the typewriter.

Scott, Malcolm wrote later, 'tended to collect in the *Manchester Guardian* journalists with strong opinions and violent prejudices: they wrote better, could be paid less and were altogether more adventurous and enterprising than weaker brethren' (*New Statesman*, 16 March 1957). Malcolm himself came into this category. It was not the case, as he liked to insist years later, that the *Guardian* leaders were woolly-minded and pious, invariably expressing the hope that 'moderate men of all shades of opinion' would rally round to each and every crisis. His own comments tended to be highly provocative and even sensational, particularly on his pet subject of India, e.g. 'We simply cannot allow Winston Churchill to stage a new and improved version of the Black and Tan drama in India. No doubt it would be thrilling enough and all the eyes of the world would be upon it. But the cost is too great – in money, in blood, and in shame – and even if we were less squeamish about investing in murder, massacre and demoralization we should like a better guarantee than Mr Churchill's for his sanguinary speculations.' (29 July 1931)

Such writing was not at all to the taste of the news editor W. P. Crozier. Son of a Methodist minister and life-long teetotaller, Crozier was a grammatical pedant who had no love of over-statement. But from the start Malcolm had a firm ally in the (nominal) editor Ted Scott. Ted was a very different character

from his father whose shadow he had lived in for so long. 'The
son was as direct and simple as the father was diplomatic and
complex,' Kingsley Martin wrote. 'Ted Scott had no time for
political parties and distrusted most political leaders. He was an
economist, he was so reserved and so modest that the brashness
of his mind and the independence of character escaped the negli-
gent eye. He was of all men the most sincere and the least prejudiced.' True to his old friend Ransome's prediction, Scott
warmed to his eager and enthusiastic recruit. 'Ted Scott', wrote
A. J. P. Taylor, 'was bewitched by Malcolm's brilliance and
Malcolm could do what he liked.' He was allowed to go home
early and even got an unsolicited pay rise (an almost unheard of
happening at the *Guardian*). Ransome and Scott kept one another
informed about their special protégé – like two hens clucking
over their chick, according to Ransome's wife Genia. 'Considering how sure of himself and his opinions he is,' Scott wrote to
Ransome, 'he seems to me surprisingly modest in his general
deportment. But I remember being more than a little put out
when after they [Kitty and Malcolm] had accepted a dinner invitation he rather strongly pressed, without knowing who the
other guests were, that we should all go to hear a speech by
Sastri* which, if Malcolm hadn't mistaken the day, we should
probably have found was to be delivered about the dinner hour.
There are advantages in having been to a public school. He was
so naive and innocent about his desire to hear Sastri and so obviously assuming that he would be bored at the dinner that I for-
gave him without a great deal of difficulty. There are advantages
also to being a child in nature.'

For his part, Malcolm had taken an immediate shine to Ted
Scott, 'a man in his fifties with a large noble head, a grey
complexion, soft dark eyes and smile of great sweetness'.
Despite the difference in their age they formed the closest kind
of friendship, going for long walks together and as always
with Malcolm engaging in endless talk. 'I was fonder of him
I think', he told Ransome later, 'than of any man I have
come across.'

* A visiting Indian politician.

Scott soon found himself facing a dilemma. In August 1931 Ramsay MacDonald's Labour Government was hit by a financial crisis caused by a budget deficit in the balance of payments and, more seriously, a run on the pound. The banks insisted on a dramatic gesture, a cut in government expenditure, particularly in the unemployment benefit. An atmosphere of panic was generated and Montague Norman, the Governor of the Bank of England, gave orders that ration books should be printed in case the currency collapsed. Without waiting for proper consultation with the Labour Party, Ramsay MacDonald formed a National Government from all the three parties with four Labour ministers (MacDonald himself, Snowden, the Chancellor of the Exchequer, J. H. Thomas and Lord Sankey) continuing to serve in the Cabinet. These events provoked a ferocious debate on the left which was to last for years.

Most Liberals and 'moderates' sided with MacDonald but the bulk of Labour supporters branded him and his colleagues as traitors to their cause. The staff of the *Guardian* was as divided as everyone else. But the editor, Ted Scott, had gone on holiday leaving his deputy, Crozier, Malcolm's *bête noire* and a Liberal, in charge.

On 25 and 26 August Crozier wrote two leaders welcoming the National Government and praising Ramsay MacDonald: 'The National Government formed for a specific purpose and for a limited time, should be warmly approved by a country which is, as a rule, suspicious of a coalition. There is today an emergency of peace which is comparable to that of war.' (25 August 1931) 'Mr Snowden will be shortly able to administer to the children of his own household those few plain words which many of his opponents have endorsed, and he will do it cheerfully. Mr Thomas will bring to the Government his vigorous buoyancy. That Thomas feeling should be good for any Government.' (26 August 1931) (This last sentence was a reference to a famous advertisement of the time: 'Bovril prevents that sinking feeling'. It caused special offence with the anti-MacDonaldites.) Crozier's views provoked a rebellion among the young leader writers, Malcolm and Paddy Monkhouse. Malcolm, especially, disliked Crozier ('Scarlet face, fishy, hostile eyes') and Crozier, a tight-lipped man who seldom betrayed his feelings, was no doubt intolerant of Malcolm and envious of his special rapport with the editor Ted Scott. When Scott returned from his holiday he called a lunchtime meeting at his Withington home to which Crozier, A. P. Wadsworth, Malcolm and Monkhouse were summoned. Ted Scott was initially undecided but the eloquence of Malcolm won him round to the view of the young men of the left. From then on the *Guardian* was opposed to Ramsay Mac-Donald and the National Government. Crozier was humiliated and Malcolm returned home to Didsbury in triumph. 'He had a vision', Alan Taylor recalled, 'of leading the *Manchester Guardian* on some great campaign of liberation.' (*Guardian* 15 November 1990).

There followed a period of release for Malcolm in which he felt able to attack MacDonald to his heart's content. His sense of new-found freedom was shared by Ted Scott. On New Year's Day 1932 C. P. Scott finally died leaving his son free to edit the paper as he wished. Scott acquired a new vitality. He began to make changes in the paper. When Kingsley Martin saw him at this time he couldn't help noticing his new spirit of confidence. The experience of the 1931 crisis had braced him 'and I never saw him so eager and determined. The responsibility which had formerly been a heavy burden was at last squarely on his shoulders and easily borne. A crisis which had confused the pundits and shaken some reputations that seemed assured, had given him his opportunity and found him ready.' As for Malcolm, his future as a *Guardian* journalist looked rosy. He was the editor's closest friend and protégé. In due course, perhaps, he himself would become editor. Then suddenly it all crumbled to dust. On 22 April 1932 Ted Scott, who had gone on a sailing holiday in the Lakes with his fifteen-year-old son Richard, was drowned on Windermere. 'I drove up on the Friday morning,' Malcolm wrote. 'He had just bought a new Vauxhall car (I remember the grooves along the bonnet) and was in a particularly cheerful mood. I was to stay with some friends at Sawrey – the Spences' – for the Friday and Saturday nights, returning to Manchester on Sunday because I was working that day. Ted dined with us on the Saturday evening; we all laughed a lot and it was altogether a carefree, happy occasion. The next morning Mrs Spence drove me to Windermere where I caught a train back to Manchester. Sunday afternoon on any newspaper is fairly dreary and the *Guardian* was no exception. I was toying with the notion of proposing yet another leader on a project for the All-India Self-Governing Federation then under consideration when I was called to the telephone. It was Mrs Spence to tell me that Ted and Dick had been involved in a sailing accident on Lake Windermere and that Dick had been rescued but Ted was drowned. I found some difficulty in registering what she had said, bad news transmitted on the telephone is particularly bleak and unconvincing. "You mean it's all over; that Ted is?" "Yes," she said in a flat definite voice.'

Realizing that it would mean a crisis in the office, Malcolm went next door to tell Crozier. 'The effect was instantaneous and extraordinary. I saw, or thought I saw – the impression was very strong – some strips of bright yellow come into the scarlet of his face.' Later, Crozier came into his room to ask him to write Ted's obituary. With little to go on apart from a *Who's Who* entry, Malcolm set to work. 'When I came to Ted's editorship, I described with unnecessary gloating how he had drastically and courageously reversed the position first taken by the paper about the formation of MacDonald's National Government. As I worked on, I was aware of Crozier standing in the doorway of my room holding that particular sheet in his hand. He was looking distressed and said he thought I had over-stressed the change in the paper's attitude. Without stopping writing I said I left it to him to make any changes he considered desirable. Actually he didn't make any changes, and nor did I.* The episode, which I consider to be very discreditable, if not contemptible on my part, sealed the hostility between us.'

Crozier was in due course confirmed as editor, though the proprietor John Scott (Ted's brother) instructed him that he must

---

* Malcolm may be exaggerating here. The only reference in the obituary to the 1931 crisis is the following rather bland statement: 'He was responsible for the policy of the paper at a difficult time and, not allowing his principle to be obscured by immediate excitements, he initiated and sustained a policy which subsequent events have amply vindicated.

not deviate from the policies established by Ted, which meant consulting his special protégé, Malcolm. It was an awkward situation which neither of them relished. Malcolm, in any case, had no wish to stay, especially now that – as always – he had gone out of his way to bite the hand that fed him. In a mood of despair – grief for Ted Scott and dislike of Crozier – he decided to burn his boats and go to Russia. This suited Crozier who was as anxious to see the back of Malcolm as Malcolm was to leave. The *Manchester Guardian*'s man in Moscow, William Henry Chamberlin, was due to go on leave. It was arranged that Malcolm should take his place for a few months.

CHAPTER IV

Russia

MALCOLM'S DECISION TO go to Russia was once again made impulsively, but it had been on his mind for some time. As long ago as 1926 he had written to his father from India: 'I should like to see Russia and taste a communist despotism.' The idea had recurred during his short stay in Egypt where he conceived the idea of becoming a lecturer at a Russian University, and, with this in mind, began to take Russian lessons. It had been this possibility that made Arthur Ransome especially keen for the *Guardian* to sign him up before he might change his mind.

What was different now was the idea of staying in Russia permanently. Malcolm always maintained that this was both his and Kitty's original intention. Certainly they sold off those possessions which they considered 'bourgeois' – Malcolm's dinner jacket and Kitty's only long dress, various trinkets and oddments and most of their books. (None of these things, Malcolm decided, would be needed in a workers' state.) Yet it is hard to believe that either of them had seriously considered what might lie ahead. They had no money and had been forced to borrow from Alan Taylor (who insisted on the payment of interest). They had no idea where they were to live when they arrived in Russia. And what were they to do about their three-year-old son Leonard? Kitty, at least, had been to Russia, thanks to Mrs Webb, and knew what conditions were like there. Perhaps because of that, they decided to leave the child behind (at school in Windermere) with some vague hope that once they had settled down they would come and fetch him. Malcolm admitted later that this arrangement was 'hateful' at the time and had come to seem more hateful since.

Whatever they'd hoped, it was not quite as easy to emigrate to Russia as they might have thought. The relatively free and easy revolutionary era was over and there was now official suspicion towards foreigners, who were allowed to live in Russia only for a limited period of six months during which time they were 'on approval' as far as the regime was concerned. This rule applied especially to journalists who, if they left the country for a short time, were compelled to re-apply for a visa.

It was, in any case, an extraordinary moment at which to pledge one's life to Russian communism. In 1929, only three years prior to Malcolm's arrival, Stalin had embarked on his first Five Year Plan to turn Russia into a fully industrialized state. His ruthless scheme entailed the total abolition of private trade and private factories and the taking into state control of every single area of economic activity. Such a revolution could only be achieved by the enforced starvation of millions of peasants and assassination or imprisonment of dissenters, suppression of all forms of political opposition, the censorship of the press and the accumulation of vast powers by the dictator Stalin himself. It involved also the widescale use of near-slave labour on a number of vast industrial projects – the construction of power stations, dams, mines, etc. To ensure the subordination of the masses Stalin relied on non-stop party propaganda and the arbitrary use of terror on an enormous scale *'pour encourager les autres!'* Power on such a scale (over an estimated 160,000,000 people at that time) is something that had never been known before in the history of the world. Stalin maintained it until his death in 1953.

Yet it was in this brutal dictatorship, with its contempt of morality and freedom, that the left in Britain (and elsewhere) had invested all its hopes. To someone like Malcolm's father (and therefore to Malcolm) the Russian Revolution had been an inspiration and Lenin a hero. Without enquiring too closely about the facts, members of the Labour Party and many Liberals, the *Manchester Guardian* included, wove a remarkable dream of Russia as a promised land where the Bolsheviks were creating a new and classless society without all the inequalities and superstitions of the old world. (To many such people, the attempted suppression of Christianity in the Soviet Union was especially welcome.) Such views were reinforced at the time of the great depression of 1929 which seemed to show that *laisser-faire* capitalism had merely created unemployment and widescale poverty in the West. In America especially, where the effects of the depression were most marked, there was a correspondingly greater enthusiasm for Russia. But for the young, many of whom, like Malcolm, decided to emigrate to Russia at this time, political issues were not really relevant. J. M. Keynes commented that it was the relative success of capitalism rather than its apparent failure which had disillusioned young people: 'The idealistic young play with communism', he wrote, 'because it is the only spiritual appeal which feels to them contemporary.' In exactly this frame of mind, Malcolm wrote to Crozier shortly before his departure: 'What takes me to Russia is not communism but the birth of a new kind of civilization. Communism is as irrelevant as Catholicism or Protestantism: it will, like any other religion, have its day. The essential thing is the new values it embodies; and these once enunciated, cannot come to nothing. At least, so it seems now.'

In Britain, Stalin had no keener apologists than Mr and Mrs Sidney Webb. All their lives they had advocated the need for greater state control to remedy irregularity and many of their ideas had been adopted by the Labour Party. But it was in Russia, particularly since the depression and the collapse of the Labour Government, that they came to invest their hopes for the future. It was therefore entirely natural that, before setting off for Russia, Kitty and Malcolm should visit the Webbs at Passfield to receive their blessing. Mrs Webb strongly approved. 'Sidney and I have become icons in the Soviet Union,' she told Malcolm. She agreed to lend them money to help them adapt to their new way of life. She introduced them to the Russian ambassador in Britain, Sokolnikov (later to be a victim of the 1937 purge) who invited them to call when they arrived in Moscow. She confided in her diary:

Malcolm and Kitty are among the most gifted and certainly the most 'proletarian' of my nephews and nieces. They are intent on going to Russia for two or three years to qualify

Malcolm for British politics and I am going to give them a hundred pounds out of the remnants of Kate Courtney's estate to smooth their way – so that they may see how the land lies for earning a livelihood. It is characteristic of Kitty that she proposes to leave the little boy, aged three years, with the respectable lower-middle-class family in the adjacent flat. It is also characteristic that she and Malcolm and the child join up with the family for cooking purposes and share a 'char' and a room for the children to play in. So far, they seem devoted to each other; but Kitty definitely holds 'free love' opinions though apparently she feels no urge to practise what she preaches! Malcolm has a strain of mysticism and a trend towards puritanism in morals. Both of them are ascetic in their daily life. They live hard and despise 'show' and deny themselves what the well to do call comfort. In all these ways they would suit Russian conditions.

Kitty and Malcolm set sail from London on the Russian ship *Kooperatsia* which Malcolm found disappointingly similar to any other ship, apart from the portraits of Lenin and Stalin in the dining saloon rather than those of the King and Queen. On board were a number of fellow pilgrims – intellectuals and Labour politicians for the most part – all eagerly addressing the members of the crew as 'comrade' and providing Malcolm with a foretaste of what was to come. Shortly after sailing, these people held a meeting at which it was decided not to tip the crew but instead to hold a collection, the proceeds of which would be used to buy books for the ship's library. They also enacted for the benefit of the Russian sailors a comic version of the Genesis story which, Malcolm observed, 'seemed to please the players better than the audience'.

After docking in Leningrad, Malcolm and Kitty proceeded by train to Moscow where they put up at the newly built Moscowskaya Hotel. Perhaps aware that what was happening was of historical and also great personal significance, Malcolm began to keep a diary. Starting on 16 September 1932, he wrote: 'Today I arrived in Moscow. Already I have made up my mind to call this the Diary of a Journalist and not the Diary of a Communist.

Moscow is an exquisite city. All the time I alternate between complete despair and wild hope. Walking by the Kremlin and seeing the Red Flag float over the golden domes, I reflected that what made the revolution so attractive to a certain type of person was that, like revivalist religion, it exalts the humble and the meek.'

All his life, wherever he went in the world, Malcolm was a compulsive walker. In India, Egypt, America, Manchester – and later when he finally settled in Sussex – a large part of his day was given to walking, through the streets or across the countryside, in an attempt to overcome his almost manic restlessness. So now on arriving in Moscow he adopted his familiar routine, setting off from the Intourist Hotel and padding across the town. 'The streets feel good,' he wrote on the very first day, 'and six years in the East convinced me that mere inefficiency, even mere brutality, are not in themselves a condemnation of anything . . . Lenin's tomb is remarkable. For the two hours that it is open daily a constant procession of people file past the embalmed body. They take off their hats when they go and they do not talk; otherwise there is no ceremonial. No one kisses the glass round him or makes the sign of the Hammer and Sickle, or anything like that. They just stare . . .'

But Malcolm had a prophetic gift which often vouchsafed him startling insights which were completely at odds with his day-to-day thoughts and impressions. He had wanted to go to Russia to settle there permanently but at the same time he told Alan Taylor: 'I shall hate it.' So now, on his first day in Moscow, watching with admiration the crowds at Lenin's Tomb he was simultaneously seized with the idea that 'one day an enraged mob would tear him from his place and trample him underfoot'. As he wandered through the Russian capital he was alternately exhilarated and cast down. 'We went to Red Square yesterday,' he wrote; 'it seems to be perfect.' Some days later in a market he saw a peasant vomiting over a piece of sausage and it came to him that the man was actually starving. 'The doubt haunted him on the way back to his hotel', he wrote of himself in his novel *Winter In Moscow*. 'He saw hunger everywhere. In the faces that hurried past him, and in the patient queues and in the empty shops, dimly lighted and decorated with red streamers, whose windows contained only busts of Marx and Lenin and Stalin. Stone busts exposed to ravenous eyes . . .'

Such doubts could initially be countered. 'Conditions are bad,' said one official to Malcolm, 'but the comparison should be with an oriental country.' Another powerful argument advanced against evidence of hardship, famine and even terror was that such things were merely temporary, but also necessary if progress with the Five Year Plan was to be made. It was an argument succinctly expressed by the regime's most dedicated apologist among the Western correspondents, Walter Duranty of the *New York Times*, who repeatedly used the formula 'You can't make an omelette without breaking eggs' (an opinion first advanced in a long and extraordinarily banal poem about Red Square published in the *New York Times* in September 1932).

Malcolm soon found that the pressures on the representatives of the Western press were considerable. There is a regrettable tendency in any case for journalists in such a situation to fall in line and rely on official briefings or stories in the local press rather than pursue independent lines of enquiry. Pressmen are prone to form themselves, voluntarily, into clubs or 'lobbies' and to cherish the close contact they are given with authorities in exchange for co-operation. In Moscow such a process was accelerated by the operation of a strict censorship. When Malcolm first arrived in Moscow journalists had to take their reports in person to be scrutinized, queuing up like schoolboys to hand in an essay. If such a system was not sufficient there were other pressures. Those who had been some time in Russia (of whom there were many) had usually formed relationships with Russian women which could be exploited by the authorities. Malcolm later instanced what happened at a time when agitation had arisen in Britain about the use of political prisoners as forced labour in timber camps. For commercial reasons the government found the controversy inconvenient and Premier Molotov made a speech denying the existence of forced labour and inviting journalists to go and see for themselves. A train trip was organized but, unfortunately for Molotov, one correspondent managed to get hold of a government order to the GPU (the equivalent of the

KGB) telling them to withdraw all political prisoners from the railway zone. This he sent to his paper by diplomatic bag. He was then summoned to the Foreign Office and told that he must either contradict the report or leave the country within thirty-six hours:

'Well, he was married to a Russian,' Malcolm wrote, 'and he had a living to earn and did what most of us would have done in similar circumstances – telegraphed to his newspaper that he had been misinformed.' (*Time and Tide*, 26 May 1934) 'Nearly all foreign journalists in Russia', Malcolm wrote in his diary for 1 December 1932, 'are frightened of the Government and frightened to write anything that seriously displeases the bosses.' This did not mean they were unaware of what was going on. Malcolm was fortunate in that one of the best-informed journalists was the man he had been sent out to replace but who did not immediately leave: William Henry Chamberlin (he was always referred to by both Christian names), an American who contributed to the *Christian Science Monitor* as well as the *Manchester Guardian*. Malcolm immediately warmed to him: 'I like him very much, we have become friends,' he wrote to Crozier (27 October 1932).

Chamberlin had arrived in Moscow in 1922 with his Russian wife Sonya as a keen supporter of the revolution, but, like many reporters, had since become disillusioned. He was a short, podgy man who neither smoked nor drank but claimed to consume his weight annually in chocolate. (It was said that he even had a special dispensation from the Russian Government to import his own favourite chocolate.) A highly intelligent and industrious journalist, Chamberlin had a better grasp of what was going on in Russia at that time than almost any other reporter. His book *Russia's Iron Age*, published after he returned to the West (1935), remains an authoritative contemporary account of Stalinist Russia in its early stages. Chamberlin also had a highly developed sense of humour. He delighted Malcolm every week by cutting out an advertisement from the *Manchester Weekly Guardian* for a private mental home and posting it off to a public figure of whom he disapproved. One week it would be Mr Roosevelt, the next Bertrand Russell or the Indian poet Rabindranath Tagore.

A. T. Cholerton (known as Chol) was another correspondent with whom Malcolm immediately became friendly. A fellow of King's College, Cambridge, he was, when Malcolm came to Russia, the *News Chronicle* correspondent; later he joined the *Telegraph*. Bearded, consumptive and cynical, Cholerton lived in an untidy flat littered with books (mostly French) where Malcolm would find him stretched out on the sofa with a bottle of Red Caucasian wine beside him. Like Chamberlin, he had a Russian wife, Katerina Georgevna, with whom Malcolm later carried on a brief flirtation. Cholerton's attitude to the Russians was detached and satirical and he did much to foster Malcolm's speedy disillusionment with the regime. It was Cholerton who coined the phrase '*Habeas Cadaver*' as the Russian version of *habeas corpus*; Cholerton, who, when asked by an American tourist if the confessions in the show trials were true, gave the memorable reply: 'Everything is true except the facts.'

It was thanks to William Henry Chamberlin that Malcolm and Kitty were finally able to find somewhere to live. There was an acute housing shortage in Moscow. A Viennese businessman friend, Herr Fremnde, offered to rent them his dacha at Kliasma, a summer resort for middle-class Muscovites and foreigners about 35km from Moscow. This was a stroke of luck and for a short time Malcolm's spirits rose. 'The air is dry and exhilarating', he wrote, 'and we look over a lovely wide plain covered with pine trees.' He went for long walks through the forest and began to take Russian lessons from Klaudia Lvona, and even to look forward to having their baby son reunited with them under the same roof.

The difficulty was that he had hardly any money coming in. Crozier's plan that he should replace Chamberlin as the *Manchester Guardian* correspondent fell through when Chamberlin changed his plans. Malcolm was forced therefore to become a freelance for the time being. To make things worse, Kitty, who was pregnant again, became seriously ill with typhus (then prevalent in Russia). The immediate worry was that it would harm the child, but a German doctor who was brought to the house of Herr Fremnde reassured them. There was nothing to be done but to remain in bed. Malcolm wondered whether Kitty should go to hospital, whereupon the doctor gave him a look of absolute horror and silently crossed himself – another vivid indication of conditions in Russia being rather different from what they had imagined. For the next few days Malcolm nursed Kitty, washing her, administering enemas, reading Shakespeare to her and sleeping on the floor beside her bed. His worry was that he himself would become infected.

> I believe I'm going to have this fever myself but am saying nothing to Kit in the hope that she may be more or less recovered before I sicken. She said there was nothing in life except love and work. I agree. When I looked at her face, flushed with fever, and with my child stuck in her belly, my inside melts. Mere passion is only the beginning of love. People who don't have children and don't go through troubles together can't really love.

In desperation at the lack of journalistic work and housebound because of Kitty's illness, Malcolm started work on a novel based on his time in Manchester and eventually published under the title of *Picture Palace*. It was his second attempt at a novel – the first, *Autumnal Face* (1931), was a study of suburban life set in Croydon, the characters based partly on his own family and the Pitmans. Where the mood of *Autumnal Face* was one of unrelieved gloom – one reviewer, L. P. Hartley (author of *The Go-Between*), described it, with justification, as 'the most depressing book I have ever read' – *Picture Palace* was an altogether superior attempt, the writing bold, flowery and satirical. Malcolm pinned great hopes on the book, though it ought to have been plain to him from the beginning that without at least an attempt to disguise the characters there was bound to be a risk of libel.

The centrepiece of the story, which like all of Malcolm's novels was really a series of inter-related sketches, was a satirical picture of C. P. Scott, who from the remote perspective of Russia had no doubt come to seem more unattractive and irrelevant than ever. He was portrayed as 'Old Savoury', a bearded, ruddy-cheeked humbug in the Dickensian tradition. The book opens with the old man at the age of eighty still at his desk leafing through the press cuttings which celebrated his eightieth birthday.

> The press cuttings were a solace to him. As the future dwindled, they became more precious. Phrases from them lingered in his mind – 'a great editor' – 'integrity and courage' – 'powerful and beneficial influence on English journalism'. He played with such phrases, using them like bricks to rebuild the past, to recreate its triumphs and certainties, its happiness and fulfilled ambition.
> Bending closely over his press cuttings he read them through yet once more, turning each word over and over in his mind to enjoy its full flavour:
>
>> Both those who disagree and those who agree with Mr John Savoury's political views – and the former are, and always have been more numerous – will rejoice to hear that he celebrated his eightieth birthday yesterday, still in full possession of his faculties, still at work. British journalism owes much to him. His name will live . . .
>
> His name would live! The old man rubbed his hands gently together. If his name lived, then death lost much of its terror. Cold eternity glowed with the radiance of his name: and the future became suddenly familiar, friendly, because it contained his living memory.

Apart from the picture of C. P. Scott, the main interest of the book lies in the picture it gives of the early life of Kitty and Malcolm. Malcolm's novels, not all of which were published, were an uneasy mix of realism and satire – the realism consisting invariably of a self-portrait of the author as a tormented soul, wracked by frustration and guilt and desperately seeking the meaning of life. Like all unsuccessful novelists, Malcolm was incapable of imagining fictional characters; his men and women are real people, thinly disguised, viewed with a satirist's rather than a novelist's eye. In *Picture Palace* he introduces, in addition to Scott, various friends and colleagues from his time in Manchester. They include his fellow leader writer Kingsley Martin, in whose house Kitty and Malcolm first stayed when they came to Manchester. Later they moved to a ground-floor flat in a house in Wilmslow Road nearby where their fellow tenants were A. J. P. Taylor and his wife Margaret. Taylor, who also appears in *Picture Palace*, was then a young don at Manchester University. He became a close friend of Malcolm and remained so for the rest of his life in spite of all their religious and political differences. Many years later Malcolm wrote to him and asked if he would speak at his funeral (Alan agreed but died shortly before Malcolm in 1990).

Aside from Malcolm himself (Pettygrew), the only rounded character in the book was Kitty. Their early life together is like something out of D. H. Lawrence. Everyone is obsessed with sex and the men's relationships with one another are as intense as those they have with women. Kitty (Gertrude) is bored with life stuck in a flat with a small baby. She and Malcolm quarrel frequently or indulge in 'lechery' (a favourite Muggeridge word). Malcolm is so absorbed by his leader-writing that he even goes to bed composing imaginary leaders about himself and his wife.

> Mr and Mrs Pettygrew got involved in another discussion about their lives yesterday. The cause, as so often has been the case in the past, was a quite trivial incident. Mrs Pettygrew gave expression in emphatic terms to her discontent, and Mr Pettygrew launched out on a long and extremely tedious exposition of its basic causes. The episode is the more regrettable in that Mrs Pettygrew is about to become a mother. As long as Mr and Mrs Pettygrew are liable to these outbursts, they cannot hope to enjoy any kind of security, or to be, in any real sense of the word, peaceful or even happy together. It is greatly to be hoped that the passage of time will dull their sensibilities, and thus enable them . . .

At this late date it is impossible to tell how much of the action in *Picture Palace* is true, how much imagined. In one scene Alan Taylor (Rattray) goes walking arm in arm with Malcolm (Pettygrew) and confides in him that he is in love with Kitty (Gertrude). Malcolm's response is magnanimous and he urges Taylor to sleep with her: 'You must, you must, it'll strengthen the bond between us'. Emboldened, Taylor then makes a pass at Kitty, whereupon Malcolm becomes insanely jealous.

There may well have been an element of truth in all this. Taylor in his memoirs describes Kitty as 'staggeringly beautiful'. However, where women were concerned, he was timid and gauche, only achieving sexual fulfilment in his third marriage – so it is highly unlikely that there was anything at all in the nature of an affair. What Taylor also describes in his memoirs, published many years later, was a true incident when Kitty left Malcolm and ran away to London – Taylor remembered Malcolm running alongside the train as it drew out of the station calling out 'Goodbye, some day perhaps our paths will cross again.' Malcolm himself had no memory of this, though the incident undoubtedly inspired the final chapters of his novel when Gertrude leaves Pettygrew to go to London. The letter she leaves behind reads as if it is a direct transcript of a letter written by Kitty:

> I've decided not to come back to Acringthorpe [Manchester] and not live with you any more. This is not because I don't love you or because I think you don't love me, or because I've fallen in love with someone else. It's because I know that, if we go on living together, we shall get to hate each other. I can't bear to think of hating you, or of you hating me. Also, as you've often said, quarrelling makes a horrible atmosphere for a child to grow up in. I'm not satisfied with being just a mother-housekeeper and I shan't be satisfied, I know, with being a secretary, or an actress, or a between-maid or whatever I have to be to earn a living. I know you so well and I love you so much, and this is the best thing to do.

In the event, according to Taylor, Kitty returned to Manchester the following day.

It is not clear from Malcolm's diary at what point he abandoned his plan to live in Russia. One can only assume that it became apparent to both of them at an early stage that it was out of the question. After Kitty's illness and what they had seen of Russian medicine it would have been equally obvious that she could not risk having a baby in Russia. She therefore decided to return to England – for the time being at least. 'I remember very vividly her face at the window as the train steamed away,' Malcolm wrote in his memoirs, 'smiling and serene as though she would be back in the evening. Actually she was leaving with practically no money and only a dubious prospect of staying with my mother.'

For the first time since they married Malcolm and Kitty were apart and Malcolm immediately began to exhibit the symptoms which were to mark all their periods of separation – increased restlessness, depression, heavy drinking and womanizing. The future suddenly seemed uncertain. 'It sometimes comes to me with a pang of horror that I am earning practically nothing . . . God help me. It crossed my mind that after all I could always commit suicide. I wonder how many suicides there are in Russia? A lot I should think.' He courted Cholerton's wife Katerina Georgevna (who eventually submitted to his advances) and wandered aimlessly around Moscow, sometimes with Sonya Chamberlin. Then to the Foreign Office to be given a copy of Stalin's latest speech. 'The whole thing was like a gangster play . . . it was all fantastic – outside, bread queues . . . and here in the Foreign Office, a crowd of villainous-looking foreign press correspondents sending off messages about an insane speech . . . Again I felt ready to die.'

He moved out of the Chamberlins' flat and into a hotel. He had very little to do except respond to Crozier's occasional demands for a piece. He finished his *Guardian* novel. He went skating with Sonya Chamberlin. And, as always, he tramped around the streets noting 'the gloom of Moscow on a cold grey day when the streets are full of slush; glaring crowds with anxious faces and shabby clothes; people leaning against a wall because too weak to stand; obscene slogans printed on buildings; queues waiting for bread; peasants wandering futilely about the streets; only soldiers well dressed and well fed with occasional vulgarly smart women; cruelty in the air.'

One idea, however, was forming in his mind. Some days before Kitty's departure a young man had knocked at the door of the Chamberlins' flat to see the correspondent of the *Manchester*

Guardian. Malcolm asked his Russian teacher and secretary Klaudia Lvovna to interpret. Terrified of being compromised in some way, she refused. Cholerton, however, asked the man to come back later, which he did, bringing a pile of newspapers and a pamphlet. He was from the North Caucasus, he said, where people were starving and being shot for storing grain, much of which was being exported. 'Ask them abroad not to buy our food. Tell them to stop buying. Otherwise we are ruined.' After he left, Cholerton and Malcolm translated the papers he had brought. Malcolm wrote in his diary, as if recording a historical event: 'The treatment of the peasants by the Soviet Government was in its way one of the worst crimes in history' – an extraordinary instance of the way he sometimes arrived at the truth spontaneously with an almost mystical intuition.

His intuition appeared to be confirmed by a meeting on 4 January 1933 with a Dr Rosen who had come to Russia from America during the Revolution to help with famine relief and had stayed to run a Jewish settlement. 'Peasants, he told us, are wandering about in their thousands with their bodies swollen by lack of food. What has happened is simply that the Government, having, by its collectivization policy, ruined agriculture is now engaged in extracting every ounce of food left in the country to feed its friends during the winter. After that it proposes to reverse policy – let the peasants pay a tax in kind, leaving them to dispose of the rest of their produce as they see fit. Meanwhile the peasants have to live through the winter as best they can. Millions of them will die.'

Rosen clearly impressed Malcolm and on 11 January he went to see him again: 'There was something exquisitely simple and ascetic about him. He spoke about the situation with a quiet despair ". . . nothing can alter the fact that horses and cattle have been, to the extent of at least 50%, destroyed." He told a characteristic story. Owing to lack of fodder an epidemic had broken out amongst such horses as still remain in the country. To deal with the situation the GPU arrested almost the entire staff of the Moscow college of veterinary studies on the grounds that they were saboteurs and had been sending infections out to the villages in order to frustrate the Government's efforts to build Socialism.'

All this made Malcolm decide that he ought to try and report what was going on in the countryside. On 14 January 1933, ten days after the meeting with Dr Rosen, he wrote to Crozier in Manchester: 'It is becoming increasingly obvious to me that the only way to write properly about the existing situation in Russia is to visit the provinces – especially the North Caucasus, Kuban and if possible, West Siberia. Would the MG be prepared to advance thirty pounds in return for, say, a five thousand word article on the condition of the peasants and of agriculture in Russia as a result of the Five Year Plan and collectivization? If so, would you please send me a telegram saying "Go", pay thirty pounds into my Manchester bank account and I'll leave at once. I'm sending this letter by someone who's travelling to England.' Crozier agreed and the single word telegram 'Go' was sent.

Before setting off Malcolm wrote to Beatrice Webb unburdening his feelings:

My Dear Aunt Bo,
   I feel very guilty about not having written to you before. As a matter of fact I've tried several times, but somehow found myself dumb. Coming here has, intellectually and in every way, turned me inside out, and in the process of being turned inside out it's difficult to express oneself except extravagantly and incoherently. I want to explain that my feelings about Soviet Russia are not based in a balancing of achievement against failure, of profit and loss, but an overwhelming conviction that the Government and all it stands for, its crude philosophy (religion if you like) is evil and a denial of everything I care for in life, everything that makes me believe, however chaotic and unhappy social circumstances become, it is still lovely to be alive and stay warm while having children to live on after I am dead.
   You'll say I haven't seen enough, haven't met enough Russians, have mixed too much with foreign diplomats, but I've seen, I know I've seen, the essence of the thing, its spirit, the mood it engenders, the kind of person in whom it invests power, the set of values – moral, aesthetic, spiritual – it encourages. And I'm more sure than I've ever been sure of

anything in my life that this is bad and that it is based on the most evil and most cruel elements in human nature.

Of course the Marxist says: 'Characteristic bourgeois-intellectual view!' Perhaps it is. I can't help it. It's my view and to pretend otherwise would be futile and dishonest. I saw the other day a physical culture demonstration in the Opera House. Lusty youths and girls, limelight playing on them, girls with shaven armpits, built socialism with imaginary hammers and shot at class enemies with imaginary rifles all to the tune of 'If you were the only girl in the world and I was the only boy'. There was the whole story – Tamerlane and big business. The whole arranged like a shop window in the best manner of Semitic salesmanship.

So you see, I've become extravagant and incoherent. But the horror of it! The humbug! Why should uncle Sidney say in Edinburgh 'I indignantly repudiate the slander that there is forced labour in the Soviet Union' when every single person in Russia knows that there is forced labour; that whole villages in the North Caucasus have been recently sent to cut timber, to dig canals for no wages and a starvation diet; when the Foreign Office officials themselves admit the facts and shrug their shoulders . . . Can you imagine, Aunt Bo, a government which boasts particular concern for the welfare of the masses offering food only for gold or foreign currency in starving cities; or taking from millions of peasants every scrap of grain they produced, leaving them without any food at all; and then announcing that the standard of life of workers and peasants has risen, proving the point by wage statistics in paper roubles? 'He must think we're children', a communist said to me after reading Stalin's speech. It's absurd to go on like this. Only I have such an admiration for the work you've done and have spent so many happy hours talking with you, and am so fond of you that I hate to think of you upholding something that I know you'd hate if you knew its real character. Please forgive this rather arrogant letter; but it's the only kind of letter I can write just now.

Famine on a massive scale was nothing new in revolutionary Russia. In 1921–23 there had been widespread famine and the

Bolsheviks had appealed for help from the West and received 66 million dollars from the USA. The difference now was that the famine was being used by Stalin as a means of smashing the opposition to his collective farm policy as well as any lingering Ukrainian resistance to communist rule. This was the point that Malcolm made: 'To say that there is famine in some of the most fertile parts of Russia is to say much less than the truth; there is not only famine, but a state of war, a military occupation.'

Malcolm had set off by train from the Russian capital one day in mid-February. He reported to the *Guardian*:

Living in Moscow and listening always to statements of doctrine and of policy, you forget that Russia is a country stretching over a sixth of the world's surface and that the lives of a hundred and sixty million people, mostly peasants, are profoundly affected by discussions and resolutions that seem, when you hear or read of them in the press, as abstract as the proceedings of a provincial debating society. 'We must collectivize agriculture', or 'We must root out Kulaks (the rich peasants)'. How simple it sounds! How logical! But what is going on in the remote villages? In the small households of the peasants? What does the collectivization of agriculture mean in practice in the lives of the peasants? What results has the new 'drive' produced? What truth, if any, is there in the gloomy reports that have been reaching Moscow? That is what I wanted to find out . . .

A little market town in the Kuban district of North Caucasia suggested a military occupation: Worse, active war. There were soldiers everywhere, in the railway station, in the streets, everywhere. Mongols with leaden faces and slit eyes: others obviously peasants, rough but not brutal; occasional officers dapper, often Jews: all differing notably from the civilian population in one respect. They were well fed and the civilian population was obviously starving in its absolute sense: not undernourished as, for instance, most oriental peasants are undernourished and some unemployed workers in Europe, but having had, for weeks, next to nothing to eat. Later, I found out there had been no bread at all in the place for three months, and such food as there was I saw for myself in the market place. The only edible thing there in the lowest European standards was chicken – about five chickens – fifteen roubles each. The rest of the food offered for sale was revolting and would be thought unfit, in the ordinary way, to be offered to animals. There was sausage at fifteen roubles the kilo; there was black cooked meat which worked out, I calculated, at a rouble for three bites; there were miserable fragments of cheese and some cooked potatoes, half rotten. A crowd wandered backwards and forwards eyeing these things wistfully, too poor to buy. The few who bought, gobbled their purchases ravenously then and there.

It is literally true that whole villages have been exiled. In some cases demobilized soldiers have moved in to take the place of the exiles. I saw myself a group of some twenty peasants being marched off under escort. This is so common a sight that it no longer even arouses curiosity.

Travelling north to Rostov-on-Don, Malcolm saw further evidence of coercion:

On the platform a group of peasants were standing in military formation, five soldiers armed with rifles guarding them. There were men and women, each carrying a bundle. Somehow, lining them up in military formation made the thing grotesque – wretched-looking peasants, half-starved, tattered clothes, frightened faces, standing to attention. These may be Kulaks, I thought, but if so they have made a mightily poor thing of exploiting their fellows. I hung about looking on curiously, wanting to ask where they were to be sent – to the north to cut timber, somewhere else to dig canals – until one of the guards told me sharply to take myself off.

The Ukraine is a more separate country than the North Caucasus. It has a language of its own and an art of its own; Southern rather than Eastern, with white good houses and easy-going people. Even now you can see that it has been used to abundance. There is nothing pinchback about the place; only, as in the North Caucasus, the population is starving. 'Hunger' was the word I heard most. Peasants begged a lift on the train from one station to another, sometimes their bodies swollen up – a disagreeable sight – from lack of food. There were fewer signs of military terrorism than in the North Caucasus . . . Otherwise it was the same story – cattle and horses dead; fields neglected; meagre harvest despite moderately good climate conditions; all the grain that was produced taken by the Government; now no bread at all, no bread anywhere, nothing much else either; despair and bewilderment. The Ukraine was before the revolution one of the world's great wheat-producing areas and even Communists admit that its population, including the poor peasants, enjoyed a tolerably comfortable standard of life; now it would be necessary to go to Arabia to find cultivators in more wretched circumstances.

Malcolm's report (printed in three separate articles in the *Guardian*, 26, 27 and 28 March 1933) was the first contemporaneous account of the famine by a Western journalist. It created considerable alarm in Moscow coming, as it did, at a time when Stalin was conducting a strenuous campaign to receive official recognition by the USA. Malcolm was denounced in the English language propaganda paper the *Moscow Daily News* as a liar and a ban was quickly introduced on journalists' travel in the famine areas. It was to stay in place until the following year. Official alarm was heightened when Malcolm's account of the famine was confirmed by another writer. Gareth Jones, son of a Welsh headmaster, was a former political secretary of Lloyd George and a fluent Russian speaker who in 1933 went on a walking tour of Russia. His findings were reported in the *Guardian* on 30 March 1933. Jones quoted an expert as estimating that one million out of five million people in Kazakstan had died of hunger and gave his opinion that 'after Stalin, the most hated man was Bernard Shaw'. He described travelling in a train with a communist who denied there was any famine: 'I flung into the spittoon a crust of bread I had been eating from my own supply. The peasant, my fellow passenger, fished it out and ravenously ate it. I threw an orange peel into the spittoon, again the peasant grabbed and devoured it. The communist subsided.' (Malcolm later incorporated this story in *Winter in Moscow*.)

Coming on top of Malcolm's three reports, Jones's interview

led to an extraordinary and incredible incident involving the Moscow Press Corps. It happened that the trial was about to begin in two days' time, of a group of British engineers working for Metro-Vickers, who were accused of being spies. There was enormous interest in the trial and newspapers all over the world had sent special correspondents to cover it. Constantine Oumansky, the head of the Press Office, realizing how great was the interest in a show trial involving foreigners, proposed a deal with the press: they would only be permitted to cover the Metro-Vickers trial so long as the Muggeridge/Jones stories about the famine were immediately repudiated. A deal on these lines was patched up and a celebration party complete with vodka and canapés ensued. On 31 March, two days before the trial was due to begin, Walter Duranty, the most prestigious of the correspondents, reported in the *New York Times* that there was no famine, repeating his famous 'omelette' tag and adding an Orwellian gloss, 'There is no actual starvation or death from starvation but there is widespread mortality from diseases due to malnutrition.' Later in the year, Duranty sailed to America with the Soviet Foreign Minister Litvinov to take part in the formal recognition of the USSR by President Roosevelt.

Thus the contemporary coverage of one of the world's most infamous crimes, involving, it is now estimated, the death of eight million people, petered out. If not actually contradicting the Muggeridge/Jones account, Duranty and the *New York Times* had succeeded in creating a smokescreen of doubt. And in the meantime, editors had focused their attention, as far as Russia was concerned, on the trial of the Metro-Vickers engineers. The fate of six British citizens was considered more newsworthy than that of six million or so Russian peasants.

Still, the arrest of six British engineers (one of them a cousin of Malcolm's *Guardian* colleague Paddy Monkhouse) showed how foreigners were not immune from random charges of espionage. Malcolm left Moscow as the Metro-Vickers trial was about to begin. Afterwards he was plagued by the thought that he left because he was afraid. This was certainly hinted by his Foreign Office friend from Moscow, William Strang, when he met him the following year in Geneva. It may be that he was alarmed by the arrest of the engineers on trumped up charges of espionage. But afraid of what? It is unlikely that the Russian Government would have moved against a foreign correspondent, they would simply have refused to renew his visa which had, in any case, nearly expired. He wrote in his diary: 'If I was afraid, it was not of the Bolo's, but for Kit. This episode is one of the most curious in my life. I came away from Moscow, I thought, reluctantly. There was Kit with her baby. There was Katerina Georgevna. There was the hysterical excitement of the trial . . .'

What happened, as usual with Malcolm who seldom made a calculated move in his life, was that he was again acting purely on impulse. Even before he went to the Ukraine he was thinking about leaving. 'It's no good my staying in Russia,' he wrote on 27 January 1933, adding, two days later after a ticking off by the Press Censor, Nehman, 'As I left him, I had a yearning to get away from Russia; to leave it all to come to its wretched end without me watching and writing about it.' Once again, his relationship with Crozier in Manchester had become strained. Malcolm's articles on the famine were a major scoop, but Crozier's reaction had been lukewarm. 'I have now read your articles,' he wrote on 8 March. 'They are, I think, extraordinarily interesting and fascinating. I am rather sorry that you did not restrict yourself to a plain, matter-of-fact statement of what you saw . . . If we denounce we are apt to be in unpleasant company.' Malcolm was not in any mood to listen. He had written to Crozier the same day: 'My time here is coming to an end. Chamberlin will be back in a few weeks . . . You know the mood I came here in, and you must have gathered from what I've written about Russia, the mood that being here has engendered. For my part, I believe that every scrap of support and encouragement given by the MG to illusions and hopes, understandable enough, about what is going on here is a crime.'

Malcolm was further aggravated by the *Guardian*'s treatment of his dispatches on the Metro-Vickers arrests. 'As MGs come and I realize how you've cut my messages about the Metrovick affair, I feel utterly disgusted. I took considerable trouble to send them, and even a certain amount of personal risk, and the result is that the *Guardian* has nothing that I couldn't have got from Reuters . . . The [Russian] F. O. people say, "Why should we bother about whether Muggeridge gets round the censor or not, the MG is at least as strict as we are." They laugh at you. They laugh at the kind of absurdities fed by the Embassy to your London correspondents. I'm going away in about a week.' (23 March 1933)

The *Guardian* had not given Malcolm's exclusive any great prominence – partly, to be fair, because it coincided with equally graphic reports by their German correspondent F. A. Voigt of Nazi persecution of Jews in Germany. He had a point, however, when he accused Crozier of playing down his reports. The inclination of the paper had always been to give Russia the benefit of the doubt, perhaps because the Bolsheviks were under constant attack from the right. There was also a very well organized propaganda campaign in operation by British communists and fellow-travellers who were ready to answer any hostile comment. An earlier report of Malcolm's in January referring to conditions in the Caucasus had also provoked a long letter to the *Manchester Guardian* from Bernard Shaw and other dignitaries (2 March 1933). This referred in outraged tones to a

particularly offensive and ridiculous attempt to portray the condition of workers as one of slavery and starvation. We the undersigned are recent visitors to the USSR. Some of us have travelled throughout the greater part of its civilized territory. We desire to record that we saw nowhere evidence of such economic slavery, privation, unemployment and cynical despair of betterment as are accepted as inevitable and ignored by the press as having 'no news value' in our own countries. Everywhere we saw a hopeful and enthusiastic working class, self-respecting, free up to the limits imposed on them by nature and the terrible inheritance from the tyranny and incompetence of their former rulers, developing public works, increasing health services, extending education, achieving the economic independence of women and the security of the child, and – in spite of many grievous difficulties and the mistakes which all social experiments involve at first (and which they have never concealed or denied) setting an example of industry and conduct which would greatly enrich us if our system supplied our workers with any incentive to follow it.

Another typical example of the Russian propaganda campaign and the susceptibility of the *Manchester Guardian* occurred when Gareth Jones's report confirming Malcolm's account of the famine was published. Directly below it, given almost equal length, was the account of a speech made to the Education Workers' League in Pendleton by P. A. Sloan, a former lecturer at Bangor University, criticizing correspondents in Russia for failing to make contact with workers or students. Starvation, he said 'had existed with far greater severity in pre-Revolution days and peasants now tended to complain a lot more, because they were so much better off under the new regime.'

Apart from the famine, Malcolm's most enduring memories of the Soviet Union were of prominent visitors like Shaw, taken round by Intourist guides – all blind to the nature of what was going on. These pilgrims, suitably caricatured, were to feature prominently in his novel *Winter in Moscow*, the book in which Malcolm incorporated many of his Russian experiences and in which most of his journalistic colleagues are portrayed.

Stalin attached great importance to securing favourable publicity in the West and much thought was given to the reception of foreign visitors. Hospitality was a lavish affair and special trains were provided to transport the sightseers. Model factories and prisons were laid open to inspection, though it is likely that the most fervent of the 'political pilgrims' would have enthused even without such sights.

They were determined to see nothing but good and had an answer for even the slightest criticism. Thus when Kitty complained to Beatrice Webb about the poor quality of the food – worse, she said than that which unemployed men in Manchester would expect – Mrs Webb replied: 'Well, my dear Kitty, if you don't like the food you can always order rice pudding – I do.'

William Henry Chamberlin reported Bernard Shaw, on the Metro-Vickers engineers, to the effect that they would get a fairer trial in Russia than anywhere else. An even more idiotic suggestion was made by Shaw to Sonya Chamberlin during his visit to Moscow in July 1931. Shaw had announced in a speech that as he had approached the Russian frontier he threw out of the train window all the hampers which anxious friends – convinced of a shortage of food in the Soviet Union – had given him prior to his trip. Later, Mrs Chamberlin remarked to him that Russians would have been grateful for the food. She herself, she said, could get enough milk for her four-year-old daughter because she was a foreigner. But if she had been dependent on Soviet milk ration, the little girl would have had milk only once or twice during the month. 'You could nurse her yourself,' Shaw said. 'I think she is a little bit old for that.' 'Nonsense,' said Shaw. 'The Eskimos nurse their children until they are twenty years old.'

Such was the extraordinary credulity of these visitors that at one stage the correspondents (notably Malcolm and his friend Cholerton) devised a contest to see who could circulate the most improbable story. Malcolm was considered to have won after an exchange with a visiting Labour peer and friend of the Webbs, Lord Morley. When asked why it was that there were so many queues in Moscow, Malcolm replied that Stalin was so concerned about the long hours being worked by the Muscovites that he had devised queues as a means of ensuring that they were guaranteed a certain amount of leisure.

More puzzling, perhaps, was the way in which others, non-communists with no special political leanings, were prepared to buttress Stalin and his regime. The most striking example was Duranty, who had used his influence to pooh-pooh Malcolm's report of the famine. Duranty was an Englishman who for many years represented the *New York Times* in Moscow, acquiring an almost celebrity status. Portrayed as Jefferson in *Winter in Moscow* he certainly was not a Communist, merely a shrewd and observant reporter who was liked and admired by a number of colleagues – even Malcolm, who, though he took an instinctive dislike to him when they first met, later confessed to finding him a convivial and amusing companion.

Born in 1884, Duranty was the son of a Liverpool businessman. Educated at Harrow and Bedford School, he read Classics

at Cambridge and subsequently, when living in Paris, became a
protégé of the notorious Satanist Aleister Crowley, the so-called
'Beast', joining him in obscene black magic rituals, devil worship
and opium-smoking sessions (prudently he kept quiet subsequently about these episodes). He became a reporter during
the First World War, losing a leg in a railway accident, and won
rapid promotion on the *New York Times*.

He went to Moscow in 1921 and remained there on and off
until 1928, becoming the doyen of the press corps and even
winning the Pulitzer Prize in 1932. Though Duranty acknowledged in some of his later reports that there had indeed been a
large number of deaths, his general tenor was one of support for
the regime. Reporting in September the same year from Rostov-
on-Don he began, 'The use of the word "famine" in connection
with the North Caucasus is a sheer absurdity. There is a bumper
crop being harvested as fast as tractors, horses, oxen, men,
women and children can work . . . Husky girls are hoisting
wheat to the threshing machines. Village markets are flowing
with eggs, fruit, poultry, vegetables, milk and butter at prices
lower than in Moscow.'

Asked later to analyse Duranty's motives by the *American
Mercury* – the article was never published because it was considered libellous – Malcolm tried to answer the question 'Why
should Duranty have devoted his considerable talents to justify-
ing the brutality and hypocrisy of a Government whose professed
aims are alien to its nature?'

He recalled, to begin with, a party given in Moscow where
he had remarked to Duranty that the scene was rather like the
ball before the Battle of Waterloo:

> He leant forward screwing up his face flushed and shiny.
> 'They'll harness peasants to the plough and drive them like
> horses!' The contempt in his voice! Peasants harnessed to
> ploughs, driven along by a whip – 'Gee up! Wo Back!' Why
> not – only peasants, Russian peasants at that, and any number
> of them available, a hundred million?
>
> That gave the key to his character. Power – that was what
> he worshipped. Other governments had to flatter, bribe, cheat,

trick, cajole; but here, whip in hand, the Government just drove. Here the Government's power was limitless, unrestricted by the suffering which its exercise might inflict on individual men and women, by any considerations whatsoever. He liked that. He rubbed his hands gleefully over that. It was good.

In the end the same explanation applied to the Webbs. Though they professed admiration for Stalin's economic and industrial achievements, it was ultimately his immense power that commanded their respect and even reverence. Malcolm never forgot how, on his farewell visit to Passfield Corner just before he and Kitty sailed for Russia, Mrs Webb had suddenly pronounced, as she sat warming her hands by the fire, 'It's true that in the USSR people *disappear*.' It was said, Malcolm reflected, more in an envious than accusatory tone. 'Clearly she would have been well content to promote the disappearance of tiresome people in the same expeditious way, with no questions asked. Some of the more difficult and obscurantist figures in local government for instance. Among trade union leaders, no lack of candidates. Yes, people *disappeared*.'

Apart from power there was also a strong religious element involved – though this is not often referred to. Even if they did not say so publicly, supporters of the Soviet Government welcomed its strenuous efforts to impose atheism and eradicate Christianity almost more than anything else that had been done. Typical in this respect was A. J. P. Taylor, who had been appalled by Malcolm's *Guardian* articles. In a long letter, he outlined to him what had been achieved by the Bolsheviks, instancing 'the marriage laws which have destroyed the humble Christian family and made people, for the first time, free in their personal relations. Then think of the fact that a new generation is growing up free from Christianity – that's something worthwhile.'

As her diary shows, Beatrice Webb was by nature a spiritual person who searched, often despairingly, for some kind of religion. (It was this side to her that, despite their political differences, endeared her to Malcolm in the end.) Yet, brought up as

75

she had been under the influence of her parents' friend, the agnostic Herbert Spencer, she could not give credence to Christianity. There is no doubt that in the end communism became for her, and for others, a substitute for religion.

The truth is, that although Mrs Webb read carefully the reports of the Ukraine famine by Malcolm and Gareth Jones, this woman who set such great store by facts, figures and statistics, was not really disturbed by them. She was incapable of absorbing the information and adjusting her view. She comforted herself with the thought that Malcolm was not objective – he had become anti-Semitic. She noted in her diary that Sidney, at any rate, was undaunted: 'The thought that there may be famine in some districts in the USSR does not disturb his faith in the eventual triumph of the Soviet Economic Principle of planned production for the needs of the whole community.'

Another curious incident which remained in Malcolm's mind took place on a subsequent visit by Kitty and Malcolm to Passfield Corner. As they were leaving, Beatrice Webb asked Malcolm to come upstairs. She opened the door of a small and otherwise empty room. There, on show like an icon, with special lighting from below, was a portrait of Lenin (presented to her by the Soviet Government). It was not a very good likeness, but the way in which it was displayed and lit made it look dramatic: 'The Mongolian features, the high cheek bones, the cruel mouth, all stood out as if they were illuminated from within as well as from without . . . For her I realized, the place was a shrine; she looked positively exalted there – uplifted, worshipful in an almost frightening way, like someone possessed. A frail, aged, bourgeois lady, wearing, as she usually did, a grey silk dress and pretty lace cap on her head, prostrating herself, metaphorically speaking, before the founding father of the 20th-century totalitarian state, the arch terrorist of our time.' The scene stayed with him as an important and vivid symbol of materialism triumphant.

CHAPTER V

India Again

THE ABRUPT END of his Russian experiment after only nine months left Malcolm high and dry. He had by now burned his boats with the *Guardian* and had no job prospects of any kind. Above all, the socialist beliefs in which he and Kitty had been brought up (by his father and the Webbs) had been exposed, to his way of thinking, as a sham. By temperament he remained, as always, a man of the left. Yet he had now seen that a central element of the socialist creed (relating to Soviet Russia) was fraudulent. Not only that, but when its fraudulence was exposed, as it had been by his eye-witness reports, he saw that even the most intelligent and politically sophisticated people like the Webbs or A. J. P. Taylor preferred to shut their eyes to reality. Nor was this a temporary phenomenon. For the rest of his life Malcolm was to be part of an intelligentsia, a large proportion of whom continued to pin their faith in a system which he knew to be corrupt and inhuman on an almost unimaginable scale. Only now that the system is finally in ruins is it possible to realize the extraordinary persistence and perversity of such beliefs.

As for Malcolm, his attitude to Russia, which was to develop into a detestation and at times an unhealthy obsession, left him increasingly isolated. Anthony Powell, who first became aware of the name of Malcolm Muggeridge as a result of reading his anti-Russian diatribes published at this time, was comparatively rare among his contemporaries in being non-political, yet at the same time *au fait* with the literary and intellectual scene. He wrote, in his memoirs:

Disillusionment with Communism, dismay at the methods of
the Soviet Union are nowadays such familiar themes that the
force of Muggeridge's virtually one-man onslaught in the
1930s is hard to grasp for those who did not experience those
years. The Muggeridge impact, for its cogency to be appreciated, must be understood in relation to the intellectual atmosphere of the period. At that time many people were apt to
think of what was happening in Russia as no worse than a few
rich people being relieved of their surplus cash, a proceeding
of which some approved, some disapproved. True, there were
awkward stories about executions, torture, forced labour,
government-engineered famine, but the analogy of omelettes
and eggs would often be invoked by those who approved;
while those who disapproved were suspected of doing so for
the wrong reasons, that is to say, desire to keep their money.
When, from time to time, those now called dissidents, having
escaped to the West, described what was happening in Russia,
no great impression was made on left-wing intellectuals, who
by then had invested too much capital in Soviet collectivization
to adjust their portfolio without considerable loss of face; compassion being unevenly balanced against *amour propre* in most
branches of life. Muggeridge has some claim to be the first
writer of his sort to disturb this left-wing complacency in a
lively manner . . . (*Faces in My Time*, 1980)

Kitty, in the meantime, had managed, with the help of Malcolm's father, to obtain them a job running a hostel in Switzerland for the Workers Travel Association, a Labour Party tourist
agency. It was at La Rossinière, near to Kitty's birthplace at
Château d'Oex. For about three months here in 1933 they
enjoyed a brief and relatively happy interlude. There were few
guests to accommodate and they spent much of their time walking in the mountains. Malcolm read Proust and started work on
his novel *Winter In Moscow* based on his Russian experiences.
Early in September, Kitty's parents Mr and Mrs Dobbs visited
them. 'Mrs Dobbs goes on painting,' Malcolm noted in his diary.
'She is a great woman with a core of evil. I find her company
horrifying – more particularly because of the effect she has on
Kit and the thought of her infirmity. Last night I watched her

reading *The Times* and fixed it in my mind; the flapping of sheets of printed matter; the bored following of the headlines; the sense that she had turned in desperation to the newspaper and that it did nothing towards satisfying her.'

A more welcome visitor was Alec Vidler who came at about the same time. In what was obviously intended to be an anti-Russian gesture, Malcolm asked him to baptize his two sons Leonard and John. Alec, however, refused when Malcolm declined to give an assurance that he would bring the boys up as Christians. Nevertheless, Mrs Dobbs reported to her sister Beatrice Webb that Malcolm was 'turning to religion'. 'That is good news', Beatrice wrote in her diary in one of those passages which shows her astonishing insight into character:

> If you see much of the Devil and idiot in human society, you had better believe in a god to set it right. And confession and absolution would suit poor Malcolm's complexes; he needs spiritual discipline and he would find peace in religious rites. 'Malcolm would do well in the Roman Catholic Church,' I suggested. 'But that would be a complete denial of all his former faith in democracy and free thought,' said Rosy, 'and Kitty is such an atheist and rebel.' She might go too; she also is devil-ridden in her anger and contempt of other human beings; that is a bearable though deteriorating state of mind during the insolence and opportunities and irresponsibilities of youth, but it becomes intolerably dreary in middle life, when responsibilities and frictions increase, adventures fail and friends fall off. In old age it is only faith in human destiny and kindly feelings towards fellow-travellers that compensate for decreasing strength and decaying faculties. And the compensation and delayed benefit may be more than adequate. Old age may become the most peaceful, because the least personal part of life.

In September 1933 Kitty and Malcolm moved to Geneva where Malcolm had been given a job working for the International Labour Organization. He had little interest in the work, which involved, in the first instance, compiling documentary material on handicrafts in India. He took it because it was well paid and by this stage he was desperately short of money. However, the change of scene did nothing to lift his spirits. Kitty alone preserved his sanity. 'This ILO is killing me,' he wrote. 'I sit in a room in a decayed villa near the new building (so like a hospital) leaning on papers; doing nothing. The other day I nodded off over my papers. In my heart always, whatever I do, is the sense of failure; the sense of enormous effort made, and with no result. Failure eating away like a disease. How ill I am. It is pouring with rain. Kit has gone to town because she promised Pan [Leonard] he should have a birthday party. She is amazing. She works like a horse and this evening, though she is utterly exhausted, she went into Geneva to buy crackers and toys. When we left Russia, we hadn't a penny. It's even difficult for us to get cash for this first month. I'll have to stay on at the ILO as long as they'll let me, though I hope they won't let me for long.'

The mood of gloom and disillusionment persisted throughout his Geneva period. 'All day I've been reading newspapers,' he wrote (26 October 1933). 'They're so boring, so monotonous, yet a kind of drug. I've read about all sorts of things that don't interest me in the least – the Hitler regime, by-elections; florid notice about Sir Thomas Beecham's conducting a sweepstake organized by the Duke of Atholl; recognition of the USSR by America; the Brains Trust; the ministerial crisis in France; the disarmament conference; political broadcasts; the great boost in armaments. Now my head aches. Hundreds and hundreds of words I've read. All about what's happening. Stale words. It's the thing one notices most in Geneva – people unfolding newspapers. Buying them and unfolding them; sitting or walking along by the Lake with them opened.'

Preceded by Kitty and the small boys, Malcolm returned to London in 1934 and once again set about trying to find work. He succeeded only in getting a commission from Jonathan Cape to write a book about Samuel Butler whose centenary was imminent. Cape no doubt assumed that Malcolm with his socialist background and iconoclastic articles would find Butler a sympathetic figure. If so, he was to be abruptly disillusioned. In the

H. T. Muggeridge

Annie Muggeridge

Winner of the beautiful baby contest:
Malcolm at three months

Malcolm (far left) with fellow pupils at
Selhurst Grammar School

The graduate: outside Senate House,
Cambridge, 1924 (Malcolm is on the left)

The Selwyn College Fourth Boat, 1921.
Alec Vidler, the coach, is seated at centre,
holding a loud-hailer. Malcolm stands
second from right just behind him.

The young journalist,
photographed shortly
before his departure
for Moscow in 1932

MM (centre) with
two Cambridge
friends, Sharp
(left) and
Eardley(right)

Malcolm and Kitty in Cairo, 1928

Kitty Dobbs, 1927

Malcolm in Indian attire,
Alwaye, 1925

With Indian pupils at the Union Christian College, Alwaye

With Amrita Sher-Gil (centre) and her parents, 1936

ABOVE: Edward Taylor Scott

LEFT: C. P. Scott, editor of the
Guardian from 1872-1929

Hugh Kingsmill (left) and Hesketh Pearson

Muggeridge the Liberator: Paris, 1944

With Lady Pamela Berry

With Hesketh Pearson, 1951

ABOVE: Following precedent, the new editor of Punch carves his initials on the editor's table

RIGHT: In the Punch dining room.

BELOW: With (from left) the Hon. Peter Dickinson, Anthony Powell and Basil Boothroyd

meantime, for want of anything better, Malcolm replied to an advertisement for an assistant editor on the *Calcutta Statesman* at a salary of £1,500 p.a.

Founded by Robert Knight in 1875, the *Calcutta Statesman*, originally the *Indian Statesman*, was a replica of a British paper (not unlike the *Manchester Guardian* at that time) published by and for the British community in India and businessmen in particular. Knight's family disposed of the paper in 1927. In 1934 the editor was Arthur Moore, a former *Times* man who inherited the editorship after his predecessor, Sir Alfred Watson, was shot at by a Bengali terrorist and was advised to return to England. Moore was a Liberal, a fervent anti-Nazi who sympathized with the Indian independence movement. No doubt Malcolm's credentials appealed to him.

Malcolm sailed for India in September for what was supposed to be a three-year absence. 'Kit saw me off at Victoria and I shan't see her again – unless something unexpected happens – for at least a year. There's always relief mixed up with grief at being separated from someone who's as near to me as part of myself as Kit is. Indeed I scarcely know how far, amongst a multitude of conscious and unconscious motives, that played a part.'

Once again Malcolm was 'making off', this time leaving a wife and three small children (their baby daughter Valentine had been born on 1 August 1934) to fend for themselves. But nothing in his diary suggests that he had any real qualms about his actions. He remained self-absorbed, anarchic and morbid, whereas Kitty, thanks to motherhood, was being forced to revise many of her youthful illusions, becoming in the process a more mature person than her husband. If she had any doubts about Malcolm deserting her at this critical time she did not express them. The probability is that she never doubted that, whatever happened, Malcolm would always return to her because he would never find any woman who would love him in the same utterly selfless way.

Picture Palace, Malcolm's novel about the *Guardian*, had been due to be published three days after the date of his sailing. The original publishers Puttnam's had sent the novel to Arthur Ransome for his opinion. Ransome was terribly upset. 'I find the book utterly loathsome,' he wrote, 'quite apart from its treachery towards Ted Scott (my oldest friend) and C. P. Scott.' There was a serious risk in Ransome's view that, even if the Scott family did not sue for libel, other obviously identifiable characters like Kingsley Martin and Olga, his wife, would do so. 'Caddish is the only word I can find for this book, and in the latter part of it, caddish pornography . . . My wife, I may say, has read the book and says that under no circumstances will either of the Muggeridges be invited to this house.'*

This rather emotional response by Ransome was enough to persuade Puttnam to drop the book. Surprisingly, *Picture Palace* nevertheless found another publisher in Douglas Jerrold of Eyre & Spottiswoode. A staunch right-winger and Roman Catholic, Jerrold responded favourably to Malcolm's exposé of Liberal humbug and agreed to publish, provided a number of minor changes were made. Inevitably, however, Malcolm's old enemy W. P. Crozier goaded the *Guardian* into bringing proceedings – the libel being that the high-minded *Guardian* was dependent on the profits of its sister paper, the popular and much racier *Manchester Evening News*. The publisher, Jerrold, seemed quite prepared to defend what was a perfectly justifiable allegation but he asked Malcolm for a deposit of £2,000 to do so. Malcolm was in no position to raise such a huge sum, with the result that the book, which had already gone on sale, had to be withdrawn and pulped.

To a man who had set his heart on being a writer, even a 'great writer', the total destruction of his novel ought to have been a major blow. ('I have a conviction that I shall never write a better book,' he had told Arthur Ransome when the controversy over it first began.) However, it is a sign of Malcolm's overall state of depression at this time that he seemed indifferent. He wrote (but for some reason did not send) this letter to Kitty:

* Ransome noted later (1935): 'Mug grew up and improved. When years later I met him again, I liked him. He came with his wife to dine with us and was so pleasant that I could only marvel at his blind spots that made possible his book on the *Guardian*.'

I had a telegram from Jerrold yesterday to say that he would have to settle with the *Manchester Guardian* for £700, and definitely withdraw the book unless I could put up £2000. This, of course, was impossible. I had to write back telling him so. It's left me a bit shaken. They've won haven't they – the others. Whether I'm melancholy because of this, or because of loneliness, being away from you, who are the only person I love, I don't know, but I am very melancholy. The world to me is an inhospitable place. I don't think I really care about its present chaos; even like it, since it reflects my own state of mind. What I feel all the time is a sense of being an alien, a stranger in a strange land.

A lot of my waking time here is just wishing I was with you and the children; when I was with you, and might after all, have stayed with you, I chose to come away.

The contrast between Malcolm's first Indian diary (1925–27) and his second (1934–35) is very marked. Admittedly the Alwaye journal was written as much for his father as for himself. Even so, his preoccupations are obvious: his work (lectures on English Literature), religion (both Christianity and Hinduism) and politics. In the latter diary, although he was working as a leader writer on the *Calcutta Statesman* there is scarcely a mention of the political issues of the day, and nothing at all about religion. His themes now are a general contempt for the British in India, his own health and two obsessive love-affairs with Indian women. The tone is morbid, introspective and pessimistic.

At Alwaye, Malcolm had been one of a handful of Englishmen in an academic community of Indians. In Calcutta, like it or not, he was a Sahib, one of the 14,000 strong British community established in the second-largest city of the British Empire. They were rich and affluent, with their own shops, offices and clubs – from which, in many cases, Indians were excluded – and an endless round of social activities. Even Malcolm had his own private car with driver in which he was driven through the streets, scattering the crowds of Indians.

As always, he preferred, when he could, to walk; even in the oppressive heat. He walked in the early morning through Eden

Gardens with a colleague. 'Ahead of us an Indian in a loin cloth walked along intoning from a book, his son following. Others were waking up. One sat cross-legged on the stone, his features immobile, like someone turned to stone in the middle of some sensuous dream. Outside the gardens a most characteristic of all Indians signs – bathers walking down hundreds of steps to the river.'

October was a time of Hindu festivals: 'There were large crowds everywhere. Processions kept passing by, one led by a man who every now and again faced round at his followers and let off a flare. Also a queer model of four or five women in tinsel and bright colours was held up and suggested Roman Catholic processions. There was a perpetual chant of singing, a perpetual ringing of bells, a perpetual undercurrent of incoherent rhythms. Somehow it was exciting. I stood looking up. Sellers of rings were lining the road jabbering, weighing out small quantities of sweets. Little lights everywhere and tumultuous bodies. I realized how excitable they were, how shrill, and how difficult it would be for them to manage a history that was not excitable and shrill, full of insane cruelty and unsure self-mortification.'

More often he walked in the Maidan, the vast park over two square miles in extent in the centre of the city. Everywhere the Raj had stamped its presence: 'Calcutta is full of statues and nearly all of Englishmen – their faces, bewhiskered, look down on passers-by. I imagine them to have been Governors and Commanders-in-Chief and whatnot who enjoyed their five years of autonomy in their day, and now stand, or sit on horseback, about the Maidan. Not having been able to get into Hyde Park, they are content with the Maidan . . . this is characteristic.'

The *Calcutta Statesman* was nearby in an imposing building on Chowringee, the city's main commercial thoroughfare, with white pillars at the front and an elaborate open portico. Malcolm lived in a flat above the newspaper offices which he shared with his colleague, the assistant editor W. C. Wordsworth, a Welshman whom he found deeply unsympathetic. Snobbery was rife among the Raj, Wordsworth being typical – 'He said of a man named Mackie last night: "He was at Charterhouse and Trinity, but you'd never think it!" Oh God! Oh God! He said of another

man named Holmes: "He was a Winchester boy!" He knows
everyone's school as schoolboys know makes of cars.' Malcolm
poured out his scorn on 'people who live to dress for dinner.
People who clip their words.'

He found almost all his fellow-countrymen distasteful, unsympathetic and in many cases repellent: 'There's not a person here
who attracts me or interests me.' Moore, his editor, was vain
and weak, not quite a fool but nearly. 'Wordsworth with his
inordinate vanity, finding expression in his always being busy.
If he comes to tea and the telephone rings, he says, "They can't
leave me alone for a minute." Often the call is for someone else.'

Finally he made friends with a group of Bengali intellectuals
through Shahid Suhrawardy, an Oxford friend of Hugh Kingsmill's brother Brian. Suhrawardy, artistic and sensual, was a
member of a very distinguished Bengali family who worked for a
time at the Moscow Arts Theatre. Now he was Professor of Fine
Arts at Calcutta University, 'a post,' said Malcolm, 'that made little
or no demands on his time and energies, there being few students,
and they not particularly diligent, and no arts, fine or otherwise.'

Suhrawardy introduced him to Sudhia Datta, a well-known
Bengali poet who had been Rabindranath Tagore's secretary and
later his biographer, Apurbo Chandra, a civil servant, and
Tulsi Goswami, a wealthy congress minister in the Bengal
Government.

They all met for dinner on 19 November 1934. 'I was happy
with them on the whole,' Malcolm wrote. 'They are a bit moth-
eaten I know, but then so am I a bit moth-eaten.'

It is Goswami who fascinates me most – he is a drunkard and
most of the time he says nothing. Then suddenly interpolates
a remark which is always good. He has a lovely voice. His
face is ravaged I suppose by drink, and looks unhappy. He's
a congressman of course and dresses in a Khadda dhoti. Datta
has patterned himself on the first post-war intellectuals. He
has (I should imagine with some difficulty) kept himself slim;
only his enormous teeth show how big he would have been
if nature had taken its course. A bit battered, too, and bewildered, yet holding to the fact of being a poet. Chandra is fat

and easy going; if ever aggressive, only to assert the fact that he feels a sense of inferiority through being a government official. As he drinks, his eyes mist over; their light is always a bit clouded, like street lamps through a fog.

They all play up to Suhrawardy as the great sensualist, the artist (by the way, when I went to see him he had the most beautiful Parsee woman with him who said she would sing to me sometime). He told me on the way back that he had a secret telephone at the University and implied that he used it for making assignations with mysterious women. All the same, I like him. His pose is, say, better than Wordsworth's, at least more sympathetic to me. Chandra by the way told me that Wordsworth was one of the most cunning, intriguing little men who ever breathed.

A few days later, Datta (the poet) invited Malcolm to his home – an old-fashioned Indian house with a courtyard and a large number of small rooms, and, facing the courtyard – a temple. They dined upstairs from little dishes on a brass tray, the Indian guests, who included a wrestler, taking off their shoes and sitting on the floor in the Bengali fashion, while Malcolm sat at a table vowing that he would never forget 'The spacious house, so quiet, dignified, so made for Calcutta and all it stands for.'

The five friends – Malcolm, Suhrawardy, Datta, Chandra and Goswami thereafter met regularly for dinner once a week. (At one club they had to reserve a private room as Indians were not allowed in the restaurant.) Although Malcolm was at first depressed by the way his Indian friends aped English attitudes, he found their sensuousness and melancholy very appealing and in keeping with his own mood. Sudhia Datta, perhaps because he was less European in attitudes, he found especially sympathetic.

Malcolm's generally low spirits were made worse by continuing stomach trouble which was to afflict him all his life until, in old age, he adopted a vegetarian diet. 'I've got one of my stomach attacks,' he wrote (15 October 1934), 'mind and body imprecise. I wonder if I'll ever be able to stop them coming. If not, I don't see much chance of being happy ever. I'd do anything to stop them. They poison my whole life. No one knows unless he's experienced it, the horror of this perpetual clouding of one's faculties. One day I'll write a short story called "Dyspepsia", showing someone tortured by a bad stomach, agonizingly straining to excrete, and looking at a filthy tongue; with his complement of pills and bottles of all sorts; with his syringes and suppositories and all the rest of it. The sense of being unclean that goes with the disease, the curious indecision, starting off for a walk and coming back again. Beginning to work and then petering out; the venomous resentment it engenders.'

Malcolm had now developed into a major hypochondriac, able to convince himself without much difficulty that he had contracted syphilis or some other fatal illness. He made frequent visits to doctors taking specimens of one kind or another. 'I know I'm a bit pathological where my body is concerned, doctors spot this.' In an effort to improve his health he took up riding again and went regularly first thing in the morning to the Maidan or the Jodhpur Club.

It was inevitable in these circumstances that Malcolm would embark on a love affair. Her name was Khurshed, a Parsee married to a rich businessman called Panda. Malcolm met her first at Suhrawardy's house, finding her 'ravishing despite her hardness, lovely eyes and a long straight nose and golden skin, she wore plaited gold bangles round her ankles and a red spot in the middle of her forehead.' They were immediately attracted to one another and began a love affair. For a time, Malcolm was in a state of ecstasy. 'It is the first time physical love has come my way,' he wrote, entertaining fantasies about running away. However, Khurshed, who confessed to Malcolm that she had had many lovers, probably regarded him as no more than another in a long line. Malcolm, who could never be blind to reality for too long, reflected as he was driven away from their first assignation that his Sikh taxi driver would probably have made a better job of it. Still, for a time he lived in a frenzy of excitement. He even bought himself a Wolseley car. 'Suddenly, all my life has become fabulous. I can't even sleep, let alone work. All the people here see that I've changed and their attitude towards me is different from what it was – even Shahid's [Suhrawardy].' They went to the circus and Khurshed was frightened and hid inside her sari.

They went for drives together and took enormous pleasure in devising ways of deceiving her husband who usually accompanied her on these outings. But after the initial thrills he also began to experience doubts. 'Was she so beautiful? Was it so ecstatic a moment?'

Kitty was due to arrive in Calcutta in a few weeks' time and Malcolm's feelings oscillated. 'I'm longing to see her. What I like best about her is that she somehow prevents me from getting cheap. How I so easily get cheap.' The next moment he was filled with doubts. His ardour for Khurshed increased, then cooled. It was typical of him that even when Kitty at last arrived almost the first thing he did was to take her to visit Khurshed and her husband. It was also inevitable that Kitty immediately realized what was going on. 'The moment we got into the room and saw Khurshed, Kit turned sour. After a few desultory remarks, I sweating with embarrassment, Kit's eyes filled with tears, she said she wasn't well and must go, but alone. I, of course, went with her. We sat in the car hating one another. I tried to be indignant with Kit for making such a scene but it was rather thin.'

Earlier, shortly after her arrival in Calcutta, with the same kind of instinct, Malcolm had questioned Kitty about Michal Vyvyan, a diplomat whom he had known in Moscow.* She cried, saying he was a beast; 'I remembered when I'd first met him in the embassy in Moscow, in a check suit and with an absurd sprouting moustache, how an intense hatred overcame me. From some chance expression in one of her letters I'd guessed that she was seeing quite a lot of Vyvyan and had said in a letter initially that I'd dreamed of them as lovers. "He's one of those men", Kit said, "who only want one thing; then when he's got it, he hates you." I was pompous – "All of us are so. I like Vyvyan," and so on.'

Kitty stayed in Calcutta for three weeks. Malcolm introduced

---

* Born in 1907, Vyvyan joined the Foreign Office after gaining a First in History at Oxford. He resigned in 1938 in protest against the Government's appeasement of Stalin and was elected a fellow of Trinity College, Cambridge, where he remained till shortly before his death in 1992. He married in 1941.

her to his Indian friends and took her to the races with his editor
Arthur Moore. They rode together at the Jodhpur Club and
danced at Firpo's, Calcutta's most fashionable restaurant. One
weekend they went to Santiniketan, the home of Rabindranath
Tagore, the famous Indian poet greatly admired by Yeats, who
had so impressed Mrs Dobbs when he talked to the pupils at
Bedales. 'Old Tagore was there,' Malcolm wrote in his most
jaundiced vein, 'picturesque, senile, fatuous, airing himself on
the verandah. We stayed in his son's house, very arty, and in the
evening he gave a lecture, and we saw his international following:
a German Jew dressed as a Buddhist monk, a German Jewess
who had been with Gandhi, spinning while she waited for the
old fool to begin.'

When Kitty left, Chandra, Suhrawardy and Sudhia Datta came
with Malcolm to see her off at the station and left flowers in her
compartment. Looking back at her visit, Malcolm wrote in his
diary, 'It has been a terrible three weeks, yet at the last I felt no
inexpressible love for her. We fought and fought, neither giving
way. There's never been such a fight ever between us. Then last
night she said quietly, "You'd better stick to me. No one'll love
you as I do." '

Shortly after Kitty left he went to see a drunken astrologer
who gave him the following list of observations, a copy of which
he sent to Kitty:

Versatile, sensitive, restless disposition. Later turn to philosophy. Imagination strong; up to 30th year many women,
afterwards one. Between 33 and 34 prosperous but not con-
tinuously. May change employment then, no employment to
be lasting. In boyhood ill between 2 and 3. Bad illness between
10 and 11. Quick marriage. Every chance of second marriage.
Chance of becoming a drunkard between 24 and 36 (avoid
this). Chance of estrangement from wife and myself within
36th year. Estrangement off and on from 28th. Never to be
adjusted, not a ghost of a chance of coming to agreement.
Assume cheerfulness, at heart wretched. Outside appearance
no indication of internal state of mind. Sometimes desire to
mix with gay companions, not natural but for escape. Marriage

biggest mistake man could commit. Tending to folly. Second wife, better than first, never happy though. Not understood. Prospects in life brighten after 34th year. 36–39 good period. Savings nil. Occupation in travelling. 39–40 kidney and bladder causing weakness in back (even before). Walks quickly, requires impulse. No particular religion, Christian to a later period. Illnesses: 16, 39, 44, 46. Not long illness – chance of hereditary malady (very likely).

One more son by first wife. Two sons and daughter by second wife, full of pride, dignity and truth. Her only fault, excessive frankness. She can hold up her head among thousands.

I to blame.

Within 34th and 35th year income about Rs 2000.

Spend the whole bloody lot. Conscience, full of wisdom and then lost.

Good memory.

Tendency to live in place hotter than my own country.

Plan tends to gay life – to be resisted.

Girls to figure in this particularly. Feeling of indifference comes over me sometimes. Low diet.

Malcolm, who always set store by such things, was deeply disturbed by this mixture of startling truth (notably the description of Kitty) and equally devilish lies (e.g. 'marriage biggest mistake'). It only helped to increase his mental turmoil, since Kitty had by now told him that she was pregnant by her lover Michal Vyvyan and was thinking of having an abortion. Three (undated) letters which she sent to Malcolm at about this time reveal her extraordinary strength of character, her total lack of self-pity or malice, so confirming the astrologer's insights.

Dearest Malcolm,

I'm so glad I've got your letter forwarded . . . I can face things again now – even an abortion . . . don't take your astrologer too seriously. I think he's told you what's already in your mind and what you wish. If you love me I hope you will come back to us. I wish you could let me know what your idea is about the future together. I know you don't want to think about it and want to let things turn out, only I can't live unless I have a vague picture of the future. You call that being romantic. But my life becomes chaotic and passionately unhappy and even if it's only for the children's sake so that I can make a nice home for them. I wish you could say what you feel at this moment . . .

Even at my most bitter to you it's always absolutely on the surface and I forget you can't know or remember that – all you know is what I say and what I look – and that I admit must be sweeping . . .

You might think I'm as pleased as punch with every opportunity of indulging in all the pleasures and delights and companionship life has to offer a healthy, youngish, fruitful woman – and yet I feel as lonely and despairing as a barren spinster living on £150 per year in a drab pension on the Lake of Thon. This is because my savage and bitter husband isn't about to make life sparkle. There's a picture for you!

Come back to us. I could fit your women and your drunkenness into the frame but I'd like you to be in the picture. When I first knew you, I said to you, '*Mauvais comme tu es, je t'adore.*' [Wicked as you are, I adore you.] It's still true. What a pity, isn't it, that holding this pen isn't a young and radiant creature instead of your clamouring, stale and familiar wife? It's just the kind of letter a young woman might write to the man she wants to marry!

I saw the other day a new sculpture called Christ or something by Epstein. It was rather an idiotic piece of rock 12ft high! But there were some excellent bits – one miraculous one of Beaverbrook. Well old man, don't forget I love you,
      Kit.

Dearest Malcolm,

Well, I saw the doctor who says it's too late to do an abortion safely. I don't know whether to believe her or not. I don't feel I can go through with another pregnancy and the ridicule and loneliness with a bastard at the end of it . . . I feel battered and broken and cowardly and I don't know what to do and I feel ashamed. I oughtn't to write to you like this, but I haven't anyone else I can tell. Ah – let us be opportunists!

I haven't heard from you so I suppose you're not writing – the most sensible thing to do really. I hadn't before realized the inevitability of having the child or having an abortion. It's a pity we can't change round as you would either welcome having a child or gleefully hope for the worst from an abortion. If I do have it, I shall send it to the national adoption society where it will be brought up by a couple who want it. I hope you're well and being able to work.

　　　　Kit.

P.S. I can't live without you. I feel sick and ill and desolate and I have no will left and I don't feel as though I've any strength left in my body to carry on.

People say it's never too late to mend but I find it's always too late to mend. I wish I'd never gone to India. Oh Malcolm, I do love you and I wish we could be together with our children. I saw an advert for a house near Rye to let at £100 with 7 bedrooms, and I began to plan out the sitting room, the nursery, your room, etc, and then I remembered how idiotic of me. It's so futile being so desperately unhappy and yet I don't really know how I'm going to get through the next few years. Being alone in the house I suppose makes it worse.

　　　　　　　　　　　　　　　19 Grove Terrace,
　　　　　　　　　　　　　　　NW5

Dearest Malcolm,

Please don't worry and please send me a cheerful letter so that I can collect a new pile. I burnt the others and they made such a roaring they nearly set the chimney on fire. I got quite alarmed and tried to extinguish the flames. Don't let's worry. I'm your wife, that's all. I love and am faithful to you – but my body isn't up to my mind – hasn't the same moral standing.

I've made this house look lovely and now the children are here. I wish you could have seen their arrival and them finding their old toys and recognize [sic] the place. It made me feel so happy to see that they felt this place was their home. Pan rushed all over the place shouting out 'Oh thank you, Mummy!' – I presume for bringing him back – and old

Johnny came up behind squeaking with excitement. This isn't
romantic, it's what happened. It was very hot in the sun
and Pan sat in it and said 'Oh goody – it's so hot I'm in India
land where Daddy is!' I don't know what you'll think. When
it came to the point I couldn't bring myself to have this
abortion and I'm glad, not because there was anything
between Vyvyan and myself but the most casual lechery and
because I'm alive and well and haven't had the child out of
my womb and I'm thankful. You see, when I saw the children
looking so lovely and remembered that the first abortionist
wouldn't do it because it was too late . . . and the squalor of
my hunt for visits to four abortionists all of whom had to
be ferreted out in the most obscene way – so macabre – and
the last man who agreed to do it when I asked him what I
wanted, taking down my address and said, 'Abortions! No
my dear lady, I've never done one in my life. They're not
right, what I think you mean is etc etc . . .' all this and an
absolutely instinctive insistent feeling not to have it made me
cancel my decision and I wired, 'Regret unable to undergo
treatment.' I don't know whether I've done right. I couldn't
have done anything else. I don't expect you to feel exalted
about it – but there it is – and when I think I'm landing you
with a bastard I feel it's a bit too much for you to stomach
– but I know if you come back to us it will be because you
want to and don't care about what has happened (having an
abortion couldn't undo what I've done). But the thing is,
do you mind having it nominally for your child? There's no
point in advertising its illegitimacy. I hope all this won't be
too horrible for you. Don't let it be.

Please don't let things worry you dearest Malcolm. What
is the point for the few years – especially when there's eternity
afterwards. If you ever feel a taste for family life or a span
of it, here we are. I wish I could undo everything that's added
to your unhappiness that's been due to me. Don't worry
about your work – if only you didn't worry it would go so
easily and what on earth is there to worry about, nothing!

How I love you – and when I see that it makes the children
so happy to have a home and be back here, everything that

93

was so wretched and miserable and squalid is alright again.
I hope I've done the right thing about this bastard. I know
you'll think me a coward because you'd have faced the
abortion. God I wish you could get pleasure out of
everything you do. You do such a lot you could get such a
huge amount . . .

Malcolm's replies to these letters do not survive, though
according to his diary (8 March 1935): 'I wrote and told her what
is the truth, that I love her and must always love her, till I die,
her only. But it doesn't mean I can live with her.'

Then on 10 April he writes: 'There was a letter from Kit which
gave me great relief because it showed I hadn't lost her. She is
so infinitely superior to everyone else, so brave.'

Still, he had no intention of returning to London in response
to her pleas. By now, in April, he was in Simla, the summer
home of the Viceroy, where every year between March and
October the administration of the vast Indian empire was carried
out in a little hill-top town like Malvern with its own church,
shops, cricket ground and theatre. In what seemed almost like a
repetition of his experiences with W. P. Crozier on the *Guardian*,
Malcolm had fallen out with Wordsworth and the latter was
pleased to have him out of harm's way. But there was not much
to report. The Viceroy, Lord Willingdon, arrived on 21 April
and two weeks later Malcolm was invited to Viceregal Lodge:

It was a large party. We lined up with the band playing. The
folding doors opened and someone announced: 'Their Excel-
lencies!' They walked along shaking hands with everyone.
After lunch, Lady Willingdon sent for me. She is really a fascinating creature in a way, so vulgar and full of vitality. She told
me how stingy the Commander-in-Chief was [Lord Chet-
wode, John Betjeman's father-in-law], how he had given
Rs300 to the Jubilee fund. She also said: 'The Viceroy's looking
well, isn't he?' This she said a bit anxiously as though she
feared that at any moment he might pop off . . .

After a while I passed on to a dim young man and then to
the Viceroy. He looks like the elderly beau of a Restoration

Comedy. He's very young and fresh, except that his eyes are pale, as though life was draining out of him from the top downwards (as Swift died) . . . I liked him too, though. When I went (I'd had a sip to drink) I felt quite affectionate towards them. 'Look after yourself,' the old girl said, squeezing my hand. The man in front of me in the procession stuttered and was terrified that seeing all the ladies curtsey, he might.

A few days later he started another passionate love affair, this time with a young artist Amrita Sher-Gil. She was born in Budapest in 1913. Her father was a Sikh nobleman, Umrao Singh, her mother Antoinette was Hungarian. Amrita had studied art in Florence but was expelled from the School of Santa Annunciata for drawing nude women. She went to Paris in 1929 and studied under Lucien Simon at the Ecole Nationale des Beaux Arts and under Pierre Vaillant at Grand Chaumière, being elected Associate of the Grand Salon for her painting *Conversation* (1934); she was the youngest person to be elected and the first Asian. Greatly influenced by the Post-Impressionists, she returned to India and from then on painted Indian subjects: 'I realized my real artistic mission,' she said, 'to interpret the life of India and particularly the poor Indians pictorially, to paint those silent images of infinite submission and patience: to depict their angular brown bodies, strangely beautiful in their ugliness; to reproduce the impression in their sad eyes created in scenes in the style of Picasso and the Fauves.' Her portrait of Malcolm now hangs in the National Gallery of Modern Art, Delhi.

They met at a country fair near Simla and Malcolm, who was struck by her beauty – she was small and dark with large, sad eyes – went up and spoke to her. They immediately began talking to one another with the easy familiarity of old friends, something that Malcolm had experienced with Kitty and also Hugh Kingsmill and which planted in his mind the strange idea that one has known certain chosen people in a previous existence. Later, they danced at a party at the Cecil Hotel where Malcolm was staying and he told her he would like to dance until he 'swooned'. They became lovers, Malcolm chronicling the affair in explicit and embarrassing detail in his diary. As with his previous lover

Khurshed, sex was the bond. On occasion Malcolm found Amrita 'utterly egocentric, coarse, petulantly spoilt'. Certainly she had had many previous lovers and used to read their letters out to Malcolm. But there is no doubt that in Amrita Sher-Gil he found for the first time a woman whose nature was like his own – sensuous, impulsive, prone to extremes of cheerfulness and depression. 'What I like about Amrita,' he wrote in his diary (10 June 1936), 'is that she, like myself, is a bare soul, without any allegiance or beliefs or hopes, just a sense of animality, so strong she can paint as I write, reproducing bare forms of life without idealizing upwards or downwards. By the time she's my age she'll be as ready to die as I am.'

Shortly afterwards, Malcolm received an offer from Percy Cudlipp, editor of the *Evening Standard* in London, to join the staff of the Londoner's Diary. (He had previously been submitting articles from India.) With his usual impulsiveness he accepted. Amrita took his departure in her stride, her give-and-take attitude adding to her appeal as far as Malcolm was concerned. Although she hated getting up early she made a special effort to see him off at the station, telling him when they parted that they had some '*beaux moments*' together. (They had always used this expression in their conversations.) Malcolm's prophetic insight was once again confirmed when Amrita Sher-Gil died, possibly at her own hand, seven weeks short of her twenty-ninth birthday. During the period of the affair with Malcolm she had produced some of her best paintings. Of all his love affairs this was the only one which Malcolm looked back on without remorse or even feelings of guilt.

CHAPTER VI

The Literary Life

ON 18 SEPTEMBER 1935 R. H. Bruce Lockhart, then editing the *Evening Standard*'s gossip column, Londoner's Diary, wrote in his journal: 'Malcolm Muggeridge, the author of an anti-Bolshevik book on Russia and of a suppressed novel on the *Manchester Guardian*, joined us today. Clever, nervous and rather freakish in appearance, holds strong views.'

Kitty had rented a flat in Kentish Town. Her fourth child Charles (son of Michal Vyvyan) had been born on 13 September, just before Malcolm started work at the *Standard*. Contrary to her first instinct to have him adopted, Kitty had decided to raise the child as Malcolm's, a scheme with which he went along. (Vyvyan himself would seem to have remained ignorant of his paternity.) Immaculately dressed with gloves and a rolled umbrella, Malcolm travelled into Fleet Street daily from their flat. The staff of the *Evening Standard* occupied a single large room in a building in Shoe Lane off Fleet Street. R. H. Bruce Lockhart was a brilliant Scot who became an employee of Lord Beaverbrook's after a career in the Foreign Office during which he served in Moscow (where he was briefly imprisoned for espionage, having been accused of masterminding a plot to assassinate Lenin). It was common among Beaverbrook's journalists, many of whom, like Lockhart, were highly intelligent and talented men, to experience feelings of guilt about having sold their souls to their employer. Beaverbrook, a Canadian adventurer, paid them higher salaries than other proprietors and would hand out cheques on high days and holidays. But, in exchange, journalists were robbed of their independence and forced to follow Lord Beaverbrook's line as it changed from day to day. Lockhart had these guilt feelings in common with Malcolm. He was also, like Malcolm, a womanizer and heavy drinker whose private life was chaotic and confused. Both men yearned to get away but Lockhart, unlike Malcolm, lived a very social life and despite his high salary was always in debt.

The job of editing the Londoner's Diary was one for which Bruce Lockhart was very well equipped as he had a huge range of contacts and was able to procure a number of scoops like his interview in 1929 with Kaiser Wilhelm. Other members of the *Standard*'s staff, like the film critic John Betjeman, were expected to supply paragraphs from their area of expertise ('Writing rubbish about what sort of throat pastilles Bing Crosby uses, what sort of lingerie Garbo wears, why Clark Gable has a bath in melted butter', *Sunday Times*, 23 June 1985). The novelist Howard Spring, whose career was brilliantly summarized by Malcolm in his memoirs, covered the publishing scene:

> Literary paragraphs were turned in by Howard Spring, the book critic; a former *Guardian* star reporter, with an adoring wife whose praise of him, Neville Cardus once remarked, would have been excessive even if he had been Shakespeare. In the course of writing on the Empire Free Trade meeting in Manchester for the *Guardian*, Spring referred to Beaverbrook as a pedlar of nightmares. Crozier, ever timid, found this rather strong, and altered 'nightmares' to 'dreams', thereby procuring Spring an immediate offer of a job on the *Evening Standard* at greatly increased salary, which he accepted. Later, as a successful popular novelist, he became a pedlar of dreams on his own account.

C. P. Scott, whatever his failings, had at least the merit of consistency. Beaverbrook, who Hugh Kingsmill called 'Robin Badfellow', was a Will o' the Wisp liable to change his tune overnight, often for some personal motive of his own. It was the time of the Abyssinian crisis but Bruce Lockhart noted that Beaverbrook was 'not interested in getting information . . . my theory is that he likes to test his wits and his own powers of prophecy in his papers. He takes long shots, like a punter on a horse.' Beaverbrook did not come into the *Standard* offices, but Malcolm remembered him on the phone to his manager at the *Evening Standard*, Captain Mike Wardell, dictating the line for the leader, 'You gotta say, you gotta say . . .'

In addition to his various political causes, Beaverbrook was always interested in religious issues and in particular the next world. Once, in the spring of 1936, the paper's vans drove through London placarded with the message: 'IS THERE AN AFTER-LIFE? SEE TOMORROW'S EVENING STANDARD'. It was all a far cry from the *Guardian*. 'Working for Scott', Malcolm wrote, 'was like waltzing with some old dowager at a mayoral reception in Manchester: for Beaverbrook, like taking the floor in a nightclub in the early hours of the morning when everyone is more or less drunk.' He had bought the *Evening Standard* in 1923. The paper circulated only in London and was therefore of little importance to him compared to his flagship, the *Daily Express*. Nevertheless, the Londoner's Diary served a useful purpose in keeping him in touch with social developments and allowing him to publicize the activities of his friends and acolytes and denigrate his enemies. Whatever else, a mood of optimism had to be maintained, partly, as Malcolm wisely noted, to reassure Beaverbrook himself that all would be well: that there would be, for example, no war. The result was that the Londoner's Diary was invariably dull and bland. Politicians were treated with respect, new diplomatic appointments were noted at length and the readers were kept abreast of the comings and goings of the Royal family. A not untypical paragraph from August 1936 tells us:

ETON'S NEW GROUNDSMAN

The playing fields at Eton require some looking after, and the school authorities have recently had some difficulty in finding the right man for the job.

For twenty years, Eton had the same groundsman, whose assistant succeeded him and carried on for ten years more until he died. Now Eton has had recourse to the playing fields of the City of London, increasing greatly in number, for a new groundsman. The appointment has been given to Mr W. H.

Bowlers who is at present in charge of the Westminster Bank sportsgrounds at Norbury. The bank speaks highly of Mr Bowlers' skills in the eradication of plantains and weeds with which the ground was infected. Certain changes are contemplated in Eton's fifty acres of turf, of which he will now take charge . . .

It was hardly surprising that Malcolm found writing for such a feature dispiriting. 'The *Evening Standard* is pretty grim work, revoltingly futile and yet exhausting,' he wrote at the beginning of 1936. 'Whenever I say anything to Lockhart he says he's heard it fifty times.'

His colleagues irritated him, with the exception of Lockhart's right-hand man, Leslie Marsh, who endeared himself to Malcolm once when he was searching for an idea by saying: 'Have you looked at the stiffs?' (i.e. the obituaries). Many years later when he took over at *Punch*, one of his first decisions was to recruit Leslie Marsh as his own right-hand man.

As early as January 1936, Bruce Lockhart was recording Malcolm's urge to get away. 'Gave luncheon to Muggeridge. He wants to retire to a farmhouse near Battle (which his mother-in-law will buy for him) and write his books. He will only have about £400 to do it with. But he is only 32 and I advised him strongly to take the risk. A cynic might have laughed at my presumption. Here I am with greater earning powers too cowardly myself to take the same decision – too selfish and extravagant to make the decision possible.'

The two had lunch again at the Jardin des Gourmets, Greek Street, on 8 February: 'Had a long talk with Muggeridge about his future. He is not happy and wants to get out. Thinks it ridiculous that people like himself and me should be consulted about anything and have our stuff "subbed" by some half-educated nit-wit.'

Malcolm's desire to give up his highly paid job to go and live in the country owed a great deal to the influence of his friend Hugh Kingsmill, the second son of George Dobbs's employer, Sir Henry Lunn. Through sharing rooms with Kitty's brother at Cambridge, Malcolm had got to know Kingsmill's younger brother Brian – a brilliant but highly erratic character. Sir Henry Lunn's travel business had by then expanded and he operated a number of tours in addition to the Swiss. His sons, Brian and Hugh, who both worked for him at one time or another, were encouraged to recruit their university friends during the vacations and both Malcolm and Leonard Dobbs acted as couriers for tourists in Belgium where Sir Henry had discovered the commercial possibilities of the First World War battlefields.

Born in 1889, Hugh Kingsmill Lunn (who later dropped his surname when he fell out with his father) had been educated at Harrow and Oxford. For a short time he worked for the author and editor Frank Harris, an idol of his youth, on a magazine called *Hearth and Home* – an experience which he later described in his brilliant biography of Harris (1932).

After enlisting in a regiment of cyclists he was captured in France in 1916 and sent as a prisoner to Mainz where he remained until the end of the war. In 1918 he resumed working for his father whilst at the same time writing books, the first being a satirical novel about Frank Harris. Although he wrote a number of novels, Kingsmill excelled as a literary critic and his studies of Johnson, Dickens and D. H. Lawrence are outstanding (although the sale, as of all of his books, was minuscule). He was an unworldly man who remained cheerful in spite of his misfortunes, which included two disastrous marriages. Friends remembered him as an inspired and witty talker with the capacity to inspire others. His disciples included Malcolm and the biographer Hesketh Pearson (a near contemporary).

Malcolm first met Kingsmill in 1930 when he was working on the *Manchester Guardian*, describing the occasion later in the book *About Kingsmill* (1951) on which he and Pearson collaborated as a tribute to their old friend:

He arrived quite late on a Friday night and we went to the station to meet him. You know that curious feeling one has of meeting someone with whom one is going to be intimate. You feel as though you know them already. Features, tone of voice, gestures, are all at once familiar. Thus I remember in the dark, cavernous Manchester station with people streaming through the barrier, picking out Hughie without the slightest difficulty and greeting him as though we were old friends, instead of strangers . . . I have never had so strongly this feeling of recognizing, as distinct from making the acquaintance of someone as I had it with Hughie. He came rolling into my life with that characteristic gait of his, with that always cheerful friendly voice, and I knew that he had been there all the time.

Kingsmill's habitual cheerfulness, as Malcolm found when they later visited the offices of the *Guardian*, had a mysterious way of annoying people. Colleagues shied away from the ebullient, red-faced figure with his loud laugh. Kitty likewise resented the way in which Malcolm and Kingsmill were able to engage in endless talk to the exclusion of other people with claims on their attention.

Although they were not to meet again for some time, Malcolm absorbed from this first meeting one important lesson from Kingsmill: his notion of 'Dawnism' a word that he had personally introduced into the language in his entertaining book on Matthew Arnold (1928). 'Dawnism is heralding the dawn of a new world, or the millennium, the establishment of heaven on earth. The New Jerusalem, the dictatorship of the proletariat . . . in short an excited anticipation that some form of collective action is about to solve all the troubles of the individual, is an intermittent but apparently incurable malady of mankind.' The word itself, though presumably owing something to Wordsworth's 'Bliss was it in that dawn to be alive', was derived from an observation Kingsmill made in his youth: 'In 1921 or 1922 emerging each morning from Euston Square underground on to the north side of Euston Road, I used to see, across the way, a large poster displaying a crowing cock. The poster was an advertisement for the *Daily Herald* and the cock signified the *Daily Herald*'s conviction that the dawn about to rise in Russia under Lenin's supervision would shortly cross over to England. Years passed and then one day the cock was no longer in the accustomed place.'

Although most Dawnists in Kingsmill's eyes were politicians

and revolutionaries, he also noted how many literary figures –
like Matthew Arnold – were attracted in middle age to the idea
of putting the world to rights in preference to creative work.
These too, he categorized as Dawnists, pointing out how their
inspired idealism had been brilliantly delineated in the character
of Cervantes' Don Quixote: 'Now these dispositions being made
he would no longer defer putting his design into execution, being
the more strangely excited thereto by the mischief he thought
his delay occasioned in the world; such and so many were the
grievances he proposed to redress, the wrongs he intended to
rectify, the exorbitances to correct, the abuses to reform and the
debts to discharge.'

Although at the time he met Kingsmill, which was shortly
before he went to Russia, Malcolm was himself a Dawnist with
a fervent faith in Marxism, he saw the point of the word and
eventually came to categorize as Dawnists his former masters
and heroes: the Webbs, C. P. Scott, even his father.

In 1933, after a short period spent in Switzerland, Kingsmill
returned with his second wife Dorothy to Hastings, eventually
settling at 24 Laton Road, Ore. It was partly in order to be
near Kingsmill that Malcolm now bought (with the help of Mrs
Dobbs) the Mill House, Whatlington – a village about ten miles
north of Hastings on the A21. The Mill House was situated in
a valley near the church (where Malcolm is now buried). It was
a large Georgian property, formerly an inn, with plenty of room
for their four children. But conditions were primitive. They had
no car, water had to be fetched from a nearby well, bathing was
done in a small metal bath in front of the stove.

Paying an impromptu visit to the Mill House, the novelist
Anthony Powell, who later became one of Malcolm's closest
friends, was reminded of the woman who lived in a shoe: 'Children swarming all over the steps, children's faces looking out of
every window, yet more children, one felt, concealed in the
garden at the back. In fact, there were only four Muggeridge
children, possibly reinforced at that hour of the morning by
auxiliaries from the village, but the effect was of a dozen or
more. Kitty Muggeridge, welcoming though plainly overwhelmed with domestic duties, dislodged two boys grappling

on the floor. Then, her husband appearing, hastened away to further duties in the kitchen.'

For Kitty there is nothing to suggest, however, that she once complained about her lot. It cannot have been easy. Malcolm had little or no interest in the four small children. ('Dad was not really a children's man,' his eldest son Leonard wrote in a short memoir of his father. 'I don't recall ever playing any game with him or going on outings with him.') However, the way in which Kitty coped with them served to reinforce his love and respect for her. 'When I think of Kitty,' he wrote in his diary during the war (25 March 1942).

> I think of her waking, of a clean house and well-cooked meals; of the children coming home and shouting for her, not because they have anything to say, but just to establish contact with her, who is everything to them.
>
> I think of her as the pivot of the household, as my companion for fifteen years, to be my companion until the end; on whom my thoughts and plans for the future will ever centre, to whom when I am away, I shall ever long to return. I think, particularly, of how one day, the village boys went fishing and clumsy old John came back disconsolate because he had been unable to catch anything, and how Kitty to cheer him up had promised to go to the stream with him at daybreak the next day, and how they went, and seeing them returning, side by side, along the road when the summer sun was still low in the sky; two figures very dear to me.

It would have been only natural for Kitty to resent her husband's extraordinarily close relationship with Hugh Kingsmill, but although there were moments of tension following their interminable conversations and telephone calls Kitty was no doubt relieved that Malcolm, for the time being at least, was domesticated. In fact everything suggests that the three years they spent at Whatlington before the outbreak of war in 1939 were a time of relative happiness; a foretaste of the peace they were eventually to find in the Sixties at Robertsbridge, only a few miles from the Mill House.

Even at this early stage, Malcolm was making a serious effort to live the sort of life which he knew would alone satisfy his nature and bring him some kind of contentment. He resolved to give up smoking and what he called 'fornication'; he recovered his interest in religion, re-reading the gospels, occasionally even going with Kitty to the village church:

> Kit and I went to church yesterday. There were about twelve people in the little church. And the clergyman was a quavering old fellow much bullied by his wife. I felt greatly moved by the service. After all, I thought, we twelve people assemble here and thereby signify our acceptance of the fact that life is based on a mystery. It is our tribute to the incomprehensible – worship. It binds us together. The clergyman preached a pitiable sermon. Thinking of what I knew of the Church's history, I thought '15th Century values must be true or they would never have survived it.' Kit feels very much as I do about all this, and said so just before we went to sleep. We thought we might have the children baptized. I should like to.

Nothing came of this idea, nor for that matter of Malcolm's resolution to live ascetically. Nevertheless a change had taken place partly, perhaps, as a result of growing older, but more especially due to Kingsmill's influence. In the course of his education, Malcolm had never once been inspired by any particular teacher. Hugh Kingsmill filled the gap. He opened his eyes to literature, whilst insisting always that it is not some kind of escape from life but one of the most important things that life has to offer. Though brought up in his father's Methodism, Kingsmill was no longer a practising Christian but he had a deeply religious nature (it was no accident that his son Brooke became an Anglican priest and his daughter Edmée a nun). He believed that nearly all great artists have a sense of the way in which this imperfect world mirrors some greater and more lasting reality. From his own experiences, Kingsmill had a keen awareness of the imperfections of life, but because of his mystical sense was able for the most part to view humanity with objectivity and humour and affection. He had an abiding love for Dr Johnson, a deeply religious man who had struggled against enormous handicaps but who, despite his fame, never lost his sense of the ludicrous nature of any writer's life – the great projects embarked on and the almost inevitable oblivion in store for them all, apart from a tiny band.

Malcolm inherited from Kingsmill an absorbing interest in Johnson and was helped by it to modify his own ambitions and to view the world with greater detachment than hitherto. This, in turn, gave his writing a humorous flavour especially when he was dealing with politics.

Through Kingsmill, Malcolm also made friends with another great influence on him – Hesketh Pearson. Pearson was Kingsmill's oldest friend who shared with him a passionate interest in English literature and literary biography. Born to prosperous Worcestershire parents in 1887, he started his career as an actor in Sir Herbert Beerbohm Tree's company, but later (mainly as a result of Kingsmill's influence) he turned his hand to biography, by the time of his death in 1963 producing over twenty lives including those of Oscar Wilde, Sydney Smith and Bernard Shaw. He was tall and good-looking and seemed to be in perpetually high spirits, 'a ladies' man' whose charm was irresistible.

Friendship with Kingsmill and Pearson introduced a new dimension into Malcolm's life. It involved long talks about writers and books and literary expeditions of various kinds (Pearson shared Malcolm's love of long walks). Typical, was the visit the three of them paid to Lord Alfred Douglas – Oscar Wilde's former lover – then living with his sister in a flat in Hove. Douglas, who had prepared a schoolboy spread of toast and scones and cakes, sat at the end of the table like a housemaster entertaining three boys. 'We could only guess', Pearson reflected, 'that the usual gatherings at Douglas's flat were juvenile.'

Kingsmill and Pearson spent a great deal of time laughing and, humour being something that hitherto had been lacking in his life, Malcolm derived an enormous benefit from it, as well as the absorption into the older men's literary ambience. Neither Kingsmill nor Pearson had much interest in contemporary literature – though Kingsmill was friendly with the novelist

William Gerhardi and Edwin Muir, the Scottish poet. On the other hand they were both steeped in Shakespeare and Kingsmill could recite reams of poetry by heart.

Neither Kingsmill nor Pearson was at all well off. Kingsmill's own efforts to make a living were invariably comic. Malcolm was always delighted to assist. They wrote two books of newspaper parodies together: *Brave Old World* and *Next Year's News* (neither of which had any sale). They also tried to launch a new humour magazine called *Porcupine*, advertising in *The Times* for financial backing. The response was poor, prompting Kingsmill to remark that being in the world was like being in a cold bath, 'If you lay quite still it was just tolerable, but the slightest stirring gave a shock.'

A more successful collaboration involved the short-lived magazine *Night and Day*, which Graham Greene founded and edited for six months in 1937. Malcolm and Kingsmill described a series of literary excursions together including a visit to Paris to see Wordsworth's great-great-granddaughter, a Madame Blanchet, who was descended from the poet's illegitimate daughter by Annette Vallon. They also both contributed to a book called the *Fifty Most Amazing Crimes of the Last Hundred Years*, published by the *Daily Herald* as a free gift for new subscribers. Malcolm wrote the story of an Alsatian murderer called Jean Baptiste Tropmann – 'His mouth often hung half open, giving him at times, because of his abnormally large lower lip and large teeth, a curious air of ferocity. His hands and especially his thumbs continued to be prodigiously out of proportion with the rest of his body. They have become legendary. In France people still occasionally say of his big hands, '*C'est la main de Tropmann!*'

None of these projects did much to promote the career of Kingsmill but, on the other hand, the less successful he was the more Malcolm liked him. All his life he was drawn particularly to misfits and failures or anyone, for that matter, who stood out against the consensus. His affection and loyalties extended even to Kingsmill's brother Brian (known in the family as Bee), a clever and gifted man who after a breakdown and a variety of mental difficulties had also settled in Hastings, lodging with a Mrs Pitcher. Previously in London he had practised as a barrister for some time, specializing in divorce actions, of which he had personal experience. Sometimes he would entertain Malcolm by reading him the more sensational evidence, sometimes they tried to collaborate on a film script together:

> Brian Lunn came in the evening and we worked at *Zoe*, a film scenario we're writing. Brian was moderately lit up. He said that he'd scarcely ever told a lie, which I know is true. I ran after him because he took my hat and found him, with a drink or two more inside him, thundering along with a suitcase. He told me twice he'd been to the Heath and picked up a prostitute. 'It's perfect,' he said. 'I can't understand why all London isn't there fucking. They're delightful little bits of stuff from the Elephant and most grateful for half a crown. No stuffy bedroom. You just have them then and there and then sit amongst the trees by yourself and they're lovelier than ever.'
> (19 May 1936)

Another misfit dear to the heart of Kitty and Malcolm was Kitty's brother Leonard, after whom they had named their eldest son. Born in 1902, Leonard Dobbs was brought up with Kitty in Switzerland and became a champion skier: 'the best racing strategist that I know', according to the great authority Sir Arnold Lunn. He studied science at Cambridge and subsequently tried his hand at teaching and sculpture without any success. He was an amateur inventor who loved making mechanical equipment. But his marriage to a French girl (Mlle Cantaloupe) was short-lived and when they decided to divorce, Kitty and Malcolm offered him a home at Whatlington. He stayed there for a year before moving to Hastings, proving himself useful in many ways; he could make electrical repairs and was especially welcome in helping Malcolm to clear the garden. 'His being with us is an inexpressible comfort to me,' Malcolm wrote in his diary. 'There is something gentle and saintly about him.' But there were times when Dobbs could be trying. He had inherited from his mother an argumentative streak. Hugh Kingsmill remembered: 'Leonard's favourite position was on the hearth rug in Malcolm's study, a long room which when the old mill was an inn could have accommodated three score or so of diners and which now seemed to stimulate a latent gift for oratory in Leonard. There was no subject, or at least it never fell to my lot to discover a subject which did not afford Leonard matter for a speech. On one occasion, I recall, I dropped a remark about Dungeness, something to the effect that its coastline looked very beautiful from Fairlight. Neither Malcolm nor I had much energy to spare that evening and drooped in silence while Leonard developed a theory of coast erosion, with special reference to Dungeness.'

Later, shortly before the war, Kitty's parents also moved to Whatlington to a stone bungalow up on the hill above the Mill House. 'Whatlington was their positively last port-of-call,' Malcolm wrote in one of the funniest passages in his memoirs:

For Mr Dobbs this meant being subjected to his wife's cooking, housekeeping and company without a break. There was no longer the possibility, which his job with Lunn's Tours had always provided, of being able to disengage from time to time, and, as it were, retire to a rest-camp where he could re-equip and recover his morale. I must say, he stood up manfully to a situation which might well have broken a lesser man; concentrating his efforts on maintaining a small limited area of his own in their disorderly household, from which he would emerge as spry, well-groomed and turned out, as ever.

For her part, Mrs Dobbs, in so far as was possible in their new circumstances, resumed her habitual ways . . . she did some local painting, seated on her camp-stool and dipping her brushes in the cup of water from which she occasionally absent-mindedly took a sip to drink. Her efforts in the kitchen produced the familiar concoctions, with safety pins and other foreign bodies liable to turn up in her cakes and puddings . . .
In the village Mrs Dobbs became a familiar and much-liked figure. Her eccentricities – like stretching out for a nap wherever and whenever she felt like it; under a hedge or by the roadside, and once on a tombstone in Battle churchyard – caused fewer stares among country-people than they would have in a town. Likewise, her weird apparel – like an old gypsy woman's – which, when she was travelling on the bus to Battle

or Hastings, often led some kindly fellow-passenger to offer
to pay her fare – an offer she readily accepted.

Malcolm's aim in moving to Whatlington had been finally to
make a serious attempt to be a 'writer' rather than a mere journalist. He was still relying on journalism to pay the bills. He
reviewed novels for the *Daily Telegraph* as well as contributing
to *Time and Tide*. But his hopes were pinned on novels and he
began to work on an autobiographical pilgrim's progress called
originally *The Bewildered Soul*, which was later published under
the title *In a Valley of this Restless Mind*. In the meantime, his
book on Samuel Butler, commissioned by Jonathan Cape shortly
before his departure to India, was finally published in the autumn
of 1936. Butler (1835–1902) was an obscure Victorian man of
letters who dabbled in a number of fields including Darwinian
controversy, art history, Homeric studies (he wrote a book
proving, to his satisfaction, that the *Odyssey* was written by
a woman) and rather tired satire at the expense of orthodox
religion.

He would have been forgotten today had it not been for the
publication after his death of an autobiographical novel, *The Way
of All Flesh*. This tells the improbable story of Ernest Pontifex
(Butler), the son of a tyrannical parson who beats him mercilessly
whilst instilling the Classics and Scripture into him. Ernest is in
due course ordained, serving as a curate in a poor London parish.
He is sent to prison for assaulting a young girl living in his house.
On leaving prison he renounces the Church, becomes a tailor
and marries Ellen, a former servant girl of his father's. To his
horror, he discovers that Ellen is an alcoholic, but luckily a coach-
man turns up who is already married to her. This relieves Ernest
of his responsibilities. After being left a fortune by his aunt,
Ernest lives happily ever after.

Butler's posthumous success with *The Way of All Flesh* was
due almost entirely to the assault on his father. The Rev. Theo-
bald Pontifex was a lifelike portrait of Butler's own father and
was seen as the typical Victorian paterfamilias and Butler was
hailed as a daring rebel for attacking him so savagely. Bernard
Shaw in particular acclaimed *The Way of All Flesh*, describing

the author as a 'great man' and a 'man of genius' and, as a result, his reputation grew. Annual dinners were held in his honour. His books, none of which (with the exception of the satirical *Erewhon*) had enjoyed any sale during his lifetime, were republished in uniform editions – this rehabilitation of Butler being masterminded by his friend and companion H. Festing Jones, who had carefully preserved all of Butler's writing and wrote a monumental two-volume biography of his mentor.

It was no doubt in the hope that Malcolm would identify with Butler, iconoclast and rebel, that Jonathan Cape commissioned him to write a book to coincide with the hundredth anniversary of Butler's birth (1835). However, from Cape's point of view and that of Butler's trustee, Geoffrey Keynes, they could not have made a more unfortunate choice. Malcolm found Butler a deeply unsympathetic figure. He rightly discerned that far from being a rebel Butler had been a timid bachelor with a morbid dislike of his parents, an obsession with money and a singular lack of imagination. Such genius as he had was warped by his continuing sense of grievance which never left him even after his father died.

Much of the research for the Butler book had been carried out by Kitty while Malcolm was in India, though it was Malcolm who, before leaving for Calcutta, had interviewed Mr Albert Cathie, Butler's Scottish valet. (Kitty may also have seen Cathie at some stage as she often used to imitate his description of Butler's funeral: 'Ah cremation, Mrs Muggeridge! It's the finest thing . . . in the worrrrrld!') In exchange for a fee of £50 (£5 down, and the rest on completion of the interview) Cathie told Malcolm how Butler and his companion Festing Jones used to pay weekly visits (Butler on Wednesday, Jones on Thursday) to a French prostitute, a Madame Dumas who lived in Handel Street. Jones had disclosed Butler's assignments in his biography, but omitted to mention that he also made a weekly visit.

The story appealed especially to Kingsmill who had himself written about Butler in his book *After Puritanism* and once he, Malcolm and Hesketh Pearson made an expedition to the house in Handel Street, where Kingsmill reduced them to hysterics by imagining Mme Dumas in conversation with her two eccentric clients: 'Votre Monsieur Mardi n'est pas très fort', or, 'Monsieur Jeudi reste toujours jeune n'est ce pas.'

Kingsmill, who had urged Malcolm to tone the book down, had anticipated a rough reception from the reviewers, and he was right. The leading literary critic of the time, Desmond McCarthy (who was, significantly, a leading member of the Butler fan club), devoted two whole articles in the *Sunday Times* to attacking Malcolm's book and was said to be so enraged by it that he threw his copy into the sea. E. M. Forster wrote: 'This is an attack on Butler's fame and on his friends, particularly Festing Jones. An attack so disgruntled and so persistent that it may be the result of a guilt complex.'

The reception of *The Earnest Atheist* and its author was in a way a repetition of Malcolm's Russian experience. As with his reports of the Ukrainian famine, he had offended the fashionable orthodoxy by pointing out certain things that people did not want to know. The prevailing atmosphere in literary circles was, and it still is, progressive, liberal, and, more particularly, atheist. Although his supporters may not have liked to say so, Butler appealed, as communism did to the Webbs and Alan Taylor, because he was the opponent of Christianity and the family; whereas Malcolm, though not at this time a professing Christian, sided with orthodoxy in both respects – at least in principle if not in practice.

It has to be said, too, that Malcolm upset a number of critics by making fun of Butler's homosexual attachments: to Charles Pauli, a lawyer whom he met in New Zealand, thereafter paying him £200 a year; and to Hans Faesch, an uninteresting Swiss youth befriended by Butler and Festing Jones. Malcolm had always had a strong antipathy towards homosexuals, as did Kingsmill, who once observed that 'Homosexuality, which aims at duplicating the self instead of complementing it, is the natural outlet of exaggerated self-love.' Even so, it is noteworthy that at no point in his book does he brand Butler as a practising homosexual, a tribute perhaps to the skill with which Butler, with the help of Jones, had created a smokescreen about his sex-life (see the letter below from Sir Angus Wilson). Nevertheless it was his flippant description of Butler's friendships which led Cape to reject the book, which was eventually published by Eyre & Spottiswoode. While homosexuality even between consenting adults remained a criminal offence, it was a delicate subject. But there was a strong homosexual lobby in the literary world of which E. M. Forster was a leading member. Malcolm had done nothing to endear himself to such critics. Harold Nicolson and Stephen Spender both wrote critically of *The Earnest Atheist*, while Lytton Strachey's boyfriend, Roger Senhouse, scrawled on the front of his copy: 'Drenched with excited conceit and twisted by spite.'

Not all homosexuals, however, were anti-Muggeridge and in an interesting letter sent to him in 1962 Sir Angus Wilson complimented him on an article he had written at that time about Butler:

May I say how much I enjoyed your piece about Butler? It seemed to hit the nails on all their heads. Only on details about his homosexuality would I take issue. As an expert, I have never believed in that French lady. Why did Jones want to advertise her so? It's very unlikely that a homosexual conscious of what he wanted would seek physical relief every week from a female tart (or any female really), the thing would be repellent. It happens more often the other way round, where a homosexual can get physical pleasure from groundsmen, male tarts, etc, but can make no emotional tie – he then goes around with some such figure or sister-figure – hence queers' women. But physical, no! If Butler didn't dare risk it after Wilde's debacle, which is more than likely, he would have masturbated. I should think you needn't pity the French lady – Jones and Butler probably made their well-advertised (in their circle) visits and all that happened was a jolly good hour of girls' gossip . . . I suspect that Butler's main activities went on in Sicily. Two years ago I visited Calatafimi (a small town near Segesta and Trapani where he always stayed). I have no reason to suppose that a small town so primitive was any less of a happy hunting ground for homosexuals than now – it's so unchanging a place. As a matter of fact, I met a Neapolitan lecturer who had interviewed many people there who remembered Butler (a street is named after him). Unfortunately he was too naive to ask these people the right questions, but much of their reminiscence is about Butler's kindness and interest in sons of the house.

Malcolm's next book *In a Valley of This Restless Mind* was a short, rather bleak series of vignettes in which the author tried to find some meaning for his existence in a variety of encounters. As usual with his fiction, Malcolm made little attempt to disguise real people and a number of his friends feature in the book, including Wilfred Knox, Brian Lunn and the Webbs. The latter appear as Mr and Mrs Daniel Brett and are quite savagely satirized. But Beatrice did not seem to mind this although the book confirmed certain impressions she had originally formed after reading *Winter in Moscow*. 'A month ago', she wrote (31 May 1937), 'when we visited the Muggeridges, I was puzzled by Malcolm's coldness and his refusal to *look at us*: he is usually so oncoming and personally affectionate. His latest book *In a Valley of This Restless Mind* gives the explanation. One chapter is an obvious caricature of the Webbs with their "blueprint of the good life". To me these pages are amusing and quite a harmless episode. Why, by the way, do people object to literary caricature when they don't to pictorial? The public personage is hurt if he is *not* cartooned. What distresses me about this strange autobiographical work is the horrid mixture of religious strivings and curious amatory adventure; also the obsession with dirt in body and mind might be a pathological record except that it is without scientific content or purpose. In essence, it is pornography, glossed over by a certain literary charm and cleverness . . . Malcolm is always dwelling on sadistic senility. Lust (a word he delights in) and cruelty are the background of Malcolm's mind. One wonders exactly where it will end? Could he have been cured by psychoanalysis and early treatment in the nursery and the school? Kitty has outgrown the hysterics of her youth. She is a handsome woman and a devoted wife and mother.'

Malcolm would no doubt have countered that Mrs Webb was sexually frustrated and therefore antipathetic to his viewpoint. Nevertheless it is true that the book (like Malcolm's diary) displays an obsession with sex which is morbid. It is also, unlike the later Muggeridge, almost completely lacking in humour. Rather surprisingly it found a champion in Evelyn Waugh. Reviewing it in the *Spectator* (27 May 1938), he began by welcoming Malcolm into the 'very small company of writers' whose work was not marred by bad English. 'His book gives the reader the hope that no two words mean exactly the same to him: the punctuation, though not always orthodox (commas before ands) is usually consistent: with the exception of three painful conjunctival uses of "like" there are no barbarities of grammar; there is an abundance of literary allusion and concealed quotation to flatter the reader's knowledge. It is, in fact, a highly unusual and welcome piece of workmanship.'

Waugh did not make Mrs Webb's mistake of confusing writing about sex with pornography. There was nothing spicy about such passages, he said, they betrayed the attitude of a surfeited and rather scared Calvinist. Himself a deeply religious man, Waugh recognized in Malcolm 'the loneliness of a religiously-minded man suddenly made alive to the fact that he is outside Christendom'.

It was not until *The Thirties* was published in 1940 that Malcolm finally found his form as a writer. The tone could not be more different. It is confident and, above all, humorous. A survey of the decade that had just passed, the book is remarkable for its spirit of detachment – especially remarkable when we remember that it was completed at the outbreak of war (the final chapters were written in a barracks hut at Aldershot) at a time when many writers were engaged in propaganda or were so uncertain about the future that they had given up writing altogether. Although the book was essentially concerned with politics, its style was poetic, with frequent literary and biblical quotations (often stood on their head to great effect). Image was piled on image to render individuals and institutions ludicrous:

The BBC came to pass silently, invisibly, like a coral reef, cells briskly multiplying, until it was a vast structure, a conglomeration of studios, offices, cool passages along which many passed to and fro; a society with its King and Lords and commoners, its laws and dossiers and revenue and easily suppressed insurrection; where there was marriage and giving in marriage, and where evil doers and adulteresses were punished, and the faithful rewarded. As many little rivulets empty themselves into a wide lake, all their motion is lost in its still expanse of water, so did every bubbling trend and fashion empty themselves into the BBC.

Circumstances shaped it, making it an image, pure and undefiled, of the times. It was a mirror held up to nature. Beards grew on chins, tufty rather than sparse, as inevitably as reeds in marshland; sentiments crystallized with the same slow certainty that a pearl forms in an oyster. Whatever was put in it must either take on its texture or be expelled, a waste product; though different meats were inserted, the resultant sausages were indistinguishable. Nightly, the nine million listened – 'News bulletin, copyright reserved!' – merely curious or apprehensive; gently and persuasively instructed in their own and other's misfortunes, in what they should hope for and what they should dread; music to delight them, both serious and frivolous, edifying discourses, perhaps a domestic chat from Lord Elton, or a curious encounter between a Chinese poet and a Westmoreland shepherd; prayers for the prayerful, tunes for the tuneful, instruction for those who wished to be instructed. Comfortable in armchairs, drowsing perhaps, snug and secure, the whole world was available, its tumult compressed into a radio set's small compass. Wars and rumours of wars, all the misery and passion of a troubled world, thus came into their consciousness, in winter with curtains drawn and a cheerful fire blazing; in summer often out of doors, sprawling on a lawn or under a tree, or in a motor car, indolently listening while telegraph poles flitted past. Dolfuss had been murdered, despairing Jews had resorted to gas ovens, Wall Street prices were rising or falling or stationary, Lord Runciman thought war unlikely, much of Cardiff had been disposed of by its owner, Lord Bute, for some millions of pounds, and the king and queen had received a warm welcome in Hackney – well, there it was, and now for another station, as the wave length slowly changes, fragments of music heard, sounds and sweet airs, spluttering voices, many languages and many intonations, laughter and anger and stockprices and salesmanship and oratory were all mingled together, frenzied confusion.

From now on, this was to be the distinctive Muggeridge tone of voice – Gibbon-like detachment, elegant mockery, expressed in perfect prose. If Malcolm had a text, it was 'vanity of vanities, all is vanity'. Regardless of the war that loomed, Malcolm saw clearly a civilization in decline. 'If there is any central theme in Mr Muggeridge's book,' Harold Nicolson wrote in a review, 'it is that during the ten years between 1930–1940 the people of Great Britain were seeking to console themselves for loss of faith by the fiction that life upon this earth is a creative and enjoyable thing.' George Orwell, who later became a close friend of Malcolm's, also discerned a religious theme running through the book, though he concluded: 'Unfortunately, Mr Muggeridge shows no sign of believing in God himself. Or at least he seems to take it for granted that this belief is vanishing from the human mind. There is not much doubt that he is right there, and if one assumes that no sanction can ever be effective except the supernatural one, it is clear what follows . . . wars and yet more wars, revolutions and counter-revolutions, Hitlers and Super-Hitlers – and so downwards into abysses which are horrible to contemplate, though I rather suspect Mr Muggeridge of enjoying the prospect.' (Orwell, *Collected Essays and Journalism* Vol. II)

In fact, as Orwell hinted, what made *The Thirties* more than just a gloomy Jeremiad was the high spirits in which it was written. The book is studded with telling quotations: ' "Wider still and wider shall thy bounds be set" does not indicate the desire for more territory,' Anthony Eden. 'Generally speaking, I am certainly opposed to anything in the nature of third degree or torture,' The Dean of Canterbury. Malcolm had not lost his acute sense of living in a dying civilization, but it was no longer a cause with him for morbidness or despair. This new spirit of satirical detachment was largely the outcome of his new-found friendship with Hugh Kingsmill.

CHAPTER VII

World War II

MALCOLM'S RESOLUTION to settle down and write, to give up women, drink and smoking, had long since gone by default. After only a few months he had been discussing the possibility of going to work on a South African newspaper (luckily for Kitty the idea fell through). He began an affair with the wife of a neighbour, Mrs Hallinan, whilst also travelling up on the train to London for assignations with Natalie, the wealthy wife of Ernest Davies, a left-wing journalist, later a Labour MP. When Kitty went away to Switzerland for a brief holiday in 1937, he even made a pass at Hugh Kingsmill's wife Dorothy, a woman he disliked and despised. In the meantime, he confided in his diary his confused thoughts about religion, lust ('Why do I always think, when I meet a woman, of seducing her?') and Kitty, one day rhapsodizing about his great love for her, the next deciding regretfully that they would have to separate.

The consequence was that he greeted the outbreak of war in 1939 almost with relief as it provided him at last with an excuse for making off yet again as he had done in 1934. Even before war was declared he joined the Civil Air Guard and learned to fly in the hope that when hostilities began he would be able to get into the Air Force. On the Monday following Chamberlain's declaration of war he announced to Kitty that he was off to join the army. However, when he reported at the recruiting office in Maidstone, he was told that journalism was a 'reserved occupation' and returned home feeling rather foolish. He then wrote to Lord Lloyd, whom he had met in Cairo when the latter was High Commissioner, hoping that he would use his influence to get him into the RAF, but to no avail. (This perhaps was not

surprising, as Lloyd had recommended Malcolm to the Air Ministry on the grounds that he was not only a friend but a brilliant
rider.) He was then offered a job in London at the Ministry of
Information, which had been set up under Duff Cooper in the
London University buildings in Bloomsbury. He immediately
accepted, partly because he needed the money – his novel-
reviewing on the *Daily Telegraph* had come to a halt with the
outbreak of war – but mainly in order, once again, to cut loose.
His job was to produce articles for the foreign press which would
help to raise enthusiasm for the Allied cause. A colleague was
Graham Greene, already a friend as a result of *Night and Day*.
Another was Richard Crossman, the Oxford Don who later
became a Labour Minister and editor of the *New Statesman*.

After a few months, Malcolm's wartime career changed as the
result of a tongue-in-cheek article he had written in the *Daily
Telegraph* describing his unsuccessful attempt to join the army.
A Major Davies he had known in Egypt had written to him
saying that if he was so keen to join up, why did he not consider
the Field Security Police, of which Davies was C.O. and which
had recently been advertising for foreign linguists. Malcolm
wrote back saying that he had not been bluffing and that he was
anxious to serve in any capacity. He had forgotten all about this
when he received a summons to report to Mytchett Hutments,
Ash Vale near Aldershot, the depot of FSP, shortly to be trans-
formed into the Intelligence Corps. At the recruiting office he
put down 'Independent' since all his known occupations were
still reserved. For six months he served in the ranks as a sergeant
being subjected to all the indignities of army life – drill, fatigues
and kit inspection. Kitty received £1.19 for the support of herself
and the four children, while Malcolm received 75p a week. Luckily, while he was at Ash Vale, he received news that *The Thirties*
had been selected by the Book Society, which made things easier
until he was commissioned in May 1940. To his disappointment
he was not sent abroad but kept on at Mytchett as an instructor,
giving lectures on propaganda.

In May 1940, he was commissioned. Shortly afterwards the
war began in earnest and the depot was transferred to the Isle of
Sheppey. Here on one of the courses he encountered an officer

whose large soup-strainer moustache caught his eye. It turned out that his name was Enoch Powell; he told Malcolm he had grown the moustache in order to resemble his hero, Frederick Nietzsche.

Eventually, Malcolm secured a posting to GHQ Home Forces, then housed at Kneller Hall but later in the buildings of St Paul's School, Hammersmith (now destroyed). Malcolm described it at this time: 'a large upstairs hall at St Paul's with heavy rafters and stolid paintings of previous headmasters. Many officers sat about in the half light of an early autumn evening, waiting to hear the news. They were always waiting to hear the news, or, having heard the news, digesting it; mostly regulars, many of them booted, with strange moustaches and vacant eyes and florid cheeks.'

Here, the responsibility of his section was to secure the head-quarters against possible subversion by enemy agents. It was, as he said, an excellent brief in that almost any activity – pub-crawling, picking up girls – could be justified as essential war work. Despite the humdrum routine, Malcolm typically became involved in an incident which, though on the surface faintly comic, was of some historical importance. One day in July 1940 the officer to whom he was responsible, Colonel Ross-Atkinson, an Irishman, handed him a confidential report stating that the car of the Commander-in-Chief of Home Forces, William 'Tiny' Ironside, had been spotted for long periods outside a house in Holland Park where a number of Fascists were known to live. He duly investigated, and found that it was indeed the case that the Commander-in-Chief was paying visits to the house in question – whether for personal or political reasons it was impossible to tell. After consulting a colleague, Bobby Barclay, they decided to inform Barclay's stepfather, Lord Vansittart, who was then head of the Foreign Office. Vansittart took careful note, without committing himself to an opinion. However, the following day it was revealed that Ironside had been sacked and replaced by Sir Alan Brooke. With all official documents still 'classified' it is impossible to tell whether this was anything more than a coincidence.

It was the period of the phoney war and there was very little to do. Most of his friends had left London. Hugh Kingsmill had taken a teaching job at Marlborough. But Hesketh Pearson was still in Hampstead. In June they had dinner together in Richmond, Malcolm predicting that the war would be over in four weeks and that Lloyd George would be trotted out to do a deal with Hitler. 'We had a grand evening and laughed ourselves sick,' Pearson wrote in his diary. Shortly afterwards, they visited the House of Commons together. Pearson wrote to Kingsmill: 'Malcolm wanted to see the revolting swine in session for the last time.'

The writer Lettice Cooper also saw something of Malcolm at this time. They had both been contributors to *Time and Tide*. She found him a fascinating companion and they used to meet regularly for lunch at the Dominion, a pub in Tottenham Court Road. When Lettice Cooper discovered how poor he was, she insisted on paying her share. But Malcolm would only let her pass over money outside the restaurant, otherwise he said it would lower his standing in the eyes of the waiter. They talked a lot about religion: 'Malcolm with such obvious yearning towards the Roman Catholic Church that I was surprised that it took him so long to get there,' she remembered.

The next time I saw him, I think he was going home from training camp for a weekend's leave and asked me to meet him at Waterloo on his way through. He arrived with four other young soldiers. They had an hour to wait for their train. Malcolm led them to collect six cups of tea and handed me a shilling with which to buy six buns at the food counter. We all sat down at a long empty table in the refreshment room. Malcolm had also bought a large slab of chocolate (not yet rationed). This he divided meticulously into six shares while carrying on a religious conversation at which one or two of the soldiers looked slightly dazed. I remember that part of it was about suicide and whether it was true that people who talked about killing themselves were less likely to do it.

I can only recall one other war-time meeting which must have been after the bombing of London had begun. Malcolm asked me to meet him for supper at the Dominion. I made my way there through blacked-out streets. The approach to the entrance we had always used seemed to be different. I seemed to be at the edge of a hole. Then I heard Malcolm's voice saying, 'Lettice? Look out, it's been bombed, come away.' We got across the dark street and into the comparative warmth and light of Lyons Corner House.

I don't remember what we talked about except for one fragment of conversation. Malcolm said, 'If the Germans occupy England, are you going into the resistance?'

'I haven't thought about it, but I suppose so. Are you?'

'No, I'm learning German.'

'If you feel like that, why did you go straight into the army?'

'Oh well,' he said, 'if you saw this ceiling beginning to fall down, you'd put up your hand and try and stop it, wouldn't you?'

The Blitz, which had begun in September 1940, came to Malcolm as a relief, marking as it did the outbreak of war in earnest and also appealing to his anarchic instincts. He went out to watch almost every night when it was on, often with Andreas Mayor, a young cousin of Kitty's and the brother of Tessa, who later married Lord (Victor) Rothschild. Mayor, at this time a Captain of the Royal Fusiliers, was another of those outsiders to whom he was instinctively drawn – a melancholy intellectual of great charm, who was later recruited into intelligence. Another companion of his 'Blitz-crawls' was Graham Greene, now an air-raid warden, who like Malcolm took a perverse pleasure in seeing the buildings reduced to rubble.

In his camouflaged Austin, he toured the city inspecting the bomb damage (once driving around Piccadilly Circus the wrong way to 'celebrate the absence of all other traffic'). Later, he crashed the car after celebrating the news that he was to be posted to Salisbury.

It was thanks to Graham Greene that Malcolm was transferred, after a short spell at Salisbury, to MI6 or SIS (Special Intelligence Services) as it was then known. Greene, who had in turn been recruited by his sister Elizabeth, was already installed in SIS working in Section Five – the Counter-Espionage Section. When he was posted to Freetown, Sierra Leone, he learned that they needed someone to serve as agent in Lourenço Marques, Mozambique and suggested Malcolm's name in order, he told him many years later, 'that you should escape those wintry rides on motor cycles'. The head of the Iberian Department (dealing with Portugal and the Portuguese empire) was Kim Philby.

In 1942 Kim Philby was thirty and generally regarded as the white hope of the Secret Service. He was intelligent, very hard-working and popular with most of his colleagues. Malcolm was no exception in finding him agreeable and charming, though not particularly interesting to talk to. He appeared to have no interest in politics. For this reason, when he looked back later after Philby had been exposed as the most highly-placed Russian agent in the history of the Cold War, Malcolm refused to accept the official version of Philby as a dedicated Marxist who had for some years been building a cover for himself by appearing pro-Fascist (as was his father, the famous Arabist, Sir John Philby). Malcolm persisted in believing that Philby was a natural toady who only sided with the Russians when it was clear to him that they were going to be in the victors' camp – in other words, another version of the non-ideological Walter Duranty who faithfully served the Russian Government as a result of being drawn to and excited by the immense power of Stalin. It was very typical of Malcolm to adopt a view of this kind about a person and refuse to budge however much evidence was produced to refute it.

However, it was surprising how often Malcolm's general instincts about people were right, even when he appeared most perverse in his attitude towards facts. Thus, though it may be true that Philby was a Russian agent for some years prior to the war, it is equally true that he had the mentality of a civil servant and was prepared to serve the Soviet Union, not because of its political ideology but its immense and terrifying power.

Malcolm had met Philby at the SIS headquarters, which were in a large requisitioned country house near St Albans, Herts. Here he was told to 'put himself in the picture' and familiarize himself with intelligence work. He also spent some time at the Government Code and Cipher School (GCCS) which had moved to a Victorian mansion at Bletchley Park in Buckinghamshire.

Here a number of brilliant dons (including Wilfred Knox's brother Dilly) had succeeded in mastering the German's secret Enigma cipher machine – in its way the most important British victory of the war.

The Enigma breakthrough had altered considerably the role of British agents abroad. A priority was now to ensure that the Germans had no suspicion that the code had been cracked. Agents, therefore, had often to go through the motions, even though SIS headquarters were aware of what the Germans were up to because all their cables were being intercepted. The new situation also made life difficult for the individual agent in that once his activities were reported by German spies they automatically became known also to his superiors in England.

At Bletchley, Malcolm was taught the techniques of ciphering and deciphering by an elderly Scottish lady whose thumb had become deformed after years of using a codebook. He took pleasure in observing the dons playing rounders during their lunch hour. Subsequently, he was sent to an address in Hans Crescent, Knightsbridge, to be taught how to use invisible ink. There were various substances which could be used, his instructor told him, including a well-known brand of headache tablets. In emergencies he was advised to collect deposits of BS (bird shit).

Malcolm had first to go to Lisbon, leaving in March 1942 on a plane from Poole Harbour, in order to acquire a visa. He hung about in Lisbon for weeks, trying to learn Portuguese and experiencing his usual feelings of depression.

It was while he was in Lisbon waiting to sail for Mozambique that he heard from Kitty about his father.

> Your father now is dying. He is in the nursing home at Hastings. Your mother is staying with me. We go in the car to see him every day and stay about twenty minutes. He has lost his angry look and lies very still with a peaceful expression and I don't think he any longer has any fear of death. He does not even open his eyes, and his hands lie on the bed very lifeless. He can with difficulty speak names, Douglas, Malcolm. Your mother is distressed because he does not look at her and she tries to lift his lids and kisses his brow, but he cannot make

the effort of recognizing her. I tell her that he knows she is there but is unable to say so. Sitting by his bedside, although he cannot speak, I feel closer in touch with him than before. I suppose being near to death, H. Muggeridge is no more and he is just one of us giving up the ghost and therefore more familiar.

A few days later Kitty wrote again:

Your father died on March 25th at 6 in the morning. He died in his sleep. The funeral was on Friday, and his grave is in the churchyard here as you said it should be and Noble took the service. About twelve people came to the funeral. Mr Wimble, Goodwin Law, Berwick Sayers and one or two other Croydon relatives as well as your brothers. He was buried very quietly and the people came and had refreshments here and spoke to your mother. It was a lovely day and it did not seem a very sad occasion even for your mother, who received her guests with a great air, was more like Val at one of her parties than a bereaved widow. I think his death was a relief to him and to her, and an atmosphere of great relief seemed to hang about him when he was hoisted on trestles in the box in the church, as if the man was singing 'Ain't it grand to be blooming well dead?' We are going to plant his grave with flowers and have a stone frame with his name on it. I went up with P. A. Wilson to choose his grave and we decided to have a double grave so that your mother can be there too when she dies.

'Was somewhat stricken by my father's death,' Malcolm wrote in his diary. Inevitably, he and his father had grown apart. H. T. Muggeridge had never lost his faith in his son or his pride in his achievements, but Malcolm could no longer share his father's idealism, though he never lost his great affection for him. Already experiencing his usual feelings of depression at being apart from Kitty, Malcolm recorded no special feelings of grief in his diary, instead indulging in banal thoughts about mortality: 'Thus proceeds the irresistible current of life . . .'

*   *   *

'What I was engaged in during those war years', Graham Greene wrote, 'was not genuine action – it was an escape from reality and responsibility.' Malcolm was later to express similar feelings. Both men, one in West Africa, the other in Mozambique, felt frustrated by not being actual combatants. In fact, in the context of war as a whole, Malcolm's posting, like Greene's, was of some importance.

In May 1942 when he left for Mozambique things were not going well for the Allies. The Africa Corps under Rommel had superiority in tanks, guns and aircraft, thus posing a threat to Alexandria, Cairo and Allied oil supplies. Because of the danger to convoys sailing through the Mediterranean, reinforcements and supplies for the British Army had to come via the Cape and the Mozambique Channel (between Mozambique and Madagascar) was an obvious place for German U-boats to lie in wait for convoys leaving Durban. At this time, prior to the development of radar, the Allies had no means of detecting the presence of German U-boats. German agents in South Africa, of whom there were a number, could send messages about shipping to the German consul in Lourenço Marques, who would in turn alert the U-boats waiting in the Mozambique Channel. There was known to be a particularly good agent (also the Consul), Dr L. Werz, who had previously been the German Consul General in Pretoria and was moved to Mozambique in 1940. He was known by the British to be cabling not only political and economic information about Germany but shipping intelligence acquired through agents in Mozambique. He was also acting as a link between the Abwehr (German Secret Service) and its contacts in South Africa, where two extreme right-wing pro-Nazi organizations, the Broederbond and Ossewa Brandweg, had successfully infiltrated the police force and the civil service.

Mozambique, or Portuguese East Africa as it was generally known, was a Portuguese colony, though with a large and influential British and South African business community. The capital, Lourenço Marques (now Maputo) was a thriving port as well as a popular tourist attraction, especially for South Africans living in a puritanical, Boer-dominated society. Malcolm's first impression of the town was of a somewhat rundown Mediterranean seaside resort complete with bathing beaches and souvenir shops. Trains arrived regularly from Johannesburg disgorging South African fun-seekers at the huge and grandiose Bauhaus station, from which it was only a short distance by rickshaw to the 'Street of Sin', lined with cafés, hotels, casinos and brothels (many with attractive wrought-iron balconies). From the old town which had grown up alongside the port, wide avenues lined with frangipani and acacia led up to the more salubrious area overlooking the sea where the Portuguese had built rows of ornate villas and where the embassies and consulates were also situated. Here too, fifteen minutes' walk from the British Consulate, was the famous Polana Hotel, a huge, ugly, white wedding-cake in stone, designed by Sir Herbert Baker in 1921 and owned by a Johannesburg cinema tycoon, complete with tennis courts, swimming pool and an adjoining golf course.

The hotel was to be Malcolm's base for the next nine months, one that he was forced to share with his German and Italian counterparts, Dr Werz and Signor Campini. Werz, Malcolm noted, was a Bavarian – a rather pleasant-looking man who played the piano and enjoyed an occasional game of tennis with his fellow Germans. Malcolm once overheard him playing sentimental music to celebrate the fall of Sebastopol. On Saturdays he appeared in shorts and a small Bavarian green coat.

In the espionage game Malcolm had two advantages over his Axis enemies. The first was the generally pro-British attitude of most of the Portuguese, the second was the fact that all Werz's messages were being intercepted and decoded by the decipher department of SIS Bletchley. As a result of the interception of Axis signals it emerged that there were three German agents operating out of South Africa, including one L. J. Elferink, a professor of literature, but that having built a transmitter to send messages to Berlin, those messages were being intercepted. The improved intelligence led to a number of counter-measures, one of which was the kidnapping of Alfredo Manna, head of the shipping intelligence network operated by Campini and Werz. Manna, Malcolm discovered with the help of a Portuguese police inspector who was on his payroll, had a South African girlfriend in Lourenço Marques who was anxious to return to Johannesburg but had been denied a visa on the grounds that her way of life was considered immoral. Malcolm promised to help her with a visa if she would persuade her lover to take her on a car ride towards the border with Swaziland, then British territory. The girl agreed and as the car neared the border it was stopped by the waiting police inspector and Manna was bundled into another car and driven into Swaziland. Malcolm learned subsequently that he had been taken to England for interrogation and spent the rest of the war there. He was also relieved to learn that the girl eventually found her way back to Johannesburg, being so grateful to Malcolm that she sent him flowers.

Official British concern at events in Mozambique mounted in November 1942 following the sinking in quick succession of two ships, SS *Nova Scotia* and SS *Llandaff Castle*. The *Nova Scotia* was a British troop ship which had set out from North Africa carrying over a thousand Italian prisoners of war and a number of South African soldiers when it was torpedoed by U-boats. Such was the influence of the British and South African business communities in neutral Mozambique that a group of local well-wishers led by Francis Spence, a British shipping agent, was able to mingle freely with the South African soldiers and arranged to supply them all with civilian clothes to avoid their being interned by the Portuguese. Spence then contacted Malcolm at the Polana Hotel to see if he could arrange for taxis to transport the survivors to Namaacha on the border with Swaziland. Malcolm was happy to oblige and the South Africans were thus able to get home safely. (It is notable that in Malcolm's account of this incident in his memoirs, there is no mention of Spence and the impression is given that he himself single-handedly organized the rescue operation.)

Of all his various escapades, Malcolm was proudest of all of the plot he engaged in to capture a ship that was supplying equipment and stores to German U-boats. He had a Jewish agent from Eastern Europe named Serge who one night arranged for him to meet a Greek sailor in Marie's Place, a Lourenço Marques brothel. The sailor agreed that he could easily take over the ship; the first officer was on his side. All Malcolm would have to do, he said, would be to arrange for them to be able to sail into Durban harbour after they had 'disposed' of the captain.

Malcolm could see how eager Serge and the Greek sailor were to feed the captain to the sharks, but he could not bring himself to authorize his killing; for all that, the operation went ahead like clockwork. The ship duly sailed into Durban with the captain, one Homer Serafimides, locked in his cabin. Malcolm's decision to spare him proved not only merciful but expedient as he subsequently provided MI6 with valuable information about Campini's spy network. Malcolm later received the unusual honour of a personal telegram from 'C', the head of the Secret Service, congratulating him on the success of the operation.

In his official history of British Intelligence in the Second World War, Professor F. H. Hinsley observes that 'from the end of 1942 there was a marked increase in SIS intelligence about the German activities [in South Africa]. This improvement, he said, owed something to the recruitment by the SIS officer [Malcolm] of a well-placed member of the German community there.' His name was Baron Werner Von Alvensleben, a German aristocrat and former Nazi who had escaped to Mozambique from a British internment camp in Rhodesia. Malcolm became friends with him through his fiancée Maria Adriana de Souza Costa, known as Bibla, a Portuguese woman whom Malcolm had met, and immediately fallen in love with, at the Polana Hotel. Bibla was unhappily married to the local 'Gauleiter', Herr Leidenburg, and her sister was the mistress of Malcolm's German counterpart, Leopold Werz. 'Like her sister,' Malcolm wrote later, 'she is very sallow, even swarthy, with dark eyes and graceful movements and very fine teeth. Her expression is sad; she dresses well, often in the hot weather in shorts or trousers. Her husband is a typical German with no back to his head, a white face and an aggressive bearing.'

Malcolm went up to her when he first saw her standing at the reception desk and introduced himself. Then when they met in the hotel corridor he would smile and she would smile back:

Bibla now became an obsession. I was always looking for her, and when she used to walk up and down the terrace I'd walk up and down the garden trying to summon up the courage to go and join her. One evening, in the bar with a number of others, when I'd had a fair amount to drink, I suddenly felt I could keep away from her no longer. In the writing room I found her writing and sat down beside her. We talked and later went out on the terrace and sat down there looking down at the sea. When she got up to go I clumsily embraced her, and when she had gone the air seemed full of her presence. For some while I walked about to tranquillize myself.

I had said to Bibla when we separated that I should be at the same place on the terrace at the same time the following evening, and there of course I was, wondering if she would come. The door from the lounge opened, and I watched her walking along with the imperious swinging gait that I already knew so well. Henceforth we met often on the terrace. I remember so well, sitting there waiting for her, wondering of each footstep if it was hers; or if she was with me, starting at each footstep for fear we should be seen together. I remember so well the terrace. And the stars above it and the sea beneath it and the winds which sometimes swept it.

From their talks Malcolm learned that she was unhappily married to Leidenburg, that they slept in separate rooms in the hotel and were going to get divorced. She also spoke about her mother, who had committed suicide in Lisbon at the outbreak of war, and about her sister's unfortunate liaison with Werz, whom she detested. Now she was planning to marry Werner Von Alvensleben and go and live in South Africa.

On New Year's Eve 1942, after a party in the Polana Hotel, Malcolm and Bibla became lovers. He had been sitting drinking with a Major in the Marines when she beckoned him upstairs: 'Bibla's room – how easily I summon up a picture of it, the two chairs, the bed, the table, the large boxes, the photographs (Von A. very noticeable at her bedside), the wireless – how well I remember being there, sometimes my heart almost stopping because of a footstep on the large verandah outside, or crunching gravel below. While I was there on this New Year's Eve, Bibla's sister rang her up and as they spoke together she cried because

of their estrangement. The waiter brought us a bottle of cham-
pagne and two glasses; and just at midnight she drank to Von
A's health alone, afterwards breaking the glass, then in the other
glass we drank to each other's health. Now for the first time I
kissed her passionately on the mouth, and she responded. She
showed me photographs of a tour she had made in Germany
with Leidenburg and descriptions written underneath in his hand,
most neat, in white ink. When I left, I held her in my arms.'

Malcolm now became a partner in a rather complex ménage
à trois. As their love affair progressed, Bibla began to feel guilty
about Von Alvensleben and Malcolm therefore suggested that
they should all three meet. This they did, picking Werner up
from his house and taking him to a remote spot on the beach.
The two men took an immediate liking to each other – 'It's
Werner who's fallen in love with you,' Bibla told Malcolm. Von
Alvensleben was a tall, long-haired aristocrat who had joined the
Nazi party in his youth and even taken part in a plot to murder
an Austrian politician. Later, disenchanted with the Nazis and
regarded by them as a traitor, he fled to Africa but was interned
by the British in Rhodesia as an alien, subsequently escaping
and ending up in Lourenço Marques where he had gained the
confidence of Werz. However, Von Alvensleben was now a liberal and, like Bibla, a convinced anti-Nazi and therefore very
willing to help Malcolm in the fight against Werz and Campini
by becoming a double agent. It was he who discovered that
Werz was sending an agent into South Africa to contact pro-Nazi
elements there. Malcolm decided to go to South Africa to tip off
the police in the hope that they would arrest Werz's man. However, when he got there, the South African police chief whom
he saw merely laughed at him, pointing out that Werz's agent
would have the support of large numbers of South Africans and
that even the Minister of Justice was a member of the extremist
pro-Nazi organization known as Ossewa Brandweg. When Malcolm returned in a depressed state to Lourenço Marques he was
further disconcerted to find that his house had been broken into.
Then he remembered that he had previously arranged for Von
Alvensleben to burgle his house during his absence to offset any
suspicion on Werz's part that it was he who had tipped Malcolm

off about the agent. It turned out to have been an unnecessary precaution the two of them had concocted, though documents unearthed by the historian David Irving in 1966 show it had succeeded in muddying the waters. Following the burglary, Werz cabled Berlin: 'Further to my earlier report an agent [Von Alvensleben] has been able to purloin from Muggeridge's room documents he had left lying around during his absence. Among them were *inter alia* daily reports emanating from police spies.' A list of documents included Werz's bank statements and, according to Malcolm's account, a bogus memorandum from MI6 querying the large sums of money they were paying Campini in view of the poor quality of information he was supplying.

Meanwhile, at the same time as he was deceiving Werz and Campini with Von Alvensleben's help, Malcolm was also deceiving Von Alvensleben about his relationship with Bibla. He would arrange to meet her in his car in the evenings after work, waiting at some lonely spot with the car lights turned off. Once she was seen getting into his car and this created a great scandal at the hotel, though luckily it never reached Von Alvensleben's ears. Often Malcolm would accompany Bibla to her room and they would lie together, scarcely daring to breathe, listening to her husband undressing in the next room and waiting for his snores to begin when they would know he was asleep. At the same time, Malcolm was growing increasingly fond of Von Alvensleben. The three of them went for picnics on the Swaziland border and bathed together; later, when Malcolm had moved into a house, spending quiet evenings with Bibla sewing while the two men played chess. Sooner or later, as was inevitable, Von Alvensleben began to suspect what was happening. There was a quarrel between him and Bibla and though they all continued to see each other the romance between Bibla and Malcolm began to cool.

Malcolm was drinking heavily throughout his time in Mozambique and now started to frequent the rather seedy Café Penguin in the 'Street of Sin' where he flirted with a Portuguese dancer, Diane, often staying there until two in the morning in order to be able to take her home. Sometimes he would drive her to a fashionable Greek restaurant on the coast road, the Costa do Sol, to eat prawns and walk on the beach. But he still hankered after Bibla. One night, when very drunk after dining at the Polana with his secretary and the wife of a colleague, he saw her at a table with two Germans. 'After dinner I noticed Bibla was not in the lounge and had a great longing to see her. So, excusing myself, I went upstairs to her room. She was not in but the light was on, the blind up. I found a pencil and piece of paper and wrote her a foolish note – how I had longed to see her, how naturally now that luck was against us, she was not in, and how she understood nothing of me or my feelings for her. Then I came downstairs again and shortly afterwards was called to the telephone. It was Von Alvensleben, very angry to know what I meant by leaving a note in Bibla's room. I said if he wanted to discuss the matter further I was at his service. He rang off.'

Malcolm, by now very drunk, went home, tried to ring Bibla (who was out) and fell asleep. He awoke at 4 a.m. feeling very ill, went to the lavatory and thought he detected the first signs of syphilis. He was suddenly overcome by a feeling of the falsity of his existence, that evening's events, the deception he was practising in every area of his life. He decided to drown himself. He put on some clothes, drove to the furthest point on the coast accessible by car and waded out to sea. It was a long way before he was finally out of his depth. He could see the lights of the Costa do Sol twinkling on the shore. Then suddenly he turned back, but he was so far out and so exhausted that he nearly drowned on the return journey.

Later, via Von Alvensleben, word got back to Werz, who cabled his Abwehr superiors that Malcolm was so demoralized that he had tried to take his life. Malcolm, in turn, knowing that Werz's cables were being intercepted at Bletchley, sent a message claiming that his suicide attempt was a deliberate piece of deception to make Werz think he had completely lost heart. After a while he began to think that this might have been true. Doubt was later cast on the whole story by Malcolm's biographer, Ian Hunter, who pointed out that the description of the attempted drowning in Malcolm's memoirs bore a marked resemblance to the passage in his *Guardian* novel, *Picture Palace*, though such a coincidence would not necessarily invalidate the second personal account. All the same, it is hard to believe that the suicide attempt was a very serious one, especially since Malcolm was drunk at the time. He was always prone to severe depression and heavy drinking while separated from Kitty for any length of time and, in the rather unreal world of Mozambique, he felt additionally cut off from friends. Coincidentally, some months before this incident Hugh Kingsmill had been writing to Hesketh Pearson (then living almost next door to Kitty in Sussex) enquiring about Malcolm's well-being. 'Have you any news of Mug?' he asked on 5 October 1942. 'I have a feeling very definite, that he is not flourishing.' He asked again on 26 October: 'Any news of Mug? I continue to wonder how he is.' Eventually, in a letter dated 30 October 1942, Kingsmill explained: 'What happened was that on September 30th when I was approaching my bedroom I heard a voice saying "Hughie" – apparently in some distress. I went into the bedroom and mentioned this to Dorothy, asking if it was her. She said that it wasn't and added that she had also heard it. I said that the voice sounded like Mug and she agreed. A curious experience but if Kitty has heard since September 30th, it can't mean he is dead . . .'

Shortly after the suicide attempt in July 1943, Malcolm left Lourenço Marques for good. When the plane stopped to refuel in Kampala, Uganda, he was suddenly afflicted with acute abdominal pains and taken to hospital for an emergency operation. He stayed in hospital for five days where he wrote an account of his love affair and suicide attempt and then flew on to Lagos. He was due to fly to London the next day but a colonel with a wooden leg claimed priority and took his seat. A few hours later the plane crashed near Shannon airport in Ireland with no survivors. So, in a short space of time, Malcolm was twice preserved from death.

Back in London, Malcolm reported to MI6 headquarters, now housed in Ryder Street, where rumours were circulating among colleagues that he had left Lourenço Marques under a cloud. Graham Greene, who had himself returned to London from Sierra Leone, where he had acted in a similar capacity to Malcolm's, noted in his copy of Malcolm's memoirs (published in the early Seventies): 'As I remember it he was recalled because he was trying inefficiently to run a double-agent – Johnson? – but was giving away more important things than he got.'

With all the official records still embargoed it is impossible to verify this version of events. A more likely explanation is that, with the Allied victories in North Africa, the Mediterranean had once again become safe for convoys and his job therefore had become superfluous. In any case, British intelligence had arrived at the view that Werz's reports on shipping which they had been intercepting were almost valueless. As for Campini, he was to be sent home following the downfall of Mussolini in the summer of 1943.

In terms of visible achievements, Malcolm's short tour of duty in Mozambique had been remarkably successful. But some of his MI6 colleagues, particularly those with an Establishment background, disparaged him. Typical was Hugh Trevor Roper who, along with many other clever young dons, had been recruited into intelligence and who first met Malcolm at this time. Trevor Roper knew his name because he had been disgusted by his biography of Samuel Butler, who was a particular hero of his, vowing that he never wished to meet the author of such a dreadful book.

Like Greene, Trevor Roper subscribed to the view that Malcolm had been brought back to England in disgrace for failing to take action over a German agent. Despite their different backgrounds, however, the two became friendly and more than once Trevor Roper stayed with Malcolm and Kitty at Whatlington after the war. Later, when he had published his famous book *The Last Days of Hitler* (1947), Trevor Roper corresponded with Malcolm about Hitler's sex life (6 July 1948): 'Re Hitler's sex life. I was too discreet to announce last night the interesting fact that according to medical files allegedly seen by Dr Kersten and quoted by him, Hitler derived some sexual satisfaction from delivering speeches before great crowds of people, having confessed to experiencing orgasm at such times. I should add that this conclusion had been independently deduced by others from the style and tempo of his oratory.'

At the close of 1943 Malcolm, who had now reverted to

military rank as a Major, flew out to Algiers where the Allies were planning the invasion of Europe. His task was to liaise with French military intelligence, the Securité Militaire under Captain Paillole, which controlled some thirty German and Spanish agents in the area. They were mostly waiters, barmen and mechanics, anyone whose job entailed free movement in public places. The French and British intelligence men would seek to identify the enemy agents and then to 'turn' them against their German masters. This involved providing them with a certain amount of true intelligence ('chicken feed') in which an important nugget of false information had been inserted – the overall aim being to mislead the Germans about where the Allies would attack next in Europe. When the attack did come it was in Italy and Malcolm accompanied the Allied Forces in the slow advance northwards.

Then, on 12 August 1944 he flew with Captain Paillole to Paris, a city in a state of almost complete anarchy and chaos. For a few days he wandered about the streets 'in varying states of intoxication', taking advantage of the free hospitality which famous restaurants like Maxim's were offering to the Allied officers. Eventually he took up residence in the mansion of Victor Rothschild in the Avenue Marigny (Rothschild, married to a cousin of Kitty's, was a senior officer in MI5 at the time).

Malcolm spent six months in Paris, officially engaged in the task of identifying German agents as well as rescuing their bona fide British agents from the frightening witch-hunt – the so-called 'épuration' – in which the French were engaged. Once again he managed to antagonize many of his colleagues in intelligence, from his tendency to sympathize with and try to help those accused of collaboration. The Americans especially were resentful and Malcolm was only saved by his friend Dick White, then head of Counter-Intelligence at SHAEF, from being sent back to England. Meanwhile, the French, it was rumoured, sought to neutralize Malcolm by providing him with a very pretty secretary called Françoise with whom, predictably, he embarked on an affair.

The Americans were especially upset by the way Malcolm had befriended P. G. Wodehouse and his wife Ethel who had ended up in Paris at the end of the war. The couple had been arrested as enemy aliens in 1940 at Le Touquet where they had lived since 1934 and Wodehouse had been interned in Poland. He was released in 1941 and joined his wife (who had not been interned) in Berlin, where he made five broadcasts to America describing his life in the camp in his usual comic style. These had caused a major storm in Britain – Wodehouse was accused of having done a deal to secure his release and was denounced as a traitor on the BBC by the influential *Daily Mirror* columnist Cassandra (William Connor). Having spent some time in Berlin, the Wodehouses ended up at the Hotel Bristol in Paris in 1944, making their presence known to the British Army as soon as the city was liberated. In the state of general confusion no one was quite sure what action to take and Malcolm was asked to keep an eye on the couple pending the arrival of Major Edward Cussen, a lawyer working for MI5. 'Our first visitor was a most delightful Major in the SIS,' Ethel Wodehouse wrote to a friend from their hotel. It was a lucky chance for both of them, as Wodehouse was a completely unworldly character whose only concern was his books. Malcolm was able to warn him that his position was potentially a dangerous one. Even though Major Cussen, after lengthy interviews lasting several days, exonerated Wodehouse, there were a number of influential people in Britain, notably Harold Nicolson MP and Quintin Hogg MP (later Lord Hailsham) who wanted him put on trial. After talking to Cussen, Malcolm was able to give Wodehouse the advice that, in the lawyer's words, it would be prudent 'to keep out of the Jurisdiction' (i.e. England) for the time being. This was wise counsel, for although the Attorney-General accepted Cussen's conclusion that Wodehouse had been guilty merely of foolishness, his Labour successor, Hartley Shawcross, later begged to differ and seemed quite prepared to prosecute.

Malcolm was able to be of more practical help when, only a few days after their first meeting, the Wodehouses were suddenly arrested by the French police. Apparently an English guest at a dinner party given by the then Préfet de Police, M. Luiset, had remarked how scandalous it was that two such notorious traitors as the Wodehouses should still be at large. At 12.30 a.m. they were awoken in their hotel room and taken to the Palais de Justice

to the fifth floor to inform Lord Camrose of his editorial inten-
tions for the next day's paper. He came back saying that he
required two leaders, one from Malcolm on Burma and one on
Syria. His fellow leader writer J. C. Johnstone, with whom he
shared an office, asked if he minded him walking up and down
as he 'composed with difficulty'. 'Whole effect very twilit,'
Malcolm noted.

Few of his friends were surprised to see Malcolm the former
Guardian leader writer comfortably installed at the *Telegraph*.
Though by temperament and upbringing he remained on the
left, he was just as strongly inclined to oppose the status quo. It
was therefore not strange to find him, in the wake of the Labour
landslide at the election of 1945, writing leaders for a Conservative paper. Later, when the Iron Curtain descended, his anti-
Russian feelings and his hatred of fellow-travellers predisposed
him more and more to ally himself to the right on foreign affairs.

Not that he ever felt himself a *Telegraph* man. He did, however, warm to his employer, Lord Camrose. The affection was
mutual and Malcolm was one of the very few *Telegraph* staffers
ever to be invited to Camrose's country home at Hackwood Park
near Basingstoke. To Malcolm, after the humbug of Scott and
the raffish opportunism of Beaverbrook, Camrose seemed an
honest, principled man whose aspirations, in Malcolm's view,
had been satisfied merely by acquiring great wealth and a peerage. One Sunday, to the surprise of all, Camrose walked into the
editorial conference: 'I was sitting with Watson and his brother
Alfred. Camrose had been walking about the City – strange on
a Sunday afternoon, this millionaire proprietor walking about
the ruined city. He was really rather a touching figure, asking
about the American loan, and whether the terms might have
been easier, and then going off again, in appearance rather like
a superior domestic servant, a gentleman's gentleman.'

After only a few months on the *Telegraph*, Malcolm was off
again – this time to America. Denys Smith, the *Telegraph*'s Washington correspondent, was coming back to London and Malcolm
eagerly asked if he could replace him. He justified this later on
purely professional grounds: 'the calculation that, since America
had become for the time being, at any rate, the richest and most

powerful country in the world, its federal capital must necessarily be overflowing with news – as, indeed, proved to be the case.' In fact, he was merely once again 'making off' out of boredom and an urge to escape from grim, post-war Britain.

His departure from Kitty was the occasion for a major row, the consequences of which hung over his short ten-month stay in Washington. Since their earliest years together, Kitty had grown in confidence, gaining a strength of character and composure which she never lost. Aunt Bo noticed the change in her. Having said previously (August 1932) that 'Kitty has a stiff will – a certain hardness diminishes her attractiveness', she later noted with approval (31 May 1938): 'Kitty has outgrown the hysteria of her youth; she is a handsome woman and devoted wife and mother.' But her life during the war years had not been easy. Left alone at the Mill House, Whatlington with four small children at the beginning of the war she was short of money and was forced to rely on her mother for help. She was also, inevitably, lonely. However, at the end of April 1941 Hesketh and Gladys Pearson moved out of Hampstead to Wood Place – an old red-brick farmhouse reached by half a mile of cart-track directly opposite the Muggeridge home at Mill House. There were a number of disadvantages from Pearson's point of view. The house was in the 'danger zone' (an area subject to restrictions because of the real fear of a German invasion), they had to walk into the village for water, milk and post. All the same he enjoyed his wartime years in the country, growing vegetables, shooting rabbits in the woods and becoming a popular figure in the local pubs.

Pearson had married his wife Gladys in 1912 mainly because she was pregnant. Though they remained great friends there was nothing physical about their marriage. Their only son Henry was killed in the Spanish Civil War. It was almost inevitable that Pearson, who had an unhappy love affair with an actress during the Thirties, should fall in love with Kitty, especially since he had an excuse to call in to the Mill House every morning to pick up the mail – the postman being unwilling to ride his bike up the pot-holed track. From Kitty's point of view, in her wartime solitude, Hesketh was a godsend; now in his mid-fifties, very good-looking, charming, a brilliant mimic, willing to dress up as Father Christmas or take the children to the theatre. Every Tuesday night they had an outing to the Royal Oak at Whatlington. Perhaps neither of them regarded it as more than a bit of a war-time dalliance. Certainly Pearson, who dedicated his book on Dickens to Kitty ('For My Love'), was concerned that Kingsmill, with whom in 1942 he had a major row, might say something to Malcolm. Kingsmill replied (13 July 1942): 'I hope neither you nor K. would have any anxiety about me even if our late differences now ended badly. You are the last person in the world I would ever in any circumstances be indiscreet about.'

It was not until after his return from France and just before he left for America that Malcolm realized what had been happening. He and Kitty had rented a house in Battle and had invited Hesketh to spend the weekend with them. Kitty and Hesketh went ahead and when Malcolm joined them he got rather drunk and accused Kitty of infidelity, which she admitted. A few days later he sailed from Liverpool in a state of acute depression. In a letter written on board ship, he poured out his confused feelings to Kitty:

> I've tried to write to you several times on this voyage, and indeed I've written one letter which I've decided not to send . . . I have to admit there's no point in hiding such things – that the last wretched episode has preyed considerably on my mind, both sleeping and waking. Perhaps it would have been better if we'd talked more about it but I deliberately didn't because in dwelling on that sort of thing there's a morbidity, and because after all there's nothing to say . . . My affection for you has never faltered and the children have been an immeasurable satisfaction, but my dearest Kitty there's something I can't face. Is it jealousy? Perhaps more than I like to admit, going over and over that scene. That's a bad sign. Touching up all the details of it with disgusting precision – that's a very bad sign indeed. Even muttering feebly 'You might have waited till I'd gone, just another week.' That's mere self-pity. I say again that you are infinitely dearer to me than any other human being, and you know that's true, and yet the future seems darker to me than it has ever seemed, and I don't know what to do.

Like so many unfaithful husbands, Malcolm found it very hard to come to terms with his wife's infidelity. Nor could he address himself to the inconsistency of having a wife 'infinitely dearer' to him than anyone else yet one whom he was constantly abandoning as he was now, again, going off to America. Yet it remained one of Malcolm's greatest strengths that he was incapable of bearing a grudge against anyone, and he remained on the best of terms with Hesketh Pearson until his death in 1964 and even invited him to stay with them both in the South of France on a holiday. In the same way, he kept in touch with Michal Vyvyan, the father of their son Charles, and regularly looked him up whenever he was in Cambridge.

He had little time to brood on his hurt feelings as he was plunged headlong into his work. The job of foreign correspondent in Washington is an arduous one, if only because there is so much news. In fact it was here that Malcolm coined the expression 'newsak' to describe the endless flow of information from tickertapes, press conferences and communiqués. 'I've never been so sick of news and newspapers,' he wrote to Kitty. 'Unfortunately, American ones are huge and one gets six or seven every day. Then there's a horrible thing called a ticker which ticks away all day long telling me the news and which you have to watch and take bits out of.

'This job is far more strenuous than I'd envisaged and really, at any rate as it's so far worked out, leaves me time for nothing else. I just feel dog tired in the evenings, have a scotch or so and fall asleep.'

Malcolm was in fact a very conscientious journalist who despised what he considered the dilettante approach of colleagues like Colin Coote or Richard Dimbleby. But the *Telegraph* tradition of earnest news-gathering did not allow his talents much scope and it would be hard to detect the hand of Malcolm in a passage such as this:

Tarriff adjustment preparatory to the setting up of an International Trade Organization will be considered in each particular case on their merits. The Reciprocal Trade Agreement Act empowers the administration to institute adjustments without seeking Congress' approval, but Congress and therefore the Republicans still have the whip hand in that they can repeal an act which is due to expire in any case in 1948. Foreign lending will henceforth receive careful scrutiny and Congress is most unlikely to vote any further unconditional appropriations for the Export Import Bank . . .

It was the Truman era in Washington. Harry S. Truman – Malcolm never stopped reminding everyone that the S stood for nothing and called him Harry 'S-for-nothing' Truman – had taken òver as President on Roosevelt's death in April 1945, to find himself coping with the Atom bomb, the Berlin Airlift and the foundation of NATO. During Malcolm's brief period in Washington, the focus of attention, from the *Telegraph*'s point of view, was the all-important question of aid to Europe and in particular to Britain, then facing economic ruin.

'The great puzzle about America to me', he once wrote, 'has always been the contrast between its amazing economic vitality and its cumbersome government and administration. Senatorial minds moved so slowly and the traffic so fast.' Malcolm paid regular calls to the British Embassy on Massachusetts Avenue manned by the eccentric Ambassador Lord Inverchapel ('a fellow-travelling queer', according to Leonard Miall), his First Secretary the Soviet agent Donald Maclean and his press secretary Phillip Jordan, a former journalist who became a close friend to Malcolm. It was very important for any correspondent to avoid being in the pocket of the Embassy and inevitably Malcolm soon fell foul of them over his reporting of the American loan for Palestine which the British Government was trying to negotiate. When he was summoned by Inverchapel to explain himself, he pointed out that if the press attaché didn't see fit to provide him with the official version of the story he had to fish around for what he could get. The Ambassador began to laugh, saying he was sure something satisfactory could be worked out for the future and everyone should help themselves to a drink.

As always when separated from Kitty, Malcolm became easily depressed and prone to heavy drinking. In Washington, so much a contrast to post-war 'austerity' Britain, there was plenty of opportunity to drink. British correspondents formed a little colony of their own, all with offices in the National Press Building. Malcolm's special friends were Leonard Miall from the BBC, who later got him involved in television, and René McColl of the *Daily Express*. These three formed something of a gang who tried to liven up the Washington routine by playing practical jokes on one another. Miall and McColl once persuaded Malcolm that the Duke of Windsor was staying at the British Embassy and had been offered a job as head of the Anglo-Caribbean Commission. On another occasion Malcolm and Miall almost convinced McColl that Lord Beaverbrook had died.

As a single man, Malcolm found himself much in demand at the non-stop drink and dinner parties often held at the United Nations Club on 19th Street. One night at a party in Georgetown, he met up with William Hardcastle of the *Daily Mail* and his wife Constance and accompanied them home for a nightcap. It was so late that he ended up sleeping in their spare room. At about four o'clock in the morning Constance Hardcastle was surprised to be woken to find herself in bed with two men: a soundly sleeping Hardcastle and Malcolm, 'obviously not very sleepy and knowing perfectly well what he was about.' She hurled him out of bed and into the passage, stood over him while he dressed and pushed him out into the street. Hardcastle seemed unsurprised when told of this episode the following morning.

Malcolm was still very uncertain about his future. If he had considered settling permanently in America he soon realized that he had no desire to do so – quite apart from the difficulties involved in uprooting his children, all of whom were now at school in England. He had no great love for the *Daily Telegraph* and for a time he discussed with Kitty, who, with their daughter Val, joined him in Washington for a short time that autumn, the possibility of living again the kind of life they had lived before the war: a house in the country and the freedom for him to write books. He was already working on an assignment for Odhams editing the diaries of Mussolini's son-in-law Count Ciano.* Now, thanks to Graham

---

* With the help of René McColl's wife Hermione; though, as neither of them knew Italian, this was proving arduous.

Greene, he had been offered a job as literary adviser to Heinemann's at £400 a year. 'This would involve going up to London once a week and practically no work,' he told Kitty.

The money from Heinemann's, however, was not enough to live on and, in the event, Malcolm reluctantly decided to soldier on at the *Telegraph*. However he wrote to Lord Camrose in February 1947 asking if he could return to London. Camrose replied (28 February 1947):

> I am interested in what you say about returning here. I quite understand that you are not asking to be re-called, but if you are feeling in any way like returning here in the present circumstances, I should rather welcome it. In my opinion we are not too strong on the leader side and your added experience in America would make you a very welcome addition to that department of the paper.
>
> I realize in saying this that you have only had a very short spell in Washington and might not like to make another decisive change so soon – however, talk it over with Mrs Muggeridge and let me have a free expression of your feelings.
>
> By the way, I hear curious things about the Ambassador. I am told that his habits are not all they should be and that he is making a bad impression in Washington circles, including the White House. This has been told me by one or two people and incidentally by a friend of his for many years and who is very fond of him . . . I should be sorry to think this was true and should be glad if you would tell me whether there is any basis for these stories.
>
> My kindest regards to Mrs Muggeridge and yourself,
> > Yours sincerely,
> > Camrose

There are signs here of the special rapport that Malcolm enjoyed with Lord Camrose. Certainly his *Telegraph* colleagues were highly envious when the paper agreed that he could return to Britain via Japan, Hong Kong, Singapore and Rangoon, commissioning him to write a series of reports along the way. After a car journey across America, he flew into Tokyo on 20 November 1947: 'Drove in through industrial suburbs so squalid that it was difficult to see whether they'd been blitzed or not.' A few days later, along with a number of fellow journalists, he accompanied Emperor Hirohito, who had been preserved on his throne by his American conquerors, to Hiroshima. 'I was in a car immediately behind his own,' he wrote in the *Telegraph* in a report that for once carried some traces of the Muggeridge humour: 'The Emperor's day was meticulously planned. A printed schedule had indicated that two minutes were to be allowed for him to step out to greet the orphans of Hiroshima War Orphanage and five minutes to "receiving citizens hail". Later, three minutes were spared for "inspection at the way of ploughing by a cow" and another three minutes for "inspecting rural life".'

Though sardonically noting that the Emperor's itinerary did not include a visit to the Red Cross Hospital where most of the victims of the atom bomb were being treated, Malcolm was impressed by the veneration accorded to Hirohito and the complete lack of any tendency to blame him for Hiroshima's terrible fate (*Daily Telegraph*, 15 January 1948):

On the contrary, the unanimity of feeling among the people has been striking. They seemed to derive immense satisfaction from the Emperor's mere presence among them and surged round him not with the idea of touching him but to sense his physical proximity.

He is a short, nervous, man whose features frequently twitch and whose eyelids lower from time to time as though the effort of holding them open for long times at a stretch is beyond his powers. Though the war has been over long enough for him to have grown accustomed to leaving the divine seclusion in which he had hitherto spent his days, he still gives an impression of being deafened by the noise and blinded by the light of the everyday world.

He seems always to be shrinking into himself, and probably returns to his palace with relief, there to devote himself quietly to marine biology, which is his single absorbing interest.

General MacArthur, the American 'Viceroy', who maintained Hirohito on the throne despite the fact that many of his generals were currently facing charges in a war crimes trial, gave Malcolm an interview on 30 November and it is interesting to contrast the picture given to the *Telegraph* readers with Malcolm's private impressions in his diary. In the *Telegraph*, MacArthur 'was kind enough to find time for a talk with me. He received me in his office seated with his back to the window, smoking an exceptionally large pipe. He looks younger than his 67 years, bright-eyed, scarcely grey at all . . . His voice is resonant and readily becomes fervid. He talks impersonally rather than intimately.'

In the diary, MacArthur was a 'large seeming (though actually short) rather shoddy man who talked at me for nearly an hour. He seemed to me like a broken-down actor of the type one meets in railway trains or boarding houses in England who complain that his recent production of *Hamlet* at Pontypool Repertory Theatre was badly attended whereas the circus was crowded. Occasionally I made feeble efforts to check the flow of words, but with no avail . . . an inconceivable performance.'

Malcolm arrived back in London in January 1948 to find Kitty already installed in a flat in Cambridge Gate (NW1); it was a long, rambling flat, the most comfortable they had so far rented. In addition to a garden, it had, from Malcolm's point of view, many advantages, being near to Regents Park where he could walk, and also round the corner from the Powells – Tony and Violet (Frank Longford's sister) – who had a house in Chester Gate.

Malcolm was now much better off, as in addition to his *Telegraph* salary he was employed as a literary advisor to Heinemann's. He was also writing regularly for the *New English Review*, a political-cum-literary monthly owned by the publishers Eyre & Spottiswoode (for whom Graham Greene worked). All this involved him very much in the literary world and there were regular lunches at the Authors' Club in Whitehall Court overlooking the Embankment, where Malcolm, Kingsmill, Graham Greene and Anthony Powell were all members. Together they formed a loose literary coterie, linked by friendship and business ties. Malcolm owed his job at Heinemann's to Graham Greene and, thanks to Malcolm, Heinemann's became

Powell's publishers. Powell in turn had introduced Malcolm to George Orwell, who had been at Eton with him. Orwell became a special ally of Malcolm's as they were both leftists (by upbringing at least, in Malcolm's case) who were wholeheartedly opposed to Soviet Communism and the fellow-travelling British writers and intellectuals who supported it. Malcolm strongly identified with Orwell after learning of the difficulties he had had when his articles on the Spanish Civil War had been rejected by the *New Statesman,* just as his own reports on the Ukraine famine had been played down by the *Manchester Guardian.* Orwell's *Animal Farm* was also rejected by the famous left-wing publisher Victor Gollancz, who disliked its obviously anti-USSR message. When the book was eventually published, it was an enormous success though Orwell remained poor until the time of his death in 1950. When Malcolm first knew him he was an unsuccessful novelist and left-wing journalist who appealed to him, as Hugh Kingsmill did, because he was an outsider in opposition to the prevailing intellectual consensus.

Tony Powell had written a number of satirical novels in the Thirties which had had little success. Having abandoned writing during the war he had recently started work on *A Question of Upbringing*, the first in his long sequence of novels subtitled *A Dance to the Music of Time*, which was to make his name. Powell read aloud the early chapters of his book to Malcolm who was most impressed. 'His talent has now come to maturity,' he wrote in his diary. Malcolm in turn read his new novel *Affairs of the Heart* to Powell who was equally complimentary. The two now went everywhere together; there were lunches at the Authors' Club, a trip to Eton to visit Powell's old school, visits to exhibitions (where Powell tried to help Malcolm evaluate paintings for the BBC radio programme *The Critics*), endless walks round Regents Park and evenings at Cambridge Gate where they discussed books and gossiped late into the night.

Hugh Kingsmill was also a frequent visitor to Malcolm's flat in Cambridge Gate and there are many references to him in Malcolm's diary at this time: 'Picked up Kingsmill at the club and brought him home to supper. The Powells came in after supper but the evening was somewhat marred by Mrs Dobbs's insistent yanging voice. The will, H.K. said of her, lays every-thing flat. For instance, he questioned her about George Gissing, whom she had known well, but she was quite unable to give any picture of him. All she could say was that Gissing had been very fond of her and that she could have married him if she had wanted to . . . but she had little to say about Gissing himself, except that he often seemed sad, as I can well believe if he spent time in her company!' (2 February 1948)

Kingsmill had spent the early years of the war as a school-master, first at Marlborough then at Merchant Taylors. Later he was made literary editor of *Punch*. But success as a writer eluded him (though Hesketh Pearson had meanwhile made his name with a best-selling biography of Bernard Shaw published in 1942). His second marriage to the beautiful Dorothy Vernon, previously a mistress of the novelist William Gerhardi, brought him no lasting happiness. To Malcolm and his friends, Kingsmill seemed to be in her thrall, Antonia White once memorably describing them as looking like 'a cobra and its next meal'. Early in 1948 the Kingsmills moved from London to a cottage in Par-tridge Green near Horsham. Almost immediately he began to be subject to attacks of vomiting, the symptoms of a duodenal ulcer which was only discovered at a post mortem.

'Very worried about Hugh Kingsmill', Malcolm noted 'who I hear continues to be very sick, with constant vomiting. As I regard his wife as completely mad, it is an alarming state of affairs but there is nothing to be done about it.'

The Berlin Air Lift and the Communist takeovers in Czecho-slovakia and Hungary in 1948 marked the first major conflicts of the Cold War and brought on one of Malcolm's apocalyptic moods. Convincing himself that war was once again imminent, he even joined the Territorial Army. 'Everything is preparing for a showdown between Communists and the rest . . . more and more one has the feeling of living on the edge of an abyss,' he wrote in his diary. He decided to fight the Communists on his home ground in the National Union of Journalists which, like many other trade unions, they had succeeded in infiltrating. He vowed to attend meetings and mobilize the anti-Communist forces. He even offered himself to the Conservative Party as a parliamentary candidate to stand against one of the many fellow-travelling Labour members. Contrary to the impression given by his diary, it appears that the initiative came from him rather than the Tories. At any rate, following a lunch with Mr J. P. L. Thomas, Vice Chairman of the Conservative Party, Malcolm wrote to him:

> The point is this. In my view, and I am sure also in yours, it is of the highest importance in the national interest, that as many fellow-traveller MPs as possible should be defeated, and that, in any case, they should be effectively attacked in their constituencies on the fellow travelling. On this point they are excessively vulnerable, provided their opponent is adequately informed. Unfortunately, I have noticed that quite often this is not the case, and people like Pritt, Driberg and Zilliacus get away with the most preposterous mis-statements. As you perhaps know, I spent a year in Russia in the early Thirties and have ever since made rather a speciality of reading about and generally following the activities of the partyliners and their camp followers. If, therefore, you were short of a man suitably equipped to oppose one of the fellow-traveller MPs, I should be happy to put myself forward for consideration and, in any case, would be prepared to help in the constituencies or otherwise towards discrediting them and, if possible, procuring their defeat.
>
> People are constantly wondering whether there is going to be a war with Russia. The truth of course is that there is a war with Russia, and has been since the revolution. Until lately, this war didn't matter enormously because Russia was weak, but now that the Soviet regime has been able so enormously to enjoy its power and extend its influence, the war has become a matter of life and death. People like Zilliacus, who is really more of a fool than a knave, are doing the same deadly work that those we spoke about did for Germany.

The response from Tory Central Office, however, was less than enthusiastic. E. D. 'Tubby' O'Brien, the Director of Information, wrote to Malcolm on 19 July 1948:

My dear Malcolm,

I have spoken to Jim Thomas about your suggestion that you should stand against Platts-Mills or other fellow travellers, but he tells me there is already a Conservative candidate in the field . . .

As the threat of war receded with the emergence of NATO and the nuclear stalemate, Malcolm's political militancy likewise waned (and in later life he conveniently forgot all about the episode, conflicting as it did with his publicly expressed contempt for all forms of political activity). He had not, however, abandoned his ambition to be a novelist and with the encouragement of Tony Powell was working on a new book, eventually published in 1949, called *Affairs of the Heart*. This was rather different from his previous efforts; on the surface it was a mystery story about a pair of literary collaborators, one of whom is found apparently murdered in the British Museum reading room. Malcolm, however, could not sustain the mystery element and the story, which peters out with an anti-climax, was more of an opportunity for satire at the expense of the literary scene – writers, publishers and agents all coming in for their share of ridicule. There were a number of Muggeridge set-pieces – a passage on obituaries (one of his favourite themes), a description of a newspaper office – and the narrative is enlivened with some typical aphorisms and observations:

'Every Man gets the girls he deserves.'

'As a general working rule it may be safely assumed that no one ever tells the truth about fornication or cash.'

'Whatever enthusiasm I have for the social revolution is derived exclusively from the prospect it offers of getting rid once and for all of social revolutionaries.'

'The smaller the participation in the world's affairs, the greater the appetite to know about them. It is in parks and clubs that newspapers are most read, the tramp painstakingly extracting a discarded newspaper from a rubbish basket, the somnolent figure in a leather armchair making his way through column after column at the slow pace of a convalescent enjoying his first stroll in the sunshine.'

Affairs of the Heart had a surprisingly favourable reception from the critics. In the *Tablet* Evelyn Waugh, while resentful of the satire at the expense of literary Catholics (including himself), nevertheless called the novel 'a clever and complete achievement'.

John Betjeman dismissed the unsatisfactory plot as an irrelevance. 'The point is', he wrote, 'that Muggeridge is a writer of stature. He is not just another imitator of Evelyn Waugh, nor a superficial cynic, nor an angry frustrated pourer out of words on paper. He is an artist in words, a lover of the human race and what is essential and sometimes forgotten, a man who knows how to be brief and interesting.' (*Daily Herald*, 30 November 1949)

As it turned out, *Affairs of the Heart* was to be Malcolm's last novel. Shortly after publication he started work with Hesketh Pearson on a tribute to Hugh Kingsmill. In spite of his apparent recovery, Kingsmill was still suffering from his undiagnosed ulcer and had been admitted to hospital in Brighton on 10 April 1949 and died there on 15 May. Malcolm saw him for the last time on 7 May.

> Went down to Brighton to see Hugh Kingsmill. When I arrived at his ward, the doctor was with him, but after a quarter of an hour I went in. Very shocked to find him so haggard and white. I tried to talk all the time, to prevent him talking, but of course, although forbidden to do so, he did talk and laugh. All the time I was with him a blood transfusion was going on . . . I stayed two hours, which was really too long, but he kept begging me to stay on.

Malcolm was always prone to certain *idées fixes* – ideas which he got in his head and which no amount of contrary evidence could dislodge. The most extraordinary example of this was the belief which both he and Hesketh Pearson firmly held that Dorothy Kingsmill had somehow murdered her husband. In Malcolm's case it had something to do with a phone call he made to the hospital shortly before Kingsmill's death when, on a crossed line, he overheard two strange voices talking. He could not distinguish what they were saying, but the impression they gave was one of malice and foreboding. Again, Malcolm always insisted that, despite the post-mortem, doctors had been unable to discover anything wrong with Kingsmill – though in fact the post-mortem revealed that an ulcer was responsible for his death.

It was certainly true that Dorothy Kingsmill had many strange ideas about diet which she foisted on Hugh, and these may have helped to hasten the end. It may also be true that she wanted him to die, as she was already by that stage in love with Tom Hopkinson, the editor of *Picture Post*, whom she later married in 1953. But it was going a bit far, to put it mildly, to brand her a murderess on the basis of so little evidence. Hesketh Pearson was probably more to blame and eventually his accusation got back to Dorothy Kingsmill and an angry correspondence ensued. (Unrepentant, Pearson later encouraged the young Michael Holroyd to portray Dorothy as a madwoman in his biography of Kingsmill published in 1964, as a result of which she threatened a libel action and the book had to be withdrawn.)

It was very typical of Malcolm that despite harbouring dark thoughts of Dorothy as a murderess he should nevertheless now do everything he could to help her financially. He pleaded in vain with the editor of *Punch*, E. V. Knox, to give her some money and even went to Downing Street to try to secure a civil list pension for her.

He also proposed a book with Hesketh Pearson, with some of the advance going to Dorothy. Published in 1951, *About Kingsmill* consisted of an exchange of letters between himself and Hesketh in which they reminisced about their mutual friend. Though he was reluctant to admit it, Malcolm's contributions to this book were among the best things he ever wrote, mainly because, for once in his life, he was writing something out of affection and enthusiasm and without the nihilism and pessimism which, as Beatrice Webb observed, marred so much of his writing. The book is also interesting for the light it sheds on his religious development. Malcolm remained a religious person by temperament though he had completely discarded the Christian beliefs he had shared with Alec Vidler at Cambridge; he did occasionally go to church with his eldest son Leonard (Pan), who later became a Plymouth brother, and in conversations with Leonard, his interest if not his belief in Christianity revived. He also re-read St Augustine's *Confessions* at this time. Kingsmill himself had never been a practising Christian but, as Malcolm wrote: 'It might surprise those who knew Hughie only slightly that he was by temperament deeply religious. His reaction against his father's non-conformity in no wise disposed him against religion as such. On the contrary, especially as he grew older, he became more and more convinced that what he had always called the "empirical" was no more than an image of some larger reality, and this earthly life was also a preparation for another in terms of eternity . . . As far as I personally was concerned, it was a view which I came increasingly to share. To a certain extent, Hughie doubtless influenced my feelings in the matter, but only, I think, to the extent of making conscious what had formerly been unconscious, if giving a shape and coherence to convictions which had formerly only vaguely and imprecisely held.'

Malcolm seemed to have acquired by this stage a more stable routine and a more reflective state of mind. He even began to think of moving to the country again. Looking back over 1949, he concluded: 'I feel middle-aged [he was now 46], with little zest for making new friends . . . reading more than ever a solace, walking agreeable . . . Family affairs reasonably satisfactory. Pan in his own peculiar way working things out – immensely diligent, wholehearted. To me, sometimes, his evangelical idiom slightly jarring, but this probably my fault . . . John steady, also hardworking, humorous, decidedly mature for his years – with his large head and ardent temperament. Val growing up fast, becoming distinctly attractive, not at all intellectual . . . Charles top of his class, brilliant at rugger, works away through the holidays in his little workshop, no reader but immensely sharp, quick. Kitty as ever infinitely dear. Hughie's death the first which hit me hard . . .'

At the beginning of April 1950 Arthur Watson retired from the editorship of the *Daily Telegraph* to be succeeded by Colin Coote. A few days later, Malcolm was summoned by Lord Camrose and offered the job as deputy editor with an increase of £500 in his annual salary (half of it to be paid in expenses). He wrote in his diary: 'Camrose very amiable and I couldn't help being somewhat excited about the whole business, though with reservations. There had been such speculation in the office about this, and everyone very nice when the news came out. Felt quite touched by it all.'

Malcolm had great respect for Watson: 'not a dazzling person, intellectually or in any other way, but a very good one who occupied an important, and often difficult post with credit and much more shrewdness and independence of judgement than people gave him credit for.' For Coote, however, he had little or no respect. Coote, a very distinguished looking man who had been a Liberal MP and later worked as a correspondent on *The Times*, was an inveterate snob who valued his connections with the aristocracy and regarded the *Daily Telegraph* as a poor second to the more prestigious *Times*.* As an editor he was a weather-cock who, at the time of the Cuban missile crisis in 1962, wrote a leader attacking President Kennedy and then, after complaints at the editorial conference, changed his tune the following day. To Malcolm, who had to deputize for him during his frequent absences, his dilettante approach was anathema: 'Oh, if only I shared the editor's utter indifference about what appears in this newspaper,' he complained to Colin Welch. He also noted, when he and Kitty met the Cootes on holiday in France, that he cheated at poker.

In his new role as deputy editor, Malcolm found himself more and more involved in the decision making and closer to the political process. There were lunches with Harold Macmillan, Hugh Gaitskell and Aneurin Bevan. He also formed an unlikely association – friendship was too strong a word – with Field Marshall Montgomery, who since the war had entertained the notion, common to many people of his ilk, that the politicians

---

* For Coote's snobbery, see his obituary of Lord Salisbury (1972): 'British political life will be the poorer for the loss of Robert Arthur Gascoyne Cecil, 5th Marquess of Salisbury who has died aged 79. Since the Cecils made such a tremendous intellectual comeback at the turn of the century they have produced scions with minds like razors, with exquisitely sensitive souls and with rugged opinions, the whole encased in curiously frail-looking corporeal tenements.' (Quoted *Private Eye's Book of Pseuds*, edited by R. Ingrams, 1973)

would fail the nation and that he himself would be called for to sort things out. Realizing that Malcolm was sound on the Russians, the Cold War and furthermore a friend of Sir James Grigg, formerly the Secretary of State for War, Montgomery for a time treated Malcolm and the *Daily Telegraph* as a conduit for his views on what ought to be done.

In January 1950 Malcolm travelled down (with Grigg) to see him at Isington Mill in Hampshire, a house 'arranged as a museum with all his trophies on display and portraits' and Monty himself 'an exhibit among exhibits'. Though, as so often, Malcolm's later verdict was harsh and dismissive, at the time he was rather taken by Monty and flattered by his attentions.

> He is really rather charming in his odd way, more impressive out of uniform than in it . . . One cannot say that he is intelligent, or even altogether 'nice' and yet there is something quite remarkable about him, and one can see that, in his way, he fits into the general category of 'great men', greatness being, I suspect, a kind of vitality and a singleness of purpose more than anything else. References to Churchill not particularly affectionate. Said that the only way to deal with him was to be firm. Despised him very much for bursting into tears when he came down to 21st Army Group on the eve of D-Day and wanted to address the officers, and Monty forbade it. He was right of course.

This was the first of several meetings which took place, always at the Field Marshall's instigation. In March 1951 Malcolm was given the good news that Monty had been appointed Eisenhower's deputy in charge of NATO. His job, he told him, was 'to binge things up'. Later, Malcolm was summoned at very short notice to Monty's château near Fontainebleu to be given a breakdown on the emergency in Malaya which Monty believed he could sort out. Malcolm, having left London without time to pack, was touched by the way Monty lent him a pair of his own thick flannel pyjamas and even laid them out in front of the fire to warm.

*   *   *

In the summer of 1949, Malcolm and Kitty went for the first time to holiday in Roquebrune, a village on the French Riviera between Monte Carlo and Mentone. ('For some mysterious reason', Kenneth Clark wrote, 'the village of Roquebrune has preserved its original character. All around it are the villas of the rich. Roquebrune itself remains squalid and poor.') Kitty and Malcolm stayed in a little villa on the sea belonging to their friend A. T. Cholerton, the *Daily Telegraph*'s correspondent in Moscow who had been so helpful to Malcolm during his brief period in Russia. Cholerton had stayed in Russia during the war but he was refused re-admission after a brief trip to London in 1945 and subsequently worked as foreign correspondent for the *News of the World*. His marriage to Katerina Georgevna had ended in divorce in 1947 and he married an Austrian widow, Charlotte Trautschold, with a villa in Roquebrune. Here he idled away the time, reading, lying in the sun and occasionally contributing as a freelance to *Life* magazine.

'For me here perfect existence,' Malcolm wrote. 'Rise about 7, drink tea, bathe, walk by the sea; for breakfast crusty bread, butter, fruit, coffee, and then sit at a little quiet shady table looking straight onto the Mediterranean, write a bit, read, think; at noon long swim and lie in the sun till 1.30; then lunch (cheese, salad, ham, red wine, fruit) and after lunch doze and read; at 4.30 bathe again and in the evening walk either to Monte Carlo or to Mentone, buy newspapers and sit in a café reading them and watching people; return leisurely at about 8.30, dine either at villa or Madame Ambert's, solidish meal and enough red wine or rosé to feel drowsy; game of gin rummy with Kitty, brief read and early asleep. That – for anyone who cares to know – is how I like to live; but I daresay, as Kitty pointed out, it wouldn't answer permanently. As a break, wonderful.'

Malcolm had enjoyed himself so much that he and Kitty returned to Roquebrune regularly over the next ten years, renting a flat, usually in the winter months, next to the Cholertons. In 1950 they also spent a few days at Portofino, as guests of the eccentric Catholic aristocrat, Auberon Herbert, bachelor brother-in-law of Evelyn Waugh. Unlike Roquebrune, Portofino was a smart resort and they found themselves mixing with the likes of Ingrid Bergman and the film director Alexander Korda ('with Korda, little court including pansyish character with Korda's passport sticking out of his pocket'). Also holidaying in Portofino was the poet Robert Graves, who had upset Herbert with his blasphemous attacks on Jesus and St Paul.

'Graves I was interested to see,' Malcolm noted. 'Large rotting face with a kind of lost beauty in it, a petulant childishness.' Kitty, as very occasionally happened, found Graves so physically repellent that she didn't want to go bathing in case she met him on the beach. Discussing Graves when they were swimming the following day, Auberon Herbert asked Malcolm whether he was going to become a Catholic. 'I said no, and left it at that. I see the force and importance of the Roman Catholic church, but I could not, in honesty accept its dogma. In reciting the creed I should have to add "not" to most items.'

The following day Kitty and Malcolm went with Auberon Herbert to have tea with Max Beerbohm at Rapallo. Beerbohm, who had lived in semi-retirement in Italy since his marriage in 1910 to American actress Florence Kahn, was now seventy-eight.

Elderly servant waiting to show us in. Max and Lady Beerbohm on the roof, he in old-fashioned, elegant linen suit, black tie with tie pin, no turn-up in the trousers; she in white dress, long, pretty, old lady effect, in her manner of speaking very much the actress. Main road goes by villa now, and conversation punctuated by hooting, noise of gears changing, braking, etc. [Max's] face very old, somehow shaggy, gentle, quite sad; affectionate, gentle, sad eyes, head bald, very browned from the sun. Speaks in a slightly tremulous way, but with perfect lucidity. No clouding of his mind . . . Of John Churchill (who painted horrors in one of the rooms in Auberon's house) he said that he felt sure he could not be a particularly good painter because he talked intelligently about painting. In his [Max's] experience, those who could talk about painting could never paint, whereas great painters made only gruff, brief remarks about their own and others' work. Lady Beerbohm keeps her hand fairly heavily upon him – she bought inferior brands of cigarettes in the hope that he might give up smoking, but he kept on; an ant crawling over his coat received her attentions; when he made a slip in talking (American instead of Irish) she corrected him . . .

He came to the door to see us off, and gallantly waved his straw hat in the air. I felt a great affection for him. In Hughie's phrase he was 'mild and cured', and by remaining true to his own world and times had remained true to himself.

On the Riviera the news in May that year of the outbreak of the Korean War caused a ripple of alarm among the rich expatriates. For Malcolm it once again brought to the fore the apocalyptic mood which he always liked to indulge. The show was over, the whole thing 'washed up', he would proclaim with glee at the first sign that all was not well. Visiting the casino in Monte Carlo with the Cholertons he felt it was 'on the whole an unedifying scene, which, like so much else, seems to be approaching its end.'

Back in London, his mood intensified: 'Strong feeling as I returned to Regents Park that it is now very nearly zero hour; the last phase in our decomposition nearing, not much time left.' When he went to the House of Commons for the *Daily Telegraph* and watched Attlee and Churchill debating the Korean crisis he felt that 'the forces of evil were going to be dominant in the world' – feelings intensified when the Labour MP Tom Driberg got up to speak: 'a face quite full of darkness and spreading darkness before it.'

He was beginning to find life at the *Telegraph* a drag, even though his routine allowed him time to do freelance writing. It was difficult to work with Coote, with whom he so often failed to see eye to eye. 'Returned late,' he recorded on 14 November 1952, 'rather depressed at having to work with someone as unsympathetic as Coote.' After lunch a few days later with some French generals Coote annoyed him by making a speech in French: 'Coote spoke French with pedantic accuracy which in my experience Frenchmen, particularly French officers, always dislike and pretend not to understand. The worse the accent, the better pleased they are.'

What Malcolm liked most was working with the *Telegraph*'s

printers and compositors which always cheered him up. For their part, the print-workers were all very fond of him and one day to everyone's great amazement they produced a Muggeridge 'lookalike' and brought him into Malcolm's office for his inspection. When he eventually left the paper they accorded him the rare honour of banging their machines in token of goodbye.

If Malcolm had chosen to stay at the *Telegraph* he could well have become editor eventually. But he had already been flirting with other jobs. Lord Rothermere, whose wife Anne (later the wife of Ian Fleming) had become a friend, toyed with the idea of making him editor of the *Daily Mail* and the *Spectator* editorship had been another possibility. In the end, when he made a break it was in a surprising direction which few would have predicted.

In 1952 the proprietors of *Punch*, the Agnew family, worried by the falling circulation, decided to look for an editor outside the magazine's magic circle. Uncertain whom to choose they sought the advice of Sir Christopher Chancellor, the head of Reuters. Chancellor recommended his friend Malcolm, who immediately accepted. It was an unlikely sequence of events, as Chancellor could scarcely have been considered an expert on humorous journalism. Nor for that matter was it clear why anyone should think that the deputy editor of the *Daily Telegraph* would be the man to revitalize a supposedly funny magazine. Editorial appointments, however, are often made in a quite arbitrary manner and, on this occasion, it turned out to be an inspired choice. But Malcolm, having accepted, was rather rueful when he learned from Ian Fleming that he was about to be offered the editorship of the *Sunday Times*.

CHAPTER IX

Punch, *Panorama* and Pamela

FOUNDED IN 1841 BY a group of men who included its first and long-serving editor Mark Lemon, *Punch*, in its early days, had retained some vestiges of the old satire of the eighteenth century – the savage knock-about of Gillray and the great English caricaturists. But as it prospered and the Victorian age progressed, *Punch* became more respectable. Max Beerbohm noted in 1899: 'When *Punch* was young he had the courage of his own levity. But *Punch* is old now, pompous and respectable, exemplary in all relations of life. No more does it hop wickedly from side to side, banging everything with its cuddled stick. He grins and squeaks and bludgeons away only in the course of law and order, and is most polite to the hangman. He has become a national institution.' Later, *Punch* was to be fatally branded as the magazine to be found in every dentist's waiting room.

Still, there were compensations – notably features like the *Diary of a Nobody* and *1066 and All That* and the standard of the artists, who included many famous names like Phil May and later Graham Laidler ('Pont'). Under the long-lasting editorship of E. V. Knox (1932–49), *Punch* had been run on cosy collegiate lines, the atmosphere reminiscent of a minor public school. The editorial staff spent only two and a half days in the office and were presumed otherwise to be working at home. There were hallowed traditions centring around the table carved with the initials of former editors and staff members. Contributors could be elected 'to the table' in the manner of boys being given their colours at school, after which they could attend, if they wished, the weekly lunch, also attended by the proprietors, at which the full page cartoon for the next issue was discussed. As for the material in the magazine, it mostly consisted of what B. A. Young called 'well-written articles about nothing in particular' or what Malcolm later described as 'Celia and the washing up'. There was little in the way of political satire, while sex as a subject for cartoonists was strictly taboo, despite the strides made in that direction by the *New Yorker*.

In the circumstances it was hardly surprising if *Punch* had failed fully to come to terms with the post-war world. After a wartime boom, the circulation had fallen from 180,000 in 1948 to 140,000 in 1953 and advertising revenue was down. Kenneth Bird, the cartoonist 'Fougasse', who had succeeded Knox in 1949, was not the man to reverse the trend. In any case he had taken on the editorship only as a temporary measure. Concerned at the decline, Alan Agnew, the managing director, who took over as chairman in 1953, decided to look outside for a new editor and by-pass the heir-apparent, H. F. Ellis.

Not surprisingly there was resentment based on what people had heard about their new editor. Judged by his articles and his appearances on radio he was acerbic, negative and anarchic. Things were not improved when he confided to one member of the table at a *Punch* lunch that he had no interest in cricket. R. G. G. Price noted in his *History of Punch* (written when Malcolm was still editor): 'He did not sound the kind of man who would consider himself a new boy amid the pannelled walls, the memoirs of Thackeray and Tenniel, the collegiate atmosphere of *Punch*.'

As things turned out, Malcolm with his charm and naturally generous spirit quickly won over the regulars. The only exception was the deputy editor H. F. Ellis, author of *Wentworth B.A.*, who had been hoping to become editor in succession to Kenneth Bird. More than the others, Ellis had been offended by Malcolm's manner and his use of four-letter words. 'Shall we fuck off then?' Malcolm once enquired at the end of an editorial discussion. 'If you have to put it like that,' Ellis had replied frostily.

Others, especially the younger contributors, were immediately enthused. There were a great many very talented people connected with *Punch* in one way or another, but their talents had never been given a free rein by reason of the deadweight of tradition and the distinctly old-fashioned approach of editors like Knox. Cartoonists in particular, like the young Michael Cummings, were delighted by the encouragement that Malcolm gave. Another old cartoonist, Leslie Illingworth, a Sussex neighbour of Malcolm's, became a personal friend. Others, like the young political writer Henry Fairlie, counted themselves as his disciples. (Fairlie, who with his wife Lisette lived in Sussex Square, Brighton, called Malcolm 'The Saint' because he was always so generous with money. Fairlie recalled the case of one writer who asked for a loan of £20 from Malcolm and was surprised to receive in an envelope £100.)

It was a tribute to Malcolm's diplomatic skills that he managed not to give offence when he began to bring outsiders on to the staff. The first to arrive was Leslie Marsh who had befriended Malcolm during his *Evening Standard* days and who was now given the job of sub-editor in charge of collating all the copy. This was something of a challenge as some of the senior staff members like A. P. Herbert were in the habit of sending their pieces direct to the printer.

A more significant recruit was Anthony Powell who accepted the job of literary editor early in 1953. Powell was a fellow-spirit: an observant novelist with an Aubrey-esque fascination with biographical gossip. Of similar build to Malcolm, with a loud laugh, he was sometimes mistaken for his brother, so alike were they in manner.

Powell, experienced not only as a novelist but as a publisher, was an invaluable ally. One of Malcolm's first requests was for him to go through a recent issue and give his comments. He replied: 'My impression is that there are too many indifferent drawings included and that it would be better, if necessary, to reduce the number of cuts in favour of perhaps rather larger ones only by artists with more decided personality. I do beg you to steer clear of Topolski . . . the standard of verse seems to me really rather high.'

It was Powell who introduced Malcolm to his Oxford friend Claud Cockburn, who at this stage was living a life of semi-retirement in Youghal, Co. Cork. A brilliant journalist, Claud became a communist during the Depression and gave up a job on *The Times* to launch a notorious cyclo-styled newsletter called *The Week* which he wrote virtually single handed. Although he never renounced communism, remaining an apologist for Stalin until his dying day, Cockburn ceased to play any active role in the Party after the war and settled in Ireland where he tried to earn a living as a novelist writing under the pseudonym of James Helvick.

Always a heavy drinker and with three sons at private school, Claud was permanently short of money, particularly now in the time of the Cold War that his communist past was regarded as a black mark in Western journalistic circles. So he welcomed an invitation from Powell to contribute regularly to *Punch* – though initially he remained wary of Malcolm, knowing his reputation as a fanatical opponent of Soviet Russia and an anti-communist campaigner in the National Union of Journalists. When they eventually met in the *Punch* office there was an instantaneous rapport between the two men. Malcolm liked anyone who refused to subscribe to the consensus. Claud was a communist, but he never expressed any desire to visit Russia and, on the contrary, adored America. He venerated de Gaulle, as Malcolm did, and was happier reading Wodehouse than Karl Marx. Above all, he had a boyish gusto which was irresistible. The two men, for a time, were almost inseparable. Claud was a frequent guest at Malcolm's home, though Kitty never really approved of him and once when he stole a bottle of whisky removed it from his bag, replacing it with an empty one. Kitty and Malcolm visited the Cockburns in their tumbledown mansion in Youghal and when the Cockburns' youngest son Patrick was struck down by polio in 1956 arranged for him to be brought over to England and operated on by Kitty's brother, a specialist in the treatment of polio. After the operation, Patrick stayed with the Muggeridges in Sussex and Malcolm used to play chess with him, even organizing a tournament with Claud and Kingsley Martin (now a Sussex neighbour).

Claud was immediately excited by the idea of Malcolm installed at *Punch*: 'You felt some life crackling behind the desk, as though someone, for a joke, had thrown a firecracker into a mausoleum.' *Punch* would be the springboard for an anti-establishment crusade, for the return of satire. Fireworks were not long in coming, notably in an attack on Winston Churchill, still Prime Minister at an advanced age. Malcolm's feelings about Churchill were ambivalent. He wrote disparagingly about him in his memoirs, but, typically, when they met for the only time in 1950 Malcolm found him 'a quite astonishing figure, very short-legged, baby-faced, immensely thick neck and oddly lovable.' Malcolm, then deputy editor of the *Telegraph*, had been summoned to Chartwell to be briefed by the Prime Minister, notably about the latest developments in the Cold War, a question on which the two saw eye to eye. 'He treated me with great respect,' Malcolm recorded, 'and kept on looking at me out of the corner of his eye to see how I was reacting to his performance. A curious mixture of cunning and animality in his face, as with so many of the very old. He obviously longs more than anything for power and therefore is only interested in the present rather than the past. In an odd way, reminiscent of my mother-in-law, Mrs Dobbs, and, curiously enough, like her he has developed a passionate affection for a dog which follows him everywhere.'

By 1954 Churchill was seventy-nine and had had a serious stroke the previous year – though details had not been made public and there had been no mention in the official bulletins. Nevertheless there were stories in the foreign press and rumours persisted. Though Churchill was sufficiently recovered to address the Tory Party Conference in October 1953 it was obvious that he was not his old self. However, such was his extraordinary status as a totem that the newspapers said nothing at all specific about the real state of his health. It was typical of Malcolm that he should decide to break the silence and state what most people felt but nobody liked to say: that Churchill was past it and should retire.

The unsigned drawing by Leslie Illingworth showed a tired, dispirited-looking Churchill sitting ponderously at his desk, his jaw sagging, his eyes vacant. The caption read: 'Man goeth forth to his work and to his labours until the evening.' On the opposite left-hand page Malcolm had written in the style of Gibbon's *Decline and Fall* the study of a Byzantine leader called Bellarius who had successfully repelled the Barbarians from the gates of the city:

> By this time he had reached an advanced age, and might have been expected to settle down to an honourable retirement in the enjoyment of the fame, the honours and the wealth he had so richly deserved. Instead, he clung to power with a tenacious intensity. His splendid faculties, which had enabled him to excel as an artist and writer as well as orator and man of action, with the years began to falter. The spectacle of him thus clutching wearily at all the appurtenances and responsibilities of an authority he could no longer fully exercise was to his admirers infinitely sorrowful, and to his enemies, infinitely derisory.

The attack produced an immediate furore. Churchill himself was greatly upset, as his doctor Lord Moran recorded in his diary (4 February 1954): 'The PM rose, went over to a table and, opening *Punch*, handed it to me. "They have been attacking me. It isn't really a proper cartoon . . . look at my hands, I have beautiful hands . . . *Punch* goes everywhere. I shall have to retire if this sort of thing goes on." ' Two days later, Moran recorded: 'The attacks in the press, the cartoons in *Punch* in particular, are still festering in his mind.' Then on 8 February Winston said, 'Christopher [Soames] wrote to that awful fellow Muggeridge, you know, the editor of *Punch*. He knows him, lives in his neighbourhood. Muggeridge wrote back saying that he was a journalist and must do his duty; said that he was one of my greatest admirers, but that I was no longer up to the job . . .'

Soames's letter, dated 10 February, read:

Dear Mr Muggeridge,
    I must write to tell you how grieved I was to see the depths into which you have dragged *Punch* by whatever motives prompted you to publish Illingworth's cartoon and your accompanying article on February 3rd.
    I was delighted when I heard you had taken on the editorship of *Punch*. I rang you up to tell you so. Unfortunately you were out and I spoke to your wife. I asked her to

congratulate you on my behalf and expressed my hope that you would revive that element of political satire for which *Punch* was once famous.

Little did I think that your magazine would be so debased.

I am sure it matters not a jot to you – but I am much grieved.

> Yours truly,
> Christopher Soames.

Meanwhile, Churchill's son Randolph, a friend of Malcolm's since their days together on the Londoner's Diary at the *Evening Standard*, had himself written to Malcolm:

My Dear Malcolm,

I have been in London the last two days and at least twenty of my friends have asked me what I thought about the cartoon of father which you put in *Punch* this week. My friends have all made it very plain how vile they think this action was, though many of them were not clever enough to realize its true evil.

I am often happy when I hear my friends attacked as usually I find it enjoyable to defend them. On this occasion I would have been embarrassed by how to do this, if I had not already realized on seeing the cartoon that you had never been a friend of mine or of anyone or anything I care about.

Please don't bother to answer.

It was typical of Malcolm that he should describe this mad, intemperate attack as 'rather touching'. He also replied at some length seeking to conciliate Churchill.

Meanwhile, letters of protest poured into the *Punch* office, so many that a letter of reply from Malcolm had to be duplicated. 'Much perturbation in office over strong reactions to Churchill cartoon. Pretend to be less perturbed than I really am, even pleased about it.'

The furore over Churchill was met with mixed feelings in the managerial department of *Punch*. For although it was clear that a great many of the traditional readers were deeply offended by the cartoon, it was equally true that the controversy had put

Punch in the news for the first time in years. The magazine was being talked about even in New York, and those people who would never previously have dreamed of buying *Punch* were giving it a look. If they did, they found a magazine radically changed. Prior to Malcolm's arrival there had been little or no political satire in *Punch*. No one on the staff had any particular interest in politics or even knowledge of the 'outside world'. Satire was now in and there was a regular political commentary written by a maverick Tory MP, Christopher Hollis. The Churchill cartoon was followed by one of Anthony Eden which caused almost as much of a furore, showing the then Foreign Secretary (at the time involved in the Vietnam Peace Conference) in the guise of Neville Chamberlain. (It upset Eden so much that he later refused to be interviewed by Malcolm for *Panorama*.)

The old cover by 'Dicky' Doyle had finally been jettisoned and articles were now signed by their authors. There were regular pieces by Malcolm himself, P. G. Wodehouse, Claud Cockburn, and J. B. Priestley. Unlikely *Punch* names like Stephen Spender and Kenneth Tynan cropped up and a young writer called John Mortimer was contributing regular features about the law under the pen-name of Geoffrey Lincoln. There were poems by John Betjeman, pieces by Fitzrovian Bohemians like Anthony Carson and J. Maclaren Ross. But it was in the art department, surprisingly, that the changes were most marked. Just as, at the *Telegraph*, he had enjoyed the company of the print-workers, Malcolm found it easier and more rewarding to work with cartoonists, finding them for the most part deeply sympathetic characters. With Powell's encouragement he invited the famous Romanian cartoonist André François to London to be fêted by the *Punch* staff. (He was to become an inspiration to many young artists like Quentin Blake.) Another youthful cartoonist whose work helped to transform the look of *Punch* was Ronald Searle. Searle could turn his hand to most things, from political cartoons to illustrations for Eric Keown's theatre reviews. Early in 1954 he and Malcolm began to collaborate on a strip cartoon series based on Hogarth called 'The Rake's Progress' which chronicled the lives of contemporary figures.

All this was enjoyable and occasionally exhilarating. At the same time, Malcolm, like any other editor, found himself burdened by chores. He had to go to the printers and attend meetings with the Agnews. He had only been in the offices a few days when a Miss Godley called on him with a story that the communists were corrupting debutantes with a new drug that resulted in moral debilitation. The following day it was the ballet critic Lady Pratt who drew his fire: 'Tiresome woman. Must get rid of her,' Malcolm wrote. Then the religious correspondent Dorothy Sayers was a constant thorn in his flesh, ringing up to complain or sending round her agent Jean Leroy to demand more money.

Malcolm was also having to cope with the consequences of being, for the first time in his life, famous, comfortably off and socially in demand. He was earning £6,000 a year from *Punch*, he had a flat in Albany (just about the most prestigious address in London) and another flat in Brighton. He was appearing more frequently on the radio as a regular contributor to *The Critics* and *Any Questions?* He and Kitty were invited to receptions, dinners and cocktail parties. To a great extent Malcolm took it all in his stride, but there is little doubt that Kitty, who never liked any kind of socializing, found it an increasing strain.

Her life was to be made wretched for some time to come by Malcolm's protracted love affair with Lady Pamela Berry, which began about this time and was to continue on and off into the early Sixties.

Born in 1914, Pamela was the youngest daughter of F. E. Smith, the first Lord Birkenhead (1874–1930), a ruthlessly ambitious Tory politician who was made Lord Chancellor in 1919 at the age of only forty-five. Smith doted on his two daughters, with the result that both of them were spoiled. 'We were encouraged to come down after dinner and be cheeky before solemn statesmen,' the elder daughter Eleanor remembered. When Pamela was only eight, one of these statesmen, Lloyd George, observed: 'His youngest kiddie Pam is a terror – utterly spoilt.' Pamela was pretty, dark-eyed and, like her father, abnormally energetic. When F. E. Smith died at the age of only fifty-six he left hardly any money and Pamela was kept going thanks to an allowance from her father's great friend Lord Beaverbrook.

Then in 1936 she married the millionaire, Michael Berry, who was to succeed his father, Lord Camrose, as editor-in-chief of the *Telegraph*. Berry was her exact opposite: quiet, shy, deeply reserved. Yet, in spite of their lack of obvious intimacy, they remained a devoted couple. Later, Pamela established herself as a political hostess in the grand style, famous for her lunch and dinner parties at the Berrys' town house in Cowley Street (a stone's throw from the House of Commons) or in their grand country seat at Oving near Aylesbury. To these she invited leading politicians from both parties, visiting pundits from the USA, pitting them against one another to create excitement, revelling in gossip while her husband hovered discreetly in the background. Journalists, especially those of a radical or satirical bent, were her favourites. A woman of enormous vivacity, she had many admirers like Richard Crossman and Evelyn Waugh who doted on her and with whom she carried on a long and gossipy correspondence. But with those whom she considered to be of little social or political importance she could be overbearing and rude, not hesitating to lie like a trooper if the need arose. (Later, Malcolm noted in his diary: '*The Liar*. I have known some outstanding ones: Harold Laski, P [Pamela Berry], Dorothy Kingsmill'.) Others went further and regarded her as cruel and even vicious – particularly towards other women. When Henry Fairlie introduced her to his wife Lisette at a *Spectator* party, she said dismissively: 'I thought you stayed in the country.'

The affair began some time in 1953, following Malcolm's departure from the *Telegraph*. From a reference in Malcolm's diary in March 1954 it seems obvious that it must have preceded this date. Here he described going with Kitty to a reception given by Pamela Berry's brother Lord Birkenhead at Carlton House Terrace: 'Went over and had a word with Pam – very pretty in red dress. She said she'd given me up for Lent, but missed me terribly and I said I'd missed her. So all was repaired.'

In all his various affairs hitherto Malcolm had called the tune. Now, however, for the first time, he was being led by a more forceful and determined lover than himself. For her part, Pamela Berry, who had had a string of lovers over the years, found herself in her early forties desperately in love with a married man ten years older than herself. For the first and perhaps the only time in her life, this rich, spoiled society hostess experienced a real and lasting passion for a man. Malcolm, she told him in one of a handful of love letters to survive the affair, had given her the greatest happiness and fulfilment any woman could ever have known; their trips abroad together to Paris and America were, she said, all the happiness she had ever enjoyed on this earth. Apart from her wish to discharge her domestic duties and to be helpful and considerate to her husband Michael she wanted only to please Malcolm, 'the old codger who is my true love', as she rather touchingly described him.

One thing was certain. Pamela Berry was not going to be content to play the role of a compliant mistress, meeting her lover for occasional assignments in secret. She resented deeply the fact that he was married to a devoted wife – a woman who was more than her match in terms of beauty, courage and charac-ter, a woman every bit as determined as herself. She therefore did all she could to make sure Kitty knew what was going on, even scrawling her name in lipstick on the bedroom mirror of the Albany flat. When Malcolm remonstrated she told him that he had failed to understand her permanent resentment of his continuing to live with someone whom she did not like. When they were together, as they had been on a trip to Paris, she had been able to forget about Kitty. Dozing on his shoulder in the aeroplane, his home life seemed remote but there were other times when she could feel quite literally consumed with rage and humiliation at the thought of Malcolm being content to live under the same roof as Kitty – even, with pleasure, occupying the same bedroom. The thought of a man with whom she was desperately in love sleeping with another woman was enough to drive her mad – however much Malcolm might try to reassure her that it meant nothing, 'habit of a lifetime' and so on and so forth. She found it all inexpressibly distasteful.

Pamela confided in their mutual friend Anthony Powell that Malcolm wanted to divorce Kitty and set up home with her but that she couldn't do it because of her children. The surviving correspondence, however, suggests that she was lying and that it was she, rather than Malcolm, who wanted divorce and remarriage. She was the one, she said, who was prepared to run away and re-make her life with Malcolm whatever it involved, but Malcolm wouldn't consider it for more than a moment or two. Early in their affair she became pregnant (not surprising, in view of Malcolm's distaste for all forms of birth control) and used the child as a powerful argument for the two of them to marry. Malcolm, however, refused to leave Kitty and Pamela lost the baby through miscarriage.

Aware of the unhappiness the affair was causing Kitty, Malcolm made several half-hearted attempts to break it off, but was unable to resist her charm, vitality and sheer force of personality. 'Difficult to say what appeals to me in her,' he wrote later in his diary. 'She is not clever, not pretty, not nice, somewhat out of the ordinary, a remarkable person. Tony [Powell] thinks she'll crop up in memoirs as a legendary figure perhaps.'

'She's such a *pirate*,' he told Patricia Cockburn. Another source of the attraction lay in the fact that she personified the world in which Malcolm was now embroiled – the world of politics, power, high society and wealth.

The affair also coincided with Malcolm's growing involvement with something that was to transform his life completely, namely television. Although it had functioned since before the war, television in Britain only took off as a result of the broadcast of the Coronation in 1953. Then anyone with a television set found himself in demand. However, at this stage there was still only one channel, run by the BBC, and the content of programmes was generally anodyne. Later that year the then Director of Television Mr Cecil McGivern (described by Michael Barsley as a 'brilliant fiery Geordie') decided to start the first news-magazine programme (with emphasis on the arts). Two outlines were proposed: one by Grace Wyndham Goldie called *Window on the World*, the other by Andrew Miller Jones called *Panorama*.

The latter was successful and the programme went on the air on 10 November 1953 introduced by Pat Murphy, a reporter on the London evening newspaper the *Star*. However, it was so bad that McGivern shouted 'disgraceful' and suspended it for a month.

In January 1954 McGivern summoned Michael Barsley, an author of humorous books, then working for the BBC, to take over as editor. Barsley was given six weeks' probation to make a success of *Panorama*. Luckily he scored a hit with his first programme, a study of the H-bomb with speakers including Bertrand Russell and the Archbishop of York. Shortly afterwards, Leonard Miall (Malcolm's old colleague from Washington days and now head of TV talks) discussed with Barsley the idea of offering Malcolm a job as an interviewer. Malcolm was no stranger to the BBC. Since 1947 he had been a regular guest on *The Critics*, a weekly radio programme (famously parodied by Peter Sellers and Irene Handl) in which a few reviewers discussed a new film, play, art exhibition and book, and in 1950 he joined the panel of *Any Questions?*, a programme he was to grace regularly for the rest of his life.

His first solo performance, a talk on the Webbs, given two years earlier on 30 May 1948, had given the BBC a taste of what they were in for by letting him loose on the airwaves.

The chairman of the Governors Lord Simon was outraged: 'I listened to his broadcast with growing horror, incredulity and anger,' he complained to his subordinates. 'The Webbs were personal friends of mine and I have a profound admiration of their work, so I am not an impartial judge. But nobody can doubt that they were very great public servants; after all, they were buried in Westminster Abbey. The Muggeridge broadcast expressed only contempt and derision, mocking their personal characteristics, mental and physical, with practically no regard for truth and decency. It was the most disgraceful piece of bad taste that I have ever heard. Why was he chosen in view of his past career? How did any producer come to pass such a scandalous script?'

Leonard Miall was keen to recruit Malcolm to television but there were risks. Although he had some experience as a broadcaster on radio as well as in television in a programme called *Press Conference*, he was known not to possess a television set and had publicly expressed his dislike of the medium. He was also a keen supporter of the campaign then being waged for commercial television and the break up of the BBC monopoly.

In the event, Malcolm took to television like a duck to water. He was, to begin with, highly nervous before any programme and when the *Daily Telegraph* editor Michael Berry (Pamela's husband) appeared on *Panorama* in 1955 he noticed that Malcolm ate practically nothing at dinner beforehand and swallowed two purple hearts washed down with two large whiskies. Once in the studio, however, he became completely relaxed, with the result that the person he was interviewing was made to feel relaxed also. From the BBC's point of view he had all the makings of a personality: a bizarre accent – a mixture of suburban Croydon and Cambridge drawl – a habit of chain-smoking, often with a Noel Coward cigarette holder; and, above all, a tendency to be outrageous. When Billy Graham replied to one of his questions, 'Only God could answer that one,' Malcolm came back with: 'And we haven't got him in the studio [casting his eyes heavenwards] – or have we?' Interviewing an expert on Siamese twins, Malcolm ran out of questions and found himself asking the man whether it would be possible to surgically join two ordinary babies together in order to make some money.

In May 1954 he did his first *Panorama* interview, with Billy Graham who was conducting an evangelical campaign at Haringey Arena at that time. But his breakthrough came in June when he took over temporarily as the front man of *Panorama* from Max Robertson. Robertson was a tennis commentator, modest, self-effacing and deferential, and the contrast with Malcolm was striking. 'If Mr Malcolm Muggeridge is not retained as "compere" of *Panorama*,' Maurice Wiggin wrote in the *Sunday Times* (27 June 1954), 'the BBC will be throwing away a golden chance. Mr Robertson is bland, deferential, often ingratiating; the embodiment of non-controversialism. Mr Muggeridge, a powerful, prejudiced personality who defers to nobody, handled the programme with real authority and roughly doubled its impact.'

When *Panorama* returned in October 1954, Malcolm had been signed up to do a regular 10–15 minute spot, usually an interview with a 'personality'. He was paid 31 guineas a programme. One of his great advantages was that of the contact man. He seemed to know everyone and, more importantly, to be able to lure them into the studio. Somerset Maugham, a shy man with a terrible stutter, agreed to come on *Panorama* only as a result of Malcolm's blandishments. (He remembered Maugham reciting the alphabet as he had his photograph taken in the studio, saying it was a trick he'd picked up from the Royal Family to overcome nerves. 'How far did the Duke of Gloucester get?' Malcolm asked.) Another scoop was an interview with Eleanor Roosevelt, thanks to Malcolm having inside knowledge of her itinerary. Salvador Dali also appeared not long afterwards, Malcolm opening the interview with typical irreverence:

'I know we're supposed to discuss modern art, and I expect we shall, but first of all may I say I'm fascinated by your moustaches. Might I ask you what happens to them at night?'

'They droop,' Dali replied.

In 1955 *Panorama* was re-launched as a more serious political programme with Richard Dimbleby as front man and the young Michael Peacock as producer. The technical side of television had become more sophisticated and *Panorama* was growing more adventurous. On 18 June 1956 Leonard Miall had arranged for an item to be broadcast live from an inventors' exhibition in Paris with the help of a French outside broadcast unit and the Eurovision link. It turned out to be an evening of high drama and farce.

Catherine Dove (later Freeman), the director of *Panorama*, was keen to do an item on Brendan Behan, then an unknown Irish writer whose play *The Quare Fellow* had just been produced by Joan Littlewood at the Theatre Royal Stratford. The difficulty, she pointed out, was that Behan was a heavy drinker who when drunk was likely to become obscene. Miall therefore decreed that Malcolm should meet him off the plane from Dublin and make sure that he was sober for the transmission.

Panorama in those early days was still a magazine programme consisting of three or four disparate items. On the evening in question there was a filmed report of the fighting in Cyprus followed by a studio discussion between two MPs (Julian Amery and Richard Crossman), then an item on finishing schools for young ladies, with interviews with a headmistress and some of her pupils. There was then to be a scene from *The Quare Fellow*

The television
personality, c1960

Interviewing
society hostess
Elsa Maxwell, 1955

LEFT: At a gathering to protest against the visit of Bulganin and Khrushchev in April 1956, with (from the left) Auberon Herbert, Lady Hesketh and Mick Wallwork, chairman of the campaign.

BELOW: Conducting a televised debate with Lord Alport, Dr Christiaan Barnard, Rt Rev. David Sheppard and Peter Hain

In full flow at the Institute of Directors Conference at the Albert Hall, 1968

With Alec Vidler

LEFT: Filming with Kevin Billington in Highgate Cemetery

BELOW LEFT: Filming in Rome with Cardinal Heenan, Archbishop of Westminster

BELOW RIGHT: Presenting the National Viewers and Listeners Association TV personality award to fellow Festival of Light campaigner Cliff Richard

Malcolm addresses an anti-abortion rally in Hyde Park, 1974

In the pulpit at
St Mary-le-Bow, 1970

Vicky's cartoon of Saint Mugg
from the New Statesman

ABOVE: Malcolm's reception into the Catholic Church, attended by (from left to right) Father Bidone, Malcolm, Bishop of Arundel, Kitty Muggeridge and Lord Longford

RIGHT: The 1981 Foyles lunch at the Dorchester, in the company of the author and Lord Longford

Filming at Robertsbridge with Svetlana Stalin, 1981

With Mother Teresa outside Park Cottage, April 1988

A gathering of the Muggeridge clan in August 1983

Malcolm with his three
brothers (from left)
Douglas, Jack and Eric

In the study at Park Cottage, 1975

LEFT: Setting off for a walk with Kitty

BELOW: Kitty at Malcolm's funeral, supported by her two sons John (left) and Leonard

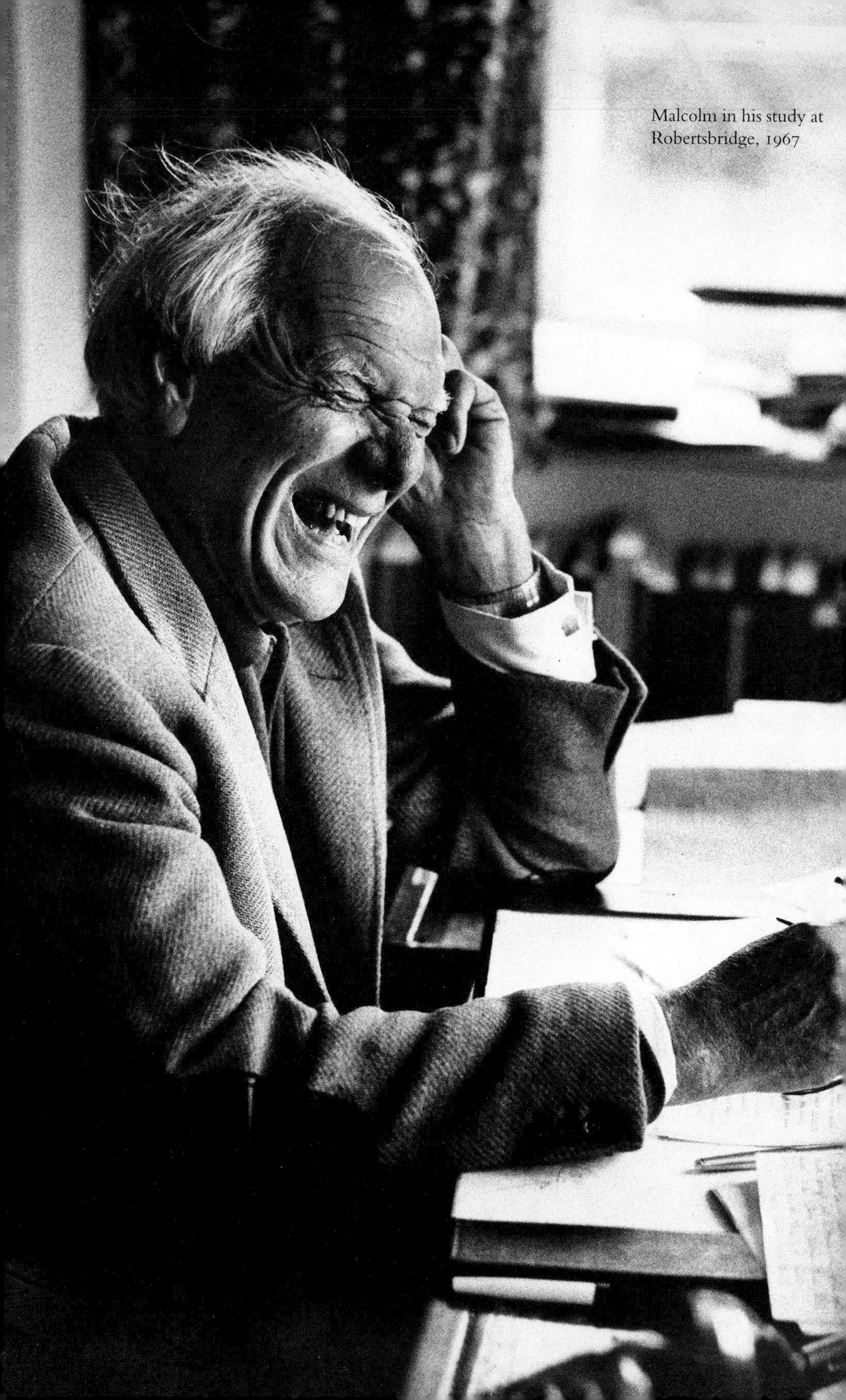

Malcolm in his study at Robertsbridge, 1967

followed by Malcolm's interview, and then the live transmission from Paris.

Miall arrived at the BBC's Riverside Studios in Hammersmith in the company of a War Office General who was keen to see the inner workings of television, to find a scene of confusion. Instead of sticking to his promise, Malcolm had taken Behan off to the Garrick Club for more drinks in addition to those he had already consumed on the plane from Dublin.

By the time they arrived at the studio Behan was well away, so much so that the conscientious Charles Wheeler, seeing his state, poured the BBC's bottle of whisky down the sink. Behan then disappeared completely, but Malcolm was on hand insisting that he had only had a few drinks and that it would be perfectly alright. Miall agreed that the interview could go ahead, on condition that if Behan said 'fuck' Malcolm was not to laugh.

The programme began. The film about Cyprus was shown, followed by the discussion with the two MPs. In the meantime, Behan, who had been found and brought to the studio, had fallen asleep in the heat of the studio lights. He awoke for a brief moment to see one of the young ladies from the finishing school wandering across the studio floor. 'I thought I saw an angel passing by,' he murmured, before falling back to sleep. Once the interview began it was obvious to everyone, including the viewers, that Behan was helplessly drunk and in the production gallery Leonard Miall gave orders to cut the interview and go on to the next item – the inventors' exhibition in Paris. But French television refused to oblige. 'You said you would be coming over to us at 8.43, it is now 8.37. We will be ready at 8.43.'

There was nothing for it; the interview had to proceed. Malcolm adopted the technique of asking a question and then answering it himself. Behan made only one coherent comment: 'I want a leak.' Eventually the French were ready to switch over and the interview came to a sudden end. Viewers rang in to complain, a BBC spokesman explained that Mr Behan had been very nervous and had had a few drinks and been affected by the heat in the studio. The following day there was some consternation in the *Panorama* office when the Director General Sir Ian Jacob rang.

He said nothing about Behan being drunk, however, and only registered his concern that the BBC should interview someone who had once been a member of the IRA.

Behan himself was delighted by the whole episode as it created enormous interest in his play. However, he told the *Johannesburg Star*: 'I am sorry if I annoyed Malcolm Muggeridge – a real English gentleman, and they are a rare breed these days.'

By this time, 1956, Malcolm's interest in *Punch* had begun to wane as he became more and more involved with television. Now he found himself caught on the fringe of politics. He had always had a special animus against Anthony Eden, saying: 'He is not only a bore, but he bores for England.' When Eden invited the Russian leaders Bulganin and Khrushchev to visit Britain in the spring of 1956, Malcolm was persuaded by his friend Auberon Herbert to lead a protest movement against them. Herbert, a devout Catholic and eccentric who had involved himself with exiled Poles and Ukrainians, was exactly the sort of quixotic character to appeal to Malcolm; his involvement in Herbert's campaign was strikingly similar to his later commitment to the anti-pornography Festival of Light organized by Mary Whitehouse – both Herbert and Whitehouse being, in his eyes, crusaders fighting futile battles against an overwhelming consensus and an apathetic British public. Herbert's organization had booked the Albert Hall for a massive anti-Communist protest, but ten days before the meeting was due to take place the management cancelled it, on the specious excuse that there was the danger of a demonstration if it took place.

Eventually the meeting was transferred to the Free Trade Hall in Manchester where Malcolm told the audience of 2,500 that 'expecting B. and K. to reform their ways as a result of seeing our free way of life is like asking two professional ladies from the Moulin Rouge to attend Roedean in the hope that they will marry Archdeacons and settle down to a life of quiet respectability.' Some days later he joined a delegation delivering a petition to Downing Street.

The anti-B. and K. campaign did not go down too well with *Punch* readers, many of whom regarded it as an irrelevance. This indifference merely helped to enhance Malcolm's feelings of frustration. He had in any case a tendency to become bored by any job he took, which made it all the more surprising that he lasted at *Punch* as long as he did (nearly five years). By this stage, he was leaving more and more of the work to Leslie Marsh and his young deputy editor Peter Dickinson, often not bothering to read articles until they appeared in print. This devil-may-care approach had resulted in another major row in March 1956 when, against the advice of his colleagues, Malcolm insisted on printing a not very well written story by Edward Hyams called 'A Taste of Wine' about an Anglo-Catholic priest who used vintage claret at communion. Hyams's joke was obscure but the *Church Times* took it to be blasphemous and attacked *Punch* openly in a leader: 'In recent years there have been several occasions when *Punch* has gone out of its way to sneer at religion. But this article is in a disgraceful class by itself. Its apparent purpose is to pour mockery on the Holy Communion. Its gratuitous offensiveness has to be seen to be believed.'

It was a sign of the extraordinary position occupied by *Punch* that the Archbishop of Canterbury, Geoffrey Fisher, should now personally write to Malcolm expressing his dismay at the turn taken by the magazine. Malcolm replied at length:

My Dear Archbishop,

It was very kind and considerate of you to write to me yourself about the question of bad taste in *Punch*. I've thought and thought about this question ever since I became editor. My own conclusion is (and you probably won't agree with it) that humour itself is in bad taste, as also, incidentally is truth. I'm sure that the Pharisees (men of taste) rightly felt our Lord was often guilty of bad taste – for instance when he said that the Sabbath was made for man and not man for the Sabbath. Equally the gargoyles that adorn our cathedrals are in bad taste, though personally I love them, and always think of them when I am trying to convince myself that editing *Punch* is a worthwhile job.

I am, alas, not myself a believing Christian. I wish I were. But one thing I can say with the utmost sincerity, and that is that I grow evermore convinced that the Christian gospel was the most wonderful thing that ever happened to the world; that it represents the nearest to ultimate truth that has ever been revealed to mankind; that our civilization was born of it, is irretrievably bound up with it and would almost certainly perish without it . . . if anything ever appeared in *Punch* which contradicted these convictions I should be ashamed indeed. I don't believe it has.

The Hyams article resulted in a further flood of angry letters and cancelled subscriptions which alarmed the *Punch* management. The final straw came in summer of 1957 in the shape of some satirical verses on the occasion of the young Prince Charles being sent to prep school at Cheam in Surrey. Peter Agnew, who was a Cheam governor, had asked Malcolm not to print anything on this subject, pointing out that it would cause him grave embarrassment. Knowing there was a veto on Cheam material one of the print workers rang up Agnew to warn him that there was a poem by Richard Usborne (who knew nothing of the veto) in the next week's issue on that very topic. Agnew gave orders for it to be taken out. Malcolm was furious. There was a row and instead of waiting only a few months for his contract to expire, the Agnews sacked him, though it was mutually agreed that for public purposes he would be resigning. His departure was reported worldwide, in almost every case with regret, though the *Guardian* pointed out that Malcolm had lasted nearly five years at *Punch*, a far longer period than he had held down any other job. When asked why he was leaving, Malcolm's stock response was to say that he wanted more time to write – particularly the biography of George Orwell which he had undertaken but was subsequently to abandon, saying that he found out too much about Orwell that he would rather not have known.

Amongst the *Punch* contributors the mood was one of sadness. John Betjeman wrote (25 September 1957):

Dear Malcolm,
    I should have written ages ago to thank you for being so kind an editor to so sparse a contributor as I am. I also

wanted to write to say how sorry I am you've given up being
editor – not that I blame you. But without you how will
Christopher [Hollis] and Tony and I be able to get along?
You were a marvellous editor – not just in introducing new
talent such as me (your greatest failure) but in keeping us
together, giving us life and JOKES. Oh dear. Back to old
APH and the cricketers down the other end. Oh hell. But
God bless you, dear Malcolm, for being such a true friend
to yours John B.

Malcolm's innovations at *Punch* and in particular his introduction of political satire had coincided with a general revolt in
intellectual circles against what was called 'The Establishment'.
The Suez crisis of 1956 helped to fan the flames of a movement
which embraced the plays and novels of the so-called Angry
Young Men and the films of the Boulting Brothers (in which
Malcolm himself was peripherally involved). A few years later
political satire became extremely fashionable with the success of
the revue *Beyond the Fringe* in 1961 and the advent of *Private Eye*
later the same year. But unaware of the 'wind of change' and
regretting the Muggeridge experiment the proprietors of
Punch reverted to type and appointed the cartoonist Bernard
Hollowood as editor and also for a time, managing director.
Hollowood was another one-time schoolmaster, a keen cricketer
and a former assistant editor of the *Economist*. Though sales rose
initially, they declined again and in 1968 the Agnews sold the
magazine to United Newspapers. By that stage *Private Eye* had
established itself as a satirical paper in opposition to *Punch* with
the help and encouragement of Malcolm, not to mention Claud
Cockburn.

Not long after his departure from *Punch*, Malcolm was again in
the news, this time with more serious repercussions. Shortly
after leaving *Punch* and while on a short tour of America, he had
agreed to write a long article on the Royal Family for the *Saturday
Evening Post*. It was an attractive assignment as he had already
written the same sort of piece for the *New Statesman* in October
1955 at the time of the controversy over Princess Margaret and

Group Captain Townsend. Headed 'Royal Soap Opera', the earlier article began in typical Muggeridge fashion: 'There are quite a lot of people – more than might be supposed – who like myself feel that another newspaper photograph of a member of the Royal Family will be more than they can bear. The Queen Mother, the Duke of Edinburgh, Nanny Lightbody, Group Captain Peter Townsend, the whole show is utterly out of hand.' Today, such an article would pass unnoticed, but at the time it was original enough to create a storm with the *Evening Standard* (owned by Malcolm's old enemy Lord Beaverbrook) printing a leader attacking him for his treasonable views.

Worse was to come. The *Saturday Evening Post* had reserved publication of Malcolm's second article to coincide with a royal tour of the USA by the Queen and Duke of Edinburgh – not surprisingly, as the piece was rather restrained in tone, consisting mainly of a historical survey of public attitudes to royalty. Malcolm's animus was directed not so much against the Queen as against those in the media who had turned the royal family into a 'soap opera' (the same expression as he had used in the *New Statesman*). His most ferocious remarks were reserved not for the Queen (about whom he was normally polite) but for his *Panorama* colleague Richard Dimbleby, famous for his commentaries on state occasions. (Dimbleby, who had taken over as compere of *Panorama* from Max Robertson in 1955, regarded Malcolm with barely concealed distaste, particularly after he ended a discussion on Orwell's *1984*, recently dramatized on the BBC, with the words: 'And now back to Big Brother.')

For his part, Malcolm could not stomach Dimbleby's unctuous manner. 'Have you ever calmly and quietly looked at his scripts?' he asked a journalist. 'He once described Big Ben as "loyal". Loyal Big Ben, the senses reel at that.'

'He is a large individual', he now wrote in the *Saturday Evening Post*, 'of eloquence which not even technical hitches can impede . . . his manner is priestly and, at the same time, in a portly sort of way, jaunty.

'What Mr Dimbleby manages to convey, by the intimacy of his observations, by his lush imagery and sedate bearing is that the subject of his commentary combines being a queen with being enchantingly "human". Seen through Mr Dimbleby's eyes, she is girlishly radiant, as well as imperiously dignified; gay and spontaneous as well as conscious of the duties and responsibilities. All this would have seemed to the Queen's forebears so much gibberish . . . to reign by courtesy of BBC television would have seemed to them preposterous.'

On 13 October two Sunday newspapers, the *Express* and the *People*, devoted most of their front pages to Malcolm's article: 'America Prints Amazing Royal Attack by English TV Idol' was the *People*'s headline, the accompanying story describing Malcolm's article as a diatribe. 'He has earned the contempt of all Britain,' the *Sunday Express* pontificated in a leader. Quite why there should be this concerted attack on Malcolm by the *People* and the *Sunday Express* was not immediately clear. However, the 'double-whammy' cannot have been wholly unconnected with the fact that during the previous week their rival the *Sunday Dispatch* had been advertising a regular forthcoming column by Malcolm Muggeridge, 'TV's most provocative personality'. The front-page attacks coincided therefore with Malcolm's first column; the *Sunday Dispatch*, panicked by the furore, dropped their new columnist like a hot potato – no doubt to the satisfaction of the paper's two rivals.

Ever the conscientious journalist with an eye for a good story, Leonard Miall arranged for the following day's *Panorama* to include a discussion with Malcolm and Bob Boothby on the Royalty row. But, on the pretext of a few angry phone calls that had come as a result of the weekend's publicity, the Director General Sir Ian Jacob (a retired general) cancelled the broadcast: 'I did not see why we should give a national platform to a man who had behaved as he had done' (letter to author, 3 September 1986).

A clear conflict now arose at the BBC between the establishment (Sir Ian Jacob, Sir Alexander Cadogan (Chairman) and most of the governors) and the professionals (broadcasters like Miall and McGivern). At issue was Malcolm's future and in particular whether the BBC should renew his contract which was about to expire. Harman Grisewood, the influential assistant to the Director General, spoke for the establishment: 'There is here and there in the BBC a marked inclination to go after any startling or showy personality,' he wrote in a memo to Jacob, 'and I think our over-use of Muggeridge must be ascribed to this journalistic urge . . . Harold Nicolson told me that if he were a member of the Board he would recommend that the BBC did not engage Muggeridge any more.'

The difficulty was that Malcolm was one of the BBC's outstanding broadcasters, that there were a number of programmes already in the pipeline and that the newly formed commercial television network was known to be after him. Sir Ian Jacob eventually agreed to see Malcolm personally for an 'off the record' discussion. However, when Malcolm subsequently gave an account of the meeting to the press, Sir Ian, already indignant at being dubbed 'General Sir Gag' by the *Daily Mirror*, decided that enough was enough and that the BBC would not renew his contract.

Muggeridge had shown that he was 'quite unreliable and not one suited to broadcast on serious matters'. The Director General's temper was not improved when he continued to read Malcolm's comments about the BBC in the press. 'It is all very well for Muggeridge to feel hurt, but he doesn't seem to absorb the idea that we might be even more affected by the insulting things he has repeatedly said to the press about us. I hope he goes elsewhere.'

CHAPTER X

Born Again

ALL THESE COMINGS and goings had been given widespread publicity throughout the world and for the first time in his life Malcolm found himself playing the part of pariah, in receipt of obscene phone calls and poison pen letters. Certain newspapers continued their campaign and the *Sunday Express* editor John Junor very nearly printed a gossip column story that Malcolm had been seen at the Oxford Union with Pamela Berry. He was only stopped when she rang Lord Beaverbrook, reminding him that he had a pact with the Berrys not to attack one another in their newspapers.

Meanwhile his cottage at Robertsbridge had been daubed with slogans by right-wing Empire Loyalists, a man spat at him when he was walking on the front at Brighton; a neighbouring land-owner told him he could no longer walk across his fields. Even his eldest brother Douglas wrote a letter to the press disassociat-ing himself publicly from Malcolm's views about the monarchy. Douglas's son, also called Douglas, by now a Talks Producer in the BBC, seriously considered changing his name as a result of the shame that his uncle had brought upon him. Most upsetting of all, perhaps, was a letter from an anonymous correspondent rejoicing in the recent death of the Muggeridges' youngest son Charles, killed while on a skiing holiday, in an avalanche near Chamonix in the Alps. He was, in fact, the son of Michal Vyvyan and turned out the most promising of the four Muggeridge chil-dren and Kitty's favourite. At the age of twenty he had just embarked on a naval career passing out top of the engineering branch at Dartmouth. Kitty was especially upset by his death and became very ill, blaming herself, an expert skier, for not warning him of the dangers of springtime avalanches. Malcolm, however, who had always regarded Charles as a cuckoo in the nest, would seem to have been almost unmoved. At any rate he did not accompany Kitty and Leonard to the funeral in Switzerland.

At the time it was comforting to have the support of friends, like John Betjeman who wrote (31 October 1957): 'Hold on old boy. There aren't many really nice and good men I know but you are one of them. So, I repeat, hold on, old boy. Love to Kitty. All will come right in the end. Meanwhile you are in the thoughts and prayers of your grateful *Punch* ex-contributor John B. '

Even so, there is no doubt that the royalty affair rattled him considerably, so much so that he even consulted a barrister about the possibility of suing the *Sunday Express* for libel. The lawyer agreed that the article was indeed defamatory but said that in the circumstances it was unlikely that the judge and jury would not be prejudiced in favour of the Queen. Following that rebuff, Malcolm made a final complaint to the Press Council accusing the *People* and the *Sunday Express* of distortion and mis-quotation. The Press Council, however, predictably rejected his complaint.

Help of a material kind came from Hugh Cudlipp who now offered him a column in the *Sunday Pictorial* with the handsome salary of £5,000 per annum. This was to be Malcolm's first and only experience of popular 'tabloid' journalism and he admitted he found it difficult: 'Anyone can write leading articles in *The Times* and the *Telegraph* or the *Manchester Guardian*,' he explained in his *New Statesman* diary, 'you get off to a good start with "Mr Macmillan's latest note to Marshall Bulganin can scarcely (or cannot, according to which newspaper) be regarded as a serious contribution to the problem of East–West relations." Then you meander on about previous notes, and statements made in a previous debate. None of this is permissible in the *Sunday Pictorial*. I notice the difference in manner in which copy is read. In Printing House Square or Peterborough Court or Cross Street they glance over the sheets. In Geraldine House they take it sentence by sentence.'

It was perhaps not surprising in view of the royalty hullabaloo that Malcolm should feel the urge to go abroad again. He may also have wished to escape, at least temporarily, from Pamela Berry. At any rate in March 1958 he flew to Australia to do a two-month stint working for the *Sydney Morning Herald* as well as doing a number of interviews for Australian television. It was not a very exciting assignment and Malcolm's articles for the Australian press lacked his normal sparkle. Although he liked Australians and the Australian landscape, he missed the intellectual stimulation he was used to in England. He wrote of Australia perceptively as if it was a gigantic desert island and the Australians themselves Robinson Crusoes: 'They are castaways-de-luxe but they have an air of expecting a ship to come in and take them away.'

A more promising journalistic opportunity came his way on his return to England. On 5 February 1959 Harold Macmillan, who had succeeded Anthony Eden as Prime Minister in 1956, announced to the surprise of everyone that he was making a visit to Moscow for talks with the Russian leader Mr Khrushchev. Though Labour Party critics accused Macmillan of merely electioneering, the announcement created enormous interest as it was the first time a British Prime Minister had visited Russia since the war. Once again Hugh Cudlipp offered Malcolm a job, this time as the *Daily Mirror*'s special correspondent in Moscow. He joined the huge pack of journalists including Randolph Churchill who set off in the wake of Macmillan, his Foreign Secretary Selwyn Lloyd and an army of officials.

Malcolm, who had regarded Anthony Eden with almost complete contempt, was more amused than disgusted by his successor. Macmillan seemed to him like a man who had strayed out of Galsworthy's *Forsyte Saga*: 'The lean, sinewy neck pulsates,' he wrote in *Life* (18 February 1957), 'the tired grey features wear a smile; the voice, soft and sibilant, emerges from the drooping moustache. A publisher? No. A civil servant? No. A Prime Minister.' For the occasion of his Russian visit Macmillan sported a distinctive ten-inch-high white fur hat which made him look, in Malcolm's eyes, even more singular.

Apart from enhancing his electoral prestige with British

voters, it was not clear what Macmillan would achieve as an independent negotiator in Moscow. Malcolm compared him to the licensed nudes at the Windmill Theatre in London: 'He is permitted to display himself but on condition that he does not move. Even an attempt at "walkabout" would be pointless. If Mr Macmillan grasps the hands of occasional members of the public, they are quite likely to be coppers.' Malcolm greatly enjoyed his excursion, which gave him an opportunity to employ his talents as a comic journalist. He particularly enjoyed briefly meeting the Russian leader Mr Khrushchev at a diplomatic reception and discussing *Krokodil*, the Russian equivalent of *Punch*. 'In your article write the truth,' Khrushchev said as he took his leave. 'Such', replied Malcolm, 'is my constant endeavour.'

In 1960 Malcolm, still banished from the BBC, began a series of half-hour interviews for Granada, the independent television company founded by the brilliant impresario Sidney Bernstein. Though *Appointment With . . .* was billed as ITV's answer to *Face to Face*, the BBC series in which John Freeman had pioneered a new no-holds-barred approach to interviewing (on one occasion he reduced Gilbert Harding to tears when he described the death of his mother), Malcolm wisely decided not to compete with Freeman and maintained his very relaxed, casual-seeming technique. Even when he interviewed W. H. Auden, Stephen Spender and Christopher Isherwood together he refrained from asking Auden and Isherwood why they had decamped together to America at the outbreak of war in 1939 – though he admitted to long agonizing about this the night before.

It was somehow typical of television that the most interesting interview in the series, with the famous Fascist leader Sir Oswald Mosley, was never shown. Even though the subject of the Jews was not once raised, Bernstein was reluctant to give offence to his community. Perhaps if Mosley had been more obviously the sinister racist, the interview might have been acceptable to Granada, but he was very careful to appear reasonable:

MALCOLM: Supposing you got into power, what would you do about people like me who would immediately criticize you?

MOSLEY: I would say 'Muggeridge, say what you like, when you like.'

MALCOLM: Are you sure about that? That wouldn't have been your view in the Thirties, you'd have locked me up.

Mosley's irrationality only became at all evident when they discussed apartheid and racial segregation. He propounded the extraordinary suggestion that the whole of Africa – not merely South Africa – should be divided into separate black and white areas. Malcolm, though guilty of anti-Semitism in his writing, was always violently against apartheid. 'Apartheid is lunacy,' he told Mosley. 'Men have 99% in common and 1% difference. Ultimately we're all the same.' When they reverted to politics Malcolm proclaimed himself a democrat: 'I prefer this ramshackle old system of democracy which staggers along.' To which Mosley replied: 'You'll believe in it until it falls about your head.'

Apart from Mosley, the series was most interesting in the evidence it gave of Malcolm's reviving concern with Christianity. He questioned Muriel Spark closely about her Catholic faith and in an interview with the Catholic Bishop of Leeds made no attempt to disguise his very personal interest in the answers that he gave. The Bishop argued that the Resurrection was just as much a historical event as the death of Nelson, but Malcolm could not begin to accept it. 'This is where a complete Iron Curtain descends,' he replied regretfully, adding that he found the whole idea of the Incarnation meaningless.

In 1960 Sir Ian Jacob retired as Director General of the BBC and was succeeded by Hugh Carleton Greene, a very different character. Whereas Jacob had been an establishment figure, Greene (the brother of Graham) was, like Malcolm, a former *Daily Telegraph* journalist; he had even been offered the editorship of *Punch* after Malcolm's dismissal. Under Greene, the BBC began to flex its muscles and experiment, notably in the field of satire with *That Was the Week That Was*. Greene gave orders that there was to be no BBC blacklist and Malcolm now found himself once again *persona grata*, while he was fêted as a hero by the young satirists. Christopher Booker, the first editor of *Private Eye* and chief script-writer of *TW3*, became a close friend and frequent visitor to Robertsbridge where he wrote much of his book *The Neophiliacs*. In the summer of 1964 Malcolm acted briefly as the guest editor of *Private Eye*. He also appeared for a time with John Wells and Eleanor Bron on a satirical television programme called *The Late Show*.

His return to the BBC coincided with a drastic change of lifestyle. Throughout the Fifties, the years at *Punch* and the BBC, he had been under enormous pressure, doing several jobs at once and coping with the conflicting demands of Kitty and his family and Pamela Berry. He was suffering from insomnia (a lifelong problem) and taking a variety of sleeping pills, smoking heavily and drinking more than ever. As a consequence, his behaviour towards women had become embarrassing and frequently out-rageous. BBC colleagues called him 'The Pouncer'. Patricia, Claud Cockburn's wife, compared him to a Russian peasant, describing an incident when during a dinner party she went upstairs to make a phone call and was pursued by Malcolm who began to assault her. Outraged, Patricia struck out at him with the telephone, knocked him down and flew into a panic, con-vinced that she had killed him.

Things came to a head in 1963 at a dinner party at Boulestin's where Malcolm, after visiting Kitty in Barts Hospital, had arranged to meet his old colleague from Washington, the *Express* correspondent René McColl, his wife Hermione and their two children. Malcolm became very drunk and began fumbling under the table, not only with Mrs McColl but with her daughter as well. Such behaviour on Malcolm's part was by no means unusual at this time, but René McColl was outraged, got to his feet, slapped Malcolm's face and stormed out of the restaurant along with his family.

The incident, which became general gossip, caused Malcolm great distress especially when McColl, who had been a very close friend, refused ever to talk to him again. It was mainly because of the Boulestin dinner that Malcolm finally decided to give up drink – something that he had previously tried to do on many occasions but without success. The decision was not, like so many of his decisions, a sudden impulsive affair. By this time he had become a very heavy drinker. The Longfords, with whom he and Kitty now dined regularly, remembered Malcolm during this period (in the late Fifties and early Sixties) drinking a great deal of whisky in the course of the evening, and having to be helped down the steps to his car when taking his leave. Yet Malcolm had always had it in the back of his mind that at the age of sixty, which he reached in 1963, he would have to give up drinking in the interests of self-preservation. Later, he would advise the *Observer*'s political correspondent Alan Watkins that he, too, when he reached the age of sixty would have to choose between drinking and working.

The Pamela Berry affair had caused him to drink more heavily, particularly because of the distress it had given Kitty. Malcolm made several half-hearted attempts to bring it to an end but to no avail. At one stage he decided never to drink when he was with her in order to have greater control over himself. He was especially exasperated by the knowledge that, while professing undying love for him, Pamela was sleeping with other men (the thought that he himself might behave in a similar way did nothing to lessen his jealousy). She tried to excuse herself by arguing that she was trying to get her own back on him because of his refusal to leave Kitty as she wanted him to do. The result was a relationship punctuated by frequent rows and recriminations. In 1960, when Pamela Berry accompanied Malcolm on a lecture tour of America (being introduced on occasion as Mrs Muggeridge), the rumour went round that they had come to blows in a New York hotel.

Perhaps because of Pamela Berry's special status as wife of a press lord – her husband Michael had by now succeeded Lord Camrose as proprietor and editor of the *Daily Telegraph* – their behaviour was quite brazen. In 1963 there was widespread amusement when Malcolm and Pamela Berry appeared one afternoon at the Labour Party Conference with straw and leaves on their clothing. Yet it was about this time that Malcolm finally broke with her. Kitty had suffered long and, for the most part, in silence. She knew that Malcolm was not to be trusted with other women but she also knew that in 99% of the cases it meant little or nothing and that he would always come back to her. The Berry affair was different not only because it lasted much longer but because for the first time it was the woman who was calling the tune. Kitty often thought about leaving Malcolm – she once told Patricia Cockburn that she was thinking of opening a tea shop in Hastings. Yet her advice to women like Mrs Henry Fairlie who were similarly troubled by unfaithful husbands (Fairlie, coincidentally, succeeded Malcolm as Pamela Berry's lover) was always to 'sit tight'.

Precisely how or where the Berry affair ended is not clear, but Malcolm's friends believed it came about because in the end Kitty asked Malcolm to choose between the two of them, telling him that she would leave if that was what he wanted. She could not bear, she said, to see him so unhappy. Faced with the option there was no doubt as to which way he would go. The decision brought an end to years of misery, and from this point it is true to say Kitty and Malcolm lived happily ever afterwards.

With drink, smoking and women put behind him, Malcolm was finally able to begin his slow rediscovery of Christianity. Ever since his Cambridge days and his near-conversion, under the influence of Alec Vidler, to a life of asceticism, he had hankered after abstinence as a means of achieving peace of mind. But the fatal combination of the World, the Flesh and the Devil intervened. How could he be reconciled to Christianity, living the kind of life he did? It was only when he finally renounced his 'pleasures' – the womanizing and the drinking in his case went hand in hand – that he was able to embrace a more spiritual outlook on life and gradually to rid himself of the morbid thoughts and preoccupations that had for so long distracted him. It was no accident that, coincidental with these various renunciations, his diary finally peters out.

In a long and revealing profile by his friend the novelist Hugo Charteris in the short-lived magazine *London Life* (December 1965) Malcolm tried to put into words his new convictions. He could not go so far as to say that he was a Christian. At this stage in his life he was still unable to subscribe to any of the dogmas in the Creed. 'All I can say is that, in all my travels, Christianity is about the best thing I have come across.' The specific appeal to him of Christianity lay in its call to the spiritual. 'I see life', he told Charteris, 'as an eternal battle between two irreconcilable opposites, the world of the flesh and the world of the spirit.'

The article was unusual in that for the first time Kitty 'went public' on the subject of Malcolm. Hugo Charteris was Ann Fleming's brother, an occasional contributor to *Punch* and, like most of Malcolm's journalistic friends, knew all about the Pamela Berry affair – to which he referred discreetly in his piece. Looking back at the last ten years, Malcolm admitted: 'That was my worst period: drinking, smoking, insomnia, barbiturates and the fleshpots – high society.'

'But Kitty', Charteris commented, 'recalls the period with the same look that Jap POWs react to mention of the Burma Road: cauterized – "It's OK now. But there were moments when I sat down here and thought I might as well buzz off."'

Kitty was to emerge as a remarkable person in her own right with the publication in 1967 of the biography of her aunt Beatrice Webb on which she collaborated with her friend Ruth Adam. It was a workmanlike and very readable book and by far the best thing in it was Kitty's own memoir of her aunt (part of which is quoted in Chapter 3).

This revealed her sharp powers of perception and her sense of humour. (She later gained an entry in the quotation books with her remark that David Frost had 'risen without trace'.) In a number of interviews to publicize her book, she spoke with the same dry humour about her marriage, though none of the journalists who visited Robertsbridge would have guessed that this beautiful and serene woman had once been as wild and anarchic as her husband, if not more so. The question of why she had put up with his absences and infidelities over the years went unasked. But the answer was simple, namely that she loved him. '*Mauvais comme tu es, je t'adore*,' Kitty had told him following her disastrous visit to Calcutta in 1935. She never really wavered from that view, though sorely tried during the Pamela Berry years. But like many others who had dealings with Malcolm, she had realized long ago that there was no point in arguing with him. 'A marriage either comes off or it doesn't,' she told

Olga Franklin in the *Daily Mail* (3 June 1967), 'but it doesn't succeed of its own accord without effort. You have to make a marriage. If things go wrong, you have to say to yourself "what attitude shall I take: am I to stick it out or have a blazing row?" Malcolm is such a persuasive arguer that I think he would be able to persuade me to agree with him on anything. Of course there were many quarrels, many, many. But then I decided I never wanted to quarrel again in my whole life. That was about ten years ago.' When another interviewer commented on her habit of always deferring to Malcolm when he butted into her conversation, she said: 'Oh, you've noticed that, have you? It doesn't mean I have no opinions or that I'm downtrodden. It merely seems easier to live that way.'

Their life together had at last begun to take on a regular routine. In 1956 they had taken a lease on Salehurst Farm, Robertsbridge. It was one of a group of buildings reached down a long cart track on the outskirts of the Sussex village which lies on the London–Hastings road, not far from Whatlington where they had lived before the war. Eventually, in 1963, they moved to Park Cottage which is right at the end of the track. It was a remote and peaceful place surrounded by farmland, which once belonged to the Cistercian Abbey of Salehurst (now a ruin). You entered the cottage by the back under a steep, sloping, windowless roof, the door opening directly into the kitchen, with a sitting room and study leading off it. A steep staircase led to the bedrooms and a bathroom, with a third bedroom and bathroom on the upper floor. Malcolm had never had the smallest interest in possessions; Kitty, as always, furnished the house comfortably but very cheaply, acquiring much of the furniture from a warehouse in Hastings Old Town. (She estimated it was the twenty-second time she had set up home with Malcolm and hoped it would be the last.) The sitting room, which looked out onto the countryside, had large comfortable armchairs and round the open fireplace Kitty hung the pictures of their children which her mother had painted during the war, along with Bernard Shaw's photograph of Beatrice Webb. The only other furniture was a large radiogram (the television set remained in Malcolm's study).

It was a perfect spot, remote, yet only a couple of miles from the village and station. The great advantage from Malcolm's point of view were the walks he could choose through the woodland and apple orchards. Gradually he adopted a routine in keeping with his new persona. He dispensed with sleeping pills (though he occasionally resorted to them at times of stress) and reconciled himself to having only a few hours' sleep a night. He would get up at about 5 o'clock and write in his study for two hours before bringing Kitty a cup of tea in bed. After a light lunch (which became lighter as the years went by) he would go for a four or five mile walk and after tea, a favourite meal with them both, would do some more writing before supper.

By now Malcolm and Kitty were grandparents. Their younger son John had married a Canadian Catholic, Anne Roche, on 4 July 1960 and was now teaching at Ontario in Canada. Their son, John Malcolm, the first of five children, was born on 31 July 1961. Leonard, who had joined the Plymouth Brethren, was married in 1965 to Sylvia, daughter of a Regular Army Sergeant. When Val married a Dutch lecturer, Gerrit Jan Colenbrander, in 1969 Malcolm wrote to his brother Jack: 'Val's marriage to this absolutely delightful young man removes my last worldly worry.' (10 May 1969)

Their life was greatly enriched when Alec Vidler moved back to Rye in 1967. Since parting from Malcolm in 1932 he had become one of the Church of England's best known theologians and the author of a number of books. He had been a Canon at Windsor and finally Dean of Kings College, Cambridge. Though his career had taken him some way from his radical beginnings in Newcastle and Birmingham, he always remained true to the vow of celibacy he had made when he joined the Oratory of the Good Shepherd. He was now, in his sixties, a patriarchal figure with a long white beard, though he seldom, if ever, wore a dog collar and was known for some rather eccentric pieces of clothing, for example, a British Rail steward's blazer. He also owned for many years a Jack Russell called Zadok over which he had little or no control.

Malcolm and Kitty had kept in touch with Alec throughout the intervening years since their marriage. Now they were in almost day to day contact with 'the Doctor' as they called him. Either they drove the ten miles or so over to Rye where Alec served tea in glass cups in his ancient house in Church Square or, more frequently, Alec would drive to Robertsbridge and they would go for long walks together. The Doctor remained an intensely reserved person who seldom, if ever, discussed religion, but Malcolm found his mere presence very calm and reassuring.

Later, when they were established at Robertsbridge, Alec, an expert apiarist, introduced Malcolm and Kitty to the joys of beekeeping, but Malcolm never really mastered the art and in the end he left it to Alec to look after his hives.

Another of Malcolm's close friendships during the last twenty-five years of his life was with Frank and Elizabeth Longford who had inherited a house in the nearby village of Hurst Green. Though they were only weekenders they made a routine of dining with the Muggeridges every Saturday night, taking it in turns to be hosts – a routine that was to be kept up until shortly before Malcolm's death in 1990. Malcolm had met the Pakenhams (as they then were) a number of times in London before the war – Longford's sister Violet was married to Anthony Powell – and while he was immediately attracted to Elizabeth, his first impression of Frank had not been very favourable (21 August 1950):

> With Tony, ran into Pakenham with the new German representative . . . Pakenham just back from Africa where he met and took a great fancy, so he said, to Dr Malan. Reflected how absurd politics are when such a character as Pakenham, believing diametrically the opposite of his colleagues in the Government, can yet remain a minister. He has to a marked degree that terrible English Upper Class trait of wanting to ingratiate himself with our enemies – Irish, German, Afrikaners etc, etc – bald-headed, slightly bloated, largely absurd.

On better acquaintance, Malcolm warmed to the eccentric peer, as he always did to anyone who failed to conform to what society expected of him. Although he became a successful politician, banker and publisher, Longford redeemed himself in Malcolm's eyes by the sincerity of his Catholicism and his lovable eccentricity. He was, like so many of Malcolm's friends, a Quixote and, like the Don, the hero of all kinds of stories. Malcolm treasured his various exploits: Longford as political campaigner being advised to address working-class women as Mother only to be told by the first woman he so greeted, 'I'm not your fucking mother!'; Longford visiting a dying colleague in the Government and deciding to cheer him up by telling him a number of cabinet secrets; above all, Longford newly created Knight of the Garter in 1971 and opening his conversation with the Queen by saying, 'You know Ma'am, Malcolm Muggeridge is a very nice man.' (The presumption being that Malcolm's *Saturday Evening Post* article had rankled with Her Majesty ever since 1957 and might have stood in the way of Malcolm being given some suitable honour himself).

These friendships with Alec Vidler and the Longfords were particularly valuable, since many of his old Fleet Street friends were finding it hard to get along with the new abstemious Muggeridge. Claud Cockburn, an inveterate atheist, could not stomach Malcolm's public pronouncements about Christianity, and Leslie Illingworth, a neighbour and friend since *Punch* days, found it impossible to adapt to Malcolm's teetotal ways.

A more serious rift had occurred in 1964 with Anthony Powell who had been, apart from Hugh Kingsmill, his closest ever friend. Malcolm had regularly reviewed Powell's novels in the *Dance to the Music of Time* sequence, and he had been instrumental in finding a publisher for it in the first place. However, when the fifth novel in the sequence (dealing with the hero's wartime career) *A Valley of Bones* was published, Malcolm's review in the *Evening Standard* (3 March 1964) came as a shattering blow to Powell. After comparing the book rather unfavourably to Evelyn Waugh's wartime trilogy *Sword of Honour*, Malcolm went on to contrast Waugh's Catholic snobbery with Powell's more Anglican version.

> Waugh's [narrator] is more involved in the sense that he actually believes for a while that the war is about something: his snobbishness is more dynamic, even crazy.

Powell's narrator [Jenkins] just takes the war for granted, as he does existing social arrangements: his snobbishness has no revivalist or mystical edge about it, but is quiet, steadfast, as it were Anglican in its flexibility and tenacity. It is Snobbishness Ancient and Modern . . . the Thirty-Nine Articles of Snobbishness

There is even at the beginning of *A Valley of Bones* an echo of another war book, *Brideshead Revisited*. Jenkins reports for duty in a place where his ancestors have lived and thriven, going back, it seems to legendary Kings. The Jenkins have thus a more ancient, if less definitive lineage than Lord Sebastian Flyte. With them it is a case of Stonehenge Revisited.

The review concluded:

Stendhal, one of Mr Powell's major admirations, prophesied how posterity would enjoy and appreciate his work, neglected by his contemporaries. The prophesy has been abundantly fulfilled.

We, Mr Powell's contemporaries, have proved less recalcitrant and done him proud. Will posterity be correspondingly less amenable? See in his meticulous reconstruction of his life at times a heap of dust? Despite strong partiality, honesty compels me to admit it might.

Powell was understandably very distressed by this devastating attack. 'I thought he was my *friend*,' he agonized to Osbert Lancaster. It was, he said, the final conclusion that upset him most, though the devastating attack on his snobbery was perhaps what really struck home. Looking back after many years, he said how Malcolm was motivated by envy of his success. It is certainly true that Malcolm, himself a failed novelist, tended to be more than usually disparaging about his contemporaries like Graham Greene and John Betjeman who had become best-sellers. It may also be true that he was personally bored by Tony Powell and had no place for him in his new, abstemious routine. The strange thing about the incident was that, when confronted by it in later life, Malcolm had no recollection at all of what had happened. He knew that Powell had rowed with him but genuinely could not remember what it had been about. Malcolm, who seldom if ever bore a grudge against anyone, even a hostile reviewer, found it difficult to understand why people sometimes took offence at what he said or wrote. The trouble was that he had a habit of sometimes expressing his thoughts without giving a moment's consideration to what effect they might have. The fact that in this instance he had only just invited himself to stay at Powell's house in Somerset suggests that he was blissfully unaware of what he was doing.

What made it worse was that so often his comments were nothing but the truth. (Malcolm was a bit like Dr Johnson who when asked why he had been so hard on Thomas Gray in his *Lives of the Poets* replied that he would like to have been kinder but that he was 'entrusted with so much truth'.) The critique of Powell's novel sequence is damning, yet at the same time his prophecy is likely to be proved true.

As so often, Malcolm, without thinking, had merely blurted out the truth and it brought to a sudden end one of his longest and most fruitful friendships. Eventually there was a reconciliation of a sort and the two men corresponded again in the late Seventies. Perhaps Powell might have been less obdurate had it not been for the fact that he, like Claud Cockburn, found himself out of sympathy with what he called in his memoirs the 'hot-gospelling, near Messianic Muggeridge promulgating an ineluctable choice between salvation and perdition.'

To many such friends, and those critics who were to attack him later, Malcolm was guilty of hypocrisy. To them it seemed as if, having taken his share of the world's pleasures, he was now preaching the virtues of abstinence. There was something in this, yet the mistake his attackers made was to think that Malcolm had only come to Christianity in old age, when in fact it had been something of a life-long obsession. It was also a mistake to imagine that Malcolm had enjoyed his years of hedonism when the truth was they had caused him a great deal of unhappiness and even torment.

Religion, however, plays a more powerful role in relationships than many people give it credit for. Malcolm himself used to say that the important division is not between left and right but between those who believe in God and those who don't. Even in his pre-evangelistic period he had the ability to excite fury among humanists and agnostics, often for no very clear reason. In a television interview with Bertrand Russell in 1957 the great philosopher became almost apoplectic with rage when Malcolm challenged his view that Christianity had caused most of the world's troubles. Another famous philosopher, Professor A. J. Ayer, took grave offence when Malcolm spoke brusquely to him on his TV discussion programme *The Question Why*. Ayer had met Malcolm during the war in Algiers and had admired his journalism but took exception to his 'growing religiosity'. When he ventured to argue on television against Malcolm's view that suffering was ennobling, Malcolm snubbed him: 'How you ever became Professor of Logic, Freddie, I shall never know.' Ayer was, for once, rendered speechless. His wife, Dee Wells, was so furious that she rang up the producer Oliver Hunkin and tore strips off him. Professor Hugh Trevor Roper was another atheist and also a fervent anti-Catholic who found himself driven into a fury by the combination of Kingsmill and Muggeridge at a dinner party, as a result of which he vowed never to have anything to do with him thereafter (though he admitted that he had thought the same before and always succumbed to Malcolm's charm when they met).

From this time – the mid-Sixties – religion was to be Malcolm's theme to the exclusion of almost everything else. He continued to write journalism, particularly in the *New Statesman*, and was later to embark on his memoirs, but his fascination with politics was beginning to wane. After Macmillan, prime ministers like Sir Alec Douglas Home and Harold Wilson never inspired the same kind of set pieces which he had devoted to their predecessors. A number of these were reprinted in a collection of articles published in 1965: *Tread Softly, for you Tread on my Jokes* (less clumsily titled in America *The Most of Muggeridge*). Malcolm was well aware of the perils of reprinting journalism but *Tread Softly* was a best-seller and received more laudatory reviews than any book he had previously written. He found himself being compared by his critics to Swift, Hazlitt, Dr Johnson and H. L. Mencken.

Though many of the pieces were literary – on Waugh, Wodehouse and D. H. Lawrence – Malcolm was always on surer ground when writing about politics and politicians. Not all of his writing was what his critics would call negative. He praised, notably, General de Gaulle whom he admired almost without qualification. Malcolm had interviewed him in Paris in 1952 during his period in the wilderness, finding in him a 'nobility, a true disinterestedness, even a sort of sublime absurdity, which overcame his physical and mental gaucherie'. Later, in 1970, he invited de Gaulle to do a BBC interview but he replied that he had no wish at that stage to 'utiliser les ondes' (use the airwaves).

Malcolm's comments on British politicians were less eulogistic, Anthony Eden being his especial *bête noire*: 'The simple fact is that nothing in Eden invited either admiration or abhorrence. He was just empty of content, like his television appearances in which a flow of banalities were presented in the persuasive manner of an ex-officer trying to sell one a fire extinguisher at the front door.'

Malcolm was especially scathing about President J. F. Kennedy, recently murdered and now the subject of a cult, especially among the young. Just as he had been the first, when editing *Punch*, to attack the idolization of Churchill, Malcolm was almost the first seriously to question the canonization of a man whom he described as 'an easy-going, amorous, rather indolent and snobbish, amiable and agreeable American patrician'. He was particularly dismissive of the historian Arthur Schlesinger, whom he had met in Washington in 1947 and whose book *The Age of Jackson* he had greatly admired. How was it possible, he asked, that a highly intelligent, sceptical, witty scholar could descend to such prose as this:

> The frenzy of August had gone though the people stood in quiet clusters at each end of the Kennedy block on Irving Avenue. The compound itself was tranquil and secluded in the drowsy sunlight. The Kennedys were out for a stroll in the dunes. In a moment they returned, Jack in a tweed jacket, sweater and slacks, hatless and tieless, swinging a cane and looking fit and jaunty, and Jacqueline, her hair slightly blown in the breeze, glowing in beauty from the walk. One could

only think: what a wildly attractive young couple. It took another minute to remember that this was the President-elect of the United States and his wife.

Schlesinger proved, in Malcolm's view, what a great mistake it was for intellectuals to attach themselves to authority. In Britain, when the newly elected Prime Minister Wilson had tried to model his appeal on Kennedy's, Malcolm singled out for ridicule the figure of C. P. Snow whom Wilson had appointed to the new Ministry of Technology, elevating him to the peerage at the same time. Perhaps because Snow, like Powell, was a highly successful novelist (though now almost completely forgotten) he became a favourite Aunt Sally for Malcolm. Reviewing Snow's book *The Corridors of Power* (a phrase he invented), Malcolm laid into the newly appointed minister: 'Let me take, by way of illustration, a single sentence which caught my fancy. Snow mentions that "during the winter the gossip began to swirl out from the clubs and Whitehall corridors". One imagines that so substantial figure, that huge moon face, unsmiling, portentous, looking across St James's Park. Then, wetting a finger, holding it up to the wind, with an expression of great gravity; yes, (head on one side), yes, sure enough he can detect a decided current of gossip swirling past him from the clubs and Whitehall corridors.'

This was the first of many pot-shots, one of which memorably described Snow as 'a kind of tragic clown of our times, stumbling Grock-like down his own phantom corridors of power.' On one such occasion Snow retaliated, telling Malcolm: 'Your mind is closed. Not only about me, I fancy, but most other things. How long is it since you had a new idea?' Malcolm, who felt no personal animus towards Snow, reminded him of H. G. Wells' reply when taxed with omitting any mention of Shakespeare from his *Outline of World History*, namely that he had contributed no new ideas. As for Kingsley Martin, whose integrity Malcolm had, in Snow's eyes, impugned: 'The whole trouble with liberalism as a governing force is that it supposes itself to have integrity. Machiavelli knew better. Will this make any sense at all to you? I doubt it. Never mind, my dear Charles.'

CHAPTER XI

Back at the BBC

LIKE MANY OTHERS who give up drink, Malcolm found himself possessed of renewed energy. He was now in constant demand from BBC producers and was eager to take on all the work that was offered.

In 1965 alone he appeared regularly on Ned Sherrin's satirical programmes *Not So Much a Programme* and *BBC3*, compered a series produced by Anthony Smith called *Let Me Speak* in which he questioned little groups of non-conformists, took part on the panel of a short-lived quiz game called *First Impressions* guessing the identity of celebrities, interviewed Cecil King about Lord Northcliffe, appeared in documentaries on Lourdes, 'The American Way of Sex', a lecture tour of the USA and a University for Blacks in Tennessee, interviewed Norman Mailer (with Jonathan Miller), Tyrone Guthrie, Cecil Beaton and Robert Graves, gave a lecture on Rudyard Kipling and produced a profile of George Orwell. It was not surprising that Kingsley Martin should complain in the *New Statesman* (4 October 1966): 'He is too fluent and omnipresent; perhaps a period of abstinence from TV would be a good idea.'

TV producers were astonished by Malcolm's vitality, his eagerness to please and his readiness to learn new techniques. In 1964 after he had recently rejoined the BBC he came up with a completely original idea in the course of talks with Alisdair Milne (later the BBC's Director General) and Donald Baverstock, a brilliant if erratic Welshman who was then the BBC's Chief of Programmes. This was a televised autobiography: six programmes in which Malcolm would re-visit Russia, India and Mozambique, etc. For this, Milne and Baverstock enlisted a

young director then working on the magazine programme
Tonight. His name was Kevin Billington and his only brief was
provided by Baverstock: 'Combine the past and present, boyo.'

It was an unlikely duo – Malcolm, whose only experience
of television at that time was doing interviews in a studio and
Billington, thirty years his junior, used to making short, newsy
films with hardened reporters like Alan Whicker and Fyfe
Robertson. Almost before they knew what was happening they
found themselves on their way to Delhi with a camera crew and
not much idea of how the film was going to develop beyond the
fact that it would describe in words and images Malcolm's two
periods in India, at Alwaye Missionary School in the Twenties
and later as a reporter in Calcutta and Simla.

To begin with, Malcolm found it difficult to adjust to working
with a director telling him what to do. There was a terrible
moment at Alwaye. Kevin Billington had arranged for a group
of Malcolm's former students to be on hand to welcome him at
the school, and, as they were travelling in two cars, impressed
on Malcolm that he must not get out of the car until the cameraman had arrived and was ready to film the emotional reunion.
Instead of which, Malcolm arrived, leaped out and rushed
towards his old friends. Billington was absolutely furious and
refused to speak to Malcolm for twenty-four hours, while
Malcolm was so agitated that he broke his vow of non-
drinking and ordered a large scotch at the hotel where they were
staying.

Apart from this, the film was extraordinarily successful. There
was a great stroke of luck when, on their arrival at the Viceroy's
summer retreat of Simla, they discovered the removal men were
just about to move into Viceregal Lodge; Billington was thus
able to film Malcolm sitting on the Viceroy's throne, still in
place, amid dust-sheets and rolled up carpets. 'Fantastic scene,'
Malcolm wrote in his diary: 'carpets rolled up, pictures removed,
leaving the blank space on walls etc. Throne Viceroy used to sit
on with silver footstool left in place . . . felt quite fabulously
exhilarated at this dismantled power; he hath put down the
mighty from their seat and hath exalted the humble and meek.
The scenery being taken away, the props sent back to store, the

stage cleared for another play. I love everything which demonstrates the transience of earthly power; never have I been served so piquant a demonstration.' Malcolm tried to read over the diaries he had kept from his previous visit to Simla 'but flagged from genuine boredom'. He walked up to Summerhill to look for Amrita Sher Gil's old house, but couldn't find it.

Billington was astonished by the speed with which Malcolm adapted to the unfamiliar task of writing a script to fit a piece of film. He discovered, too, a rapport with Malcolm that was at times uncanny. The older man seemed to have a sixth sense. Once they were driving together near Cape Comorin in Kerala when Billington noticed crowds of people walking in little processions along the streets all in the same direction, while others were busy closing the shutters on the shops. Puzzled, he woke Malcolm who had been dozing beside him and asked him what was happening. Malcolm looked out of the window and said without a moment's hesitation, 'Nehru's dead' (27 May 1964).

Even more extraordinary, when they were filming in Kerala, Malcolm told him: 'I know the girl you're going to marry. Her name is Rachel Pakenham' (daughter of the Longfords). Billington paid little attention and it only came back to him two years later when he was working in New York and got a message to ring Rachel Pakenham. They met, fell in love and were married shortly afterwards, in the presence of Malcolm's friend Cardinal Heenan.

Twilight of Empire was shown in November 1964 when Malcolm was in New York. At the BBC the reaction was one of great enthusiasm. Billington wrote to him: 'My phone was busy for about two hours after the programme with producers ringing up – including one or two I have never spoken to before. Then the meeting of Heads of Departments gave it a smash hit review and the meeting's congratulations were passed on to me.'

Originally, Alisdair Milne's idea had been to film six programmes covering Malcolm's life in the same way. But shortly afterwards Milne left the BBC and in the event Billington made only one other film with Malcolm called *A Socialist Childhood*. It was filmed in Croydon and Cambridge and Manchester. In 1969 Malcolm made *Winter in Moscow* (about his experiences in

1932) with Patricia Meehan, though it was not possible to film in Russia, Malcolm being *persona non grata* there.

Apart from *Twilight of Empire* the most successful of Malcolm's Sixties films was an account of an American lecture tour, made with another talented director, Jack Gold, called *Ladies and Gentlemen, It Is My Pleasure*. Like many writers Malcolm had done a number of lecture tours in the States and he suggested to the BBC that it would be entertaining to film him flying to Gettysburg by way of Nashville, Tennessee and the Great Lakes to Denver and the Californian coast delivering the same lecture night after night always with the same opening joke: 'I always think when I hear the Chairman introduce me I simply cannot wait to hear what I'm going to say.' Unlike *Twilight of Empire*, which had a rather lukewarm response from the critics when it was originally shown, Jack Gold's film was acclaimed: 'I cannot remember a programme which has shown so vividly a view of American life,' the critic in the *Guardian* wrote. The *Spectator* called it 'stunning television' and the *Daily Mail* 'the best documentary we have had about real America for years'.

As the Sixties progressed, Malcolm, having enjoyed himself to the full by joining the TV satirists, began to register increasing disquiet with what had become known as the 'permissive society'. These were the years of student revolt, the advent of 'porn' (in the wake of the *Lady Chatterley* verdict in 1960) and the widespread experimenting with drugs. Malcolm found himself almost accidentally involved with these issues when he was asked by Allan Frazer, an Edinburgh lawyer, to stand as rector for Edinburgh University in May 1966. The rector's office, which lasted for three years, involved him in certain ceremonial duties but, more importantly, he was required to act as intermediary between the Students' Representative Council and the university authorities. Obviously, as a busy man living in Sussex there were practical difficulties and it was left to the 'Rector's Assessor' Allan Frazer to do all the donkey-work and represent him at the various committees. All went smoothly until the student magazine printed an article about the joys of LSD. The authorities over-reacted, the university's Vice Chancellor Sir Michael

Swann informed Allan Frazer that a copy had been sent to the Home Office at the instigation of the Chief Constable of Edinburgh and at an emergency meeting of the SRC the editor of *Student* was suspended. Student unions are a notorious breeding-ground for would-be politicians and it was not long before this minor incident had developed into a major row. The students' leader Stephen Morrison (later a senior executive at Granada Television) called a meeting of the full SRC, about a hundred students, to overturn the Executive's decision to dismiss the editor, who was reinstated. The SRC then passed a resolution calling on the university to supply free contraceptive pills on demand to female students, and the next issue of *Student*, edited by Anna Coote, challenged Malcolm to support their demand. The ultimate aim behind these provocative gestures was to do away with the celebrity rector altogether and replace him with genuine 'student power'. In the short term, the ploy was 100% successful. Malcolm announced both his and Frazer's resignation in the course of his annual rectorial address and denounced the students for their sloth and self-indulgence.

> The students here in this university, as in other universities, are the ultimate beneficiaries under our welfare system. They are supposed to be the spearhead of progress, flattered and paid for by their admiring seniors, an elite who will happily and audaciously carry the torch of progress into the glorious future opening before them. Now, speaking for myself, there is practically nothing that they could do in a mood of rebelliousness or refusal to accept the ways and values of our run-down, spiritually impoverished way of life, for which I shouldn't feel some degree of sympathy, or at any rate understanding. Yet, how infinitely sad; how, in a macabre sort of way, funny that the form their insubordination takes should be a demand for pot and pills; for the most tenth-rate sort of escapism and self-indulgence ever known.

Malcolm's resignation was again given massive publicity, but it also gave rise to a certain amount of disquiet among his friends and Edinburgh supporters. His opponents were not, after all, the mass of students, but a small and unrepresentative band of Marxists whose political posturings would have been punctured more effectively by ridicule than by heavy-handed denunciations. More significantly, Malcolm, whose religious explorations in the early Sixties had been carried out in the company of Catholics like Cardinal Heenan and the Cistercian monks of Nunraw, now seemed to have joined the puritans and evangelical protestants whose air of moral certainty did not come naturally to someone of his scrupulousness.

As for his sermons on sex, the matter was perhaps best summed up by an anonymous poem in *Private Eye* (coinciding with his appearance in Jonathan Miller's TV film of *Alice in Wonderland* in 1966).

> You are old, Father Malcolm, the young man said
> And your hair has become very white
> And yet you incessantly talk about bed
> Do you think at your age it is right?
> In my youth said the sage, as he shook his grey locks
> I behaved just like any young pup
> But now I am old I appear on the box
> And tell others to give it all up.

He was on surer ground when shortly afterwards he became involved in another very public controversy. In December 1967 a brilliant South African surgeon, Dr Christiaan Barnard, performed the first heart-transplant operation at Groote Schuur Hospital, Cape Town. The breakthrough led to an immediate world-wide controversy about medical ethics. In a letter to *The Times* (5 January 1968) Malcolm wrote:

> Sir,
> There must, I feel sure, be some others who look with sick foreboding rather than ecstatic satisfaction at what is going on in Cape Town. I should like it to be put on public record that one citizen at any rate sees the liberties taken with one just expired, or about to expire, body in order to patch up another, not a step forward to further realization of human

potentialities, but a step backwards towards the final degradation of our Christian way of life. Nor is it, in my opinion, by chance that these 'experiments' should be conducted in Cape Town rather than elsewhere. Apartheid conditions people to regard large numbers of their fellows as domestic animals rather than as men with immortal souls.

Shortly afterwards Dr Barnard arrived in Britain to publicize his operation and appeared on a special BBC TV programme *Tomorrow's World* called 'Dr Barnard Faces His Critics'. For this, the BBC assembled some 200 or so doctors in the studio to debate the issue of heart transplants. In the event there was hardly any criticism of Barnard from his fellow medics – though numerous, they preferred not to voice their misgivings on TV – and it was left to Malcolm, almost alone, to question the morality of the new techniques. When he again raised the link with the apartheid system, the audience of doctors registered their clear disapproval and one eminent surgeon, Professor Calne, said he would like to disassociate all of the doctors present from what Malcolm had said.

He himself was very shaken by the experience, though comforted later to receive a letter from a doctor who said he had left Groote Schuur Hospital because he found the attitude to surgery 'veterinary' rather than medical.

In March 1968 Malcolm received a call at Robertsbridge from the BBC's Head of Religious Broadcasting Oliver Hunkin. Would he be prepared to come up to London and interview an Albanian nun involved in missionary work in Calcutta? Her name was Mother Teresa. Malcolm had never heard of her, but being warmly disposed to Hunkin he agreed to take the train to London, on the way studying the notes that Hunkin had provided. He read that Mother Teresa had been born in Skopje, Yugoslavia in 1910. She had joined the Loreto order of nuns at the age of eighteen and taught for many years at a school in Calcutta before starting her Missionaries of Charity in 1950. By now she had established centres in various countries all over the world. To the general public, however, her name was almost completely unknown and she had never been interviewed before. Malcolm was to report to a religious house in Cavendish Square where the interview had been arranged.

In retrospect, Malcolm could not see that the interview had been any different from the general run. 'I put the expected questions: When did she first feel this special vocation? Any doubts or regrets, etc?' Mother Teresa, a tiny, wizened figure, dressed in the blue and white of her Order, was nervous and halting in speech. When it was over he had no awareness that the occasion was in any way special. The interview was transmitted on the BBC's religious programme *Meeting Point* in May 1968. The critics, apart from the *Observer*'s Maurice Richardson who recognized in Mother Teresa 'an extraordinarily beautiful human being', did not take much notice. However, the critic of the *Irish Independent* noted: 'In *Meeting Point* [Malcolm Muggeridge] talked to Mother Teresa about the work for the sick of Calcutta with a degree of sympathy that almost reached personal involvement. And in a sense it was because you somehow felt that this was another minor incident drawing Muggeridge along his circuitous journey to Catholicism.'

Apart from this one very percipient reaction, the programme was mainly remarkable for the response of the viewers. Within ten days of the transmission over £9,000 had been sent, despite the fact that no appeal for money was made on the air. Malcolm himself received countless cheques and letters from viewers, nearly all of them saying the same thing, that Mother Teresa had spoken to them in a way that no one else had ever done.

The BBC was delighted. The programme was repeated shortly afterwards with an even greater response. The message seemed to be that, with the producers of religious programmes trying to interest viewers with all manner of gimmicks, there was no substitute for simple faith, however hesitant or however poorly filmed.

Malcolm was by now involved with Oliver Hunkin in a new project, a Sunday evening discussion programme called *The Question Why*. The idea was to select a topical issue and debate it live in the studio with a group of interested parties. The first programme in July 1968 was a chaotic affair with everyone talking at once, but it soon settled down and became, in the end, enormously popular. But Malcolm hankered after a full-length feature on Mother Teresa's work in Calcutta and eventually persuaded the BBC to do it. She herself, however, was initially reluctant and resisted the idea. In the end she agreed as a result of a letter from Malcolm's friend Cardinal Heenan, to whom she wrote: 'If this TV programme is going to help people to love God better, then we will have it, but with one condition – that the Brothers and Sisters be included as they do the work.' To Malcolm she wrote: 'Let us now do something beautiful for God.'

Malcolm and his crew flew out to Calcutta in March 1969. His producer was Peter Chafer and his cameraman Ken Macmillan, who had recently received plaudits for his brilliant photography in Kenneth Clark's *Civilization* series. They had only a few days in which to make the film so went immediately to 54A Lower Circular Road, a largish Calcutta house, home of the Missionaries of Charity. Mother Teresa invited Malcolm into the chapel to say a prayer and the filming began. For the next five days they followed Mother Teresa around the city filming with lepers, abandoned babies and outcast boys. In the process, Malcolm found he went through three phases: the first one of horror mixed with pity, the second 'compassion pure and simple', the third an awareness of common humanity with the lepers and the dying which he found hard to explain. Each day he attended early morning Mass with the sisters, one of them being specially posted to let him in and take him to his place beside Mother Teresa. 'I felt perfectly content to be worshipping with them,' he wrote, 'even though I could not and had no wish to partake of the sacraments.' (He had written a few years earlier in the *St Martin's Review* (1 January 1957): 'I have to confess that though the sacramental concept seems to be both comprehensive and admirable, the actual practice of taking the sacraments is meaningless and even distasteful.')

In another important way the Calcutta visit forced Malcolm to modify his views of the supernatural. He had previously written rather condescendingly about the importance Graham Greene attached to the 'magic' of religion – by which he meant miracles and strange signs like the stigmata that appeared on the hands of the Italian Priest Padre Pio – and when in 1966 Leonard Cheshire wrote to him asking if he would appear at a meeting he was organizing to discuss the mysterious Shroud of Turin, Malcolm politely declined, voicing his distaste for anything like the veneration of relics. Yet he was soon to be proclaiming his conviction of the hand of God in something that seemed equally inexplicable.

Part of the work of the Sisters in Calcutta is to pick up the people dying on the streets and bring them into a former Hindu temple, the House of Dying, so that they may die in some degree of peace looked after by the nuns. Malcolm was anxious to film here but Ken Macmillan argued that the interior was very poorly lit and that it would be pointless to try and film. Nevertheless he agreed to have a go, though as a precaution he also shot some footage outside where the inmates were sitting in the sun. When the film was eventually processed in London the interior scenes were bathed in a 'beautiful soft light', whereas the outside shots were dim and confused.

Malcolm was absolutely convinced that this was a miracle and that the light was supernatural. 'Mother Teresa's House of the Dying', he wrote, 'is overflowing with love, as one senses immediately on entering it. This love is luminous like the haloes artists have seen and made visible round the heads of their saints.' The incident had a great effect on him and for a time he spoke about it endlessly. However, as with all stories of the supernatural, most people were sceptical, including some Catholic priests to whom Malcolm told the story. Ken Macmillan was also sceptical, although he had been enormously impressed by Mother Teresa and never forgot the way, as they were taking their leave of her, she asked him a special favour: 'Mr Macmillan, will you say a prayer for me if I say a prayer for you?' He was reluctant to admit that anything out of the way had happened, attributing their success to a wonderful new film which had been recently marketed by Kodak. (However, when he used the same film in similar conditions some time afterwards in a Cairo nightclub the results were unusable.) Peter Chafer, the producer and, like Macmillan, a non-believer, wrote subsequently to the *Radio*

Times (6 May 1971) in answer to a reader's query: 'I am no authority on miracles . . . However, on purely technical grounds we were certain that the chance of producing worthwhile film in those circumstances was extremely slim. So much so, that we shot extra footage to make up for what we believed would be unusable interior material. As events showed, we were wrong.'

The film, called *Something Beautiful for God* was shown to much acclaim and later, in 1971, Malcolm published a book under the same title. Taken together, they had a far, far greater impact than anything else he did in the course of his career. The paperback edition of *Something Beautiful for God* which followed shortly was still in print in 1994 having sold over 300,000 copies, been reprinted twenty times and translated into thirteen languages. Malcolm gave away his royalty on the book to Mother Teresa, a sum amounting at the time of his death to about £60,000. Although the book consisted mainly of a transcript of an interview between Malcolm and Mother Teresa interspersed with many black-and-white photographs, it also included in a foreword and afterword by Malcolm a very personal statement by him about his religious position and in particular why he could not become a Catholic, as Mother Teresa kept urging him:

'I believe the film has brought people closer to God,' she wrote to him, 'and so your and my hope has been fulfilled. I think now more than ever that you should use the beautiful gift God has given you for His greater glory. All that you have and all that you are and all that you can be and do – let it all be for Him and Him alone. Today what is happening on the surface of the Church will pass. For Christ, the Church is the same, today, yesterday and tomorrow. The Apostles went through the same feeling of fear and distrust, failure and disloyalty, and yet Christ did not scold them. Just: "Little children, little faith – why did you fear?" I wish we could love as he did – now!'

Malcolm's religious position by this time was that of a Christian who had no commitment to any particular Church. If he had any special leaning it was towards Catholicism, but he had little sympathy for any of the trappings (confession, the rosary, the Intercession of Saints) and he was also aware of the modernizing forces which had undermined Anglicanism at work within the Catholic Church itself. In his correspondence with Mother Teresa and in what he called his unspoken dialogue conducted with her in the book Malcolm continued to harp on the imperfections of the Church: the, in his view, disastrous reforming process instigated by Pope John Paul at Vatican 2, the dangers of the ecumenical movement. (He had been greatly affected by the way that during the row at Edinburgh University the Catholic chaplain had sided with the students.) At the same time, he clung to the example of one of his heroines, the French intellectual Simone Weil, who had felt that she could best serve her church by remaining outside it.

Nevertheless, his miracle aside, the experience of filming in Calcutta had radically altered Malcolm's perception of Christianity. His dialogue hitherto had been conducted with ecclesiastics like Cardinal Heenan. Mother Teresa was completely different. She appealed to him because she was simple and unsophisticated and reduced the Christian Gospel to its bare essentials of love in action. Under her influence, his writing in *Something Beautiful for God* lost the acerbity and slight sanctimoniousness which marred so much of his religious writing (though even here he could not resist taking the odd swipe at some of his *bêtes noires* like the radical theologian John Robinson, Bishop of Woolwich and author of the best-selling *Honest to God*). The enormous success of the book and film derived not only from the example of Mother Teresa, who emerged from obscurity as a world-famous symbol of Christian love surviving in the midst of twentieth-century materialism; Malcolm himself, for once humble and enquiring, personified the quest of the modern man for faith and hope. Both of them seemed to have been chosen to fulfil a symbolic role – even though, in Malcolm's case, he was barely aware of the fact.

Later that year Malcolm set out for foreign parts again with Peter Chafer and Ken Macmillan, this time to follow in the steps of St Paul with Alec Vidler. The BBC had commissioned a series of six programmes about Paul's missionary journeys using Alec as the expert theologian and Malcolm as his disciple. It was a risky undertaking as Alec had never done any television work. In the event, however, he was his usual imperturbable self –

Jeeves to Malcolm's Wooster. Malcolm remembered in a published letter to Alec:

> I need not have worried. Where I feared your patience might be strained it was mine which gave out. Wearing a white floppy hat of the kind that used to be favoured by prep school boys, carrying your essential books in a haversack, once, I suppose, used to contain a gas mask, equipped with a small cushion to mitigate the asperities of sitting on rock faces and other uncomfortable perches, you discoursed at and with me in total disregard of the weird antics of our crew and the often gigantic gestures of our director.

In fact, Peter Chafer's only really frantic moment came prior to the filming when he was exploring Turkey by car with Alec and Malcolm, seeking out suitable sites for the filming. Peter noticed that they were running rather short of petrol but Alec, who was navigating from the back of the car, insisted that they were very near a town. When he turned round to see exactly where they were, he was alarmed to find that Alec was using an old school atlas to direct them.

Remembering his experience in the House of the Dying, Peter Chafer was not surprised and in fact rather annoyed when a slightly similar thing occurred during the making of the St Paul film. To deal with Paul's conversion on the road to Damascus, Chafer had arranged to film Malcolm and Alec walking along a lonely road in Turkey where there would be no visual distractions. His idea was to show the two figures in the distance seen through a long lens while their voices could be heard discussing St Paul. This worked very well, but when the film was processed on their return to London and Chafer was watching it in the cutting room, he noticed that at one point the two figures in the shimmering heat were joined by a third, who seemed to walk along with them before disappearing in the heat. Thinking that it would only cause confusion in the minds of viewers if it was shown, Chafer cut the sequence from the finished version of the film and it was never seen.

*   *   *

215

Malcolm's religious journey in old age took place on two very distinct levels. His more private exploration tended to be with Catholics. He had formed a friendship with Cardinal Heenan, the Irish-born Archbishop of Westminster with whom he had made a film for the BBC in 1966, directed by Kevin Billington. The following year he visited the Cistercian monastery at Nunraw in Scotland and filmed a number of interviews with the monks. The simple faith of such men was enormously appealing to him – even though at that time he could not fully share it. Later, he came into close contact with two Catholic priests, Father Bidone of the Sons of the Divine Providence and Father Gonzalo Gonzales, a Spanish priest working for Opus Dei who paid him regular visits at Robertsbridge. Both men saw in Malcolm a potential recruit to the Church whose conversion they believed could be hastened by their prayers.

On the other, public level, was the evangelical Malcolm, the twentieth century's Savanorola – what Anthony Powell called the 'hot-gospelling, near Messianic Muggeridge' who had first emerged during the row at Edinburgh University. This Malcolm tended to ally himself with Moral Rearmers, born again Christians, taking a vocal part in campaigns against abortion, euthanasia and, in the company of Mrs Whitehouse, pornography.

Malcolm's heart was never really in the anti-pornography crusade. As recently as 1960 he had written in his column in the *Sunday Pictorial* under the headline 'What's wrong with striptease?': 'To me the glory and privilege of being alive at all is to be able to do what I like, say what I like and think what I like. If ladies, for a fee, take off their clothes I may wonder why it should attract nightly audiences. But is the act itself any more or less abhorrent than any of the other ways whereby the rest of us extract from this unkindly world the means to live in it? I doubt it.' Although he railed against the exploitation of sex by the media, he could never, as one of nature's anarchists, be an advocate of censorship. At the same time, out of loyalty to his friend Frank Longford, he agreed to take part in the latter's much-ridiculed investigation of pornography and later gave his support to Mary Whitehouse when she started her clean-up television campaign – directed mainly at the BBC's Director General

Hugh Carleton Greene. Malcolm was on weak ground here, partly because he had been such an enthusiastic supporter and participant in the satire shows to which Mrs Whitehouse objected so strongly.

He never really hit it off with Mary Whitehouse. As the natural supporter of lost causes, however, and someone who could never resist the urge to have a go at the BBC he did for a time lend his voice to her campaign and it was Malcolm who, according to Mrs Whitehouse, coined the title 'Festival of Light' for her mass demonstration in 1971. The Festival of Light was launched at a meeting in Central Hall, Westminster on 10 September 1971. Although Mrs Whitehouse was the figurehead, the original impetus came from an evangelical missionary, Mr Peter Hill, who had recently returned from years in India to find himself shocked by the growth of pornography and the 'moral slide' of Britain. The Festival's backers, in addition to Mary Whitehouse, included Cliff Richard, Lord Longford and Bishop Trevor Huddleston who spoke at the inaugural meeting alongside Malcolm. Two weeks later on 25 September a mass rally took place in Trafalgar Square with a crowd estimated at 60,000 (mostly young members of Baptist and Evangelical churches). There were speeches by Malcolm and David Kossoff (the broadcaster, famous for his Bible readings), a message of good luck from Prince Charles and predictable counter-demonstrations from little groups of gays and feminists. It was a good-humoured, typically British occasion – although it was not clear exactly what it had achieved beyond generating a great deal of publicity.

That Malcolm was not really happy in the ranks of the Festival of Lighters was borne out by his extraordinary over-reaction when the BBC radio programme *The World at One* produced by his great friends William Hardcastle and Andrew Boyle, a Roman Catholic, broadcast an item on the demonstration that gave what, in his view, was unjustified prominence to the counter-protesting gays. In an angry and quite untypical letter to Andrew Boyle, Malcolm wrote:

For a long time now I've been struggling to sustain the affection and respect for you against a growing feeling of revulsion

for the programmes you edit. I have regarded you as a Christian of integrity and Bill as a journalist of the highest capacity. On both counts you've crashed in the handling by the *World at One* and *The World This Weekend* of the Festival of Light which has been unfair, dishonest and corrupt. I'm at last forced to accept the fact that in a time of great moral crisis we're on different sides; so much so that I consider all personal relations between us now being at an end.

For Malcolm, who so often outraged others with his barbs, to complain about journalistic bias was more than hypocritical. But this most untypical response to a very trivial incident shows his undue sensitivity about being involved with a movement with which he was not really in sympathy. (Needless to say, his relations with Andrew Boyle were quickly restored and the two remained great friends until Boyle's death.)

CHAPTER XII

Memoirs

IN HIS LATE SIXTIES, Malcolm began work on his memoirs, *Chronicles of Wasted Time*, two volumes of which were published: Volume I *The Green Stick* (1972) followed by Volume II *The Infernal Grove* (1973). A projected third volume was started but never completed. The books were to be highly praised by almost all the critics and even his opponents were forced to acknowledge the quality of the writing, the wit and the variety of his experiences. Yet considered as autobiography, *Chronicles of Wasted Time* could not be judged a success. This was partly because Malcolm made little or no attempt to project himself back into the past and so the reader was given the impression that all his life he had been the sort of person they knew from watching him on television – an assured, worldly-wise satirist who saw through all the politicians, churchmen and journalists with whom he came into contact. Many critics of the book made lists of Malcolm's dismissive comments on his contemporaries – Gandhi 'crafty and calculating', Nehru 'a man of echoes and mimicry', Churchill 'flabby and puffy . . . vaguely obscene', C. P. Scott 'false and phoney', T. S. Eliot 'somehow blighted, dead, extinct' – without any real awareness of the fact that there had been a time when Malcolm had revered and even, in the case of Gandhi, idolized such figures.

As always with Malcolm, the book's strength derived from his directness and admirable habit of saying what he thought about things and people. The other side of the coin were the curious omissions – not to say inaccuracies – that resulted from this uncalculating approach. Malcolm always expressed a contempt for facts, records, information of any kind. So when writing his memoirs he would seem to have made little reference to his own papers, which were very substantial (including a long diary covering the years 1925–60), and relied almost entirely on his memory. This meant that the book could not be regarded as a record of fact. Malcolm had, for example, told a long rambling story about how, during Kitty's illness in Russia, he had gone round Moscow on the day of the Red Square Parade trying to buy a bedpan with the help of his friend A. T. Cholerton. Cholerton wrote to a friend after reading *The Green Stick*:

> It is startling how he has forgotten nearly everything about his seven months in Moscow although he calls it 'the most important years of my life.' He makes a monkey out of me too, e.g. bedpan at Red Square Parade; he goes around the state pawnshops (all closed that feast day), brings the pan along to my 'ramshackle' home, my 'shabby room irradiated by a set of Stations of the Cross, very beautiful in their strength and simplicity'. (In fact, a brand new, five-room, kitchen, bathroom with parquet floors to our own planning and the pictures, Georgian kintos [bohemes] carousing in the open as they love to do by a Georgian primitive genius, in my opinion superior to Douanier . . . my 'real spiritual home was in Paris in the early twenties.' Between wars I never spent more than a few months in Paris living mainly in the Pyrenees . . . You see, I cite my case only, as M. claims to know me intimately. You can imagine what his stuff about others is like.

More serious were the gaps and omissions that occurred. Obviously Malcolm was restrained from telling the truth about his various love affairs for fear of greatly upsetting Kitty. Though the romance with Amrita Sher-Gil was described in some detail, his wartime affair in Mozambique with Bibla (described as Anna in the book) was glossed over. Various old friends like Alan Taylor and Hesketh Pearson were hardly referred to at all, while Alec Vidler his oldest and closest friend had to make do with three cursory mentions. Alec, who had kept all Malcolm's letters, offered to show them to him when he started work on the book but to his disappointment Malcolm was not in the least interested. He had no particular wish to confront his youthful self, his passionate enthusiasms, his eagerness to conform to the public-school ethos of Cambridge, his romantic hero-worship of Alec Vidler. Malcolm had a view of things – including his own life – which he arrived at almost by instinct and it was difficult if not impossible to alter his perceptions by the application of logic or consultation with records or evidence. In many instances, like the quarrel with Tony Powell, he even had no memory of what had happened and certainly no wish to examine the evidence.

Though Malcolm wrote some ten thousand words of his pro-jected third volume, he never managed to complete it. He had, in Volume II, reached the end of the war and his account fizzled out with a description of life at the *Daily Telegraph*. There were several reasons for his failure to bring the story up to date. One was the purely practical one that he could not scatter his grape-shot so freely when so many of the people he was writing about were still alive. Even if he avoided libel he was bound to give offence. He certainly could not go into his affair with Pamela Berry which had so complicated his life between 1954 and 1964.

More crucially, by this time, Malcolm was finding it increas-ingly difficult to write. Even in Volume II there are signs of strain, evidence of padding and a tendency to produce mere waffle. The long years of working in television had finally taken their toll. This was not merely in practical terms, namely that it was much easier and more lucrative for him to appear briefly on television than to labour at a book. Television had turned Mal-colm into a personality. He was paid to be dogmatic and provoca-tive (he always remembered a television producer during one of his many discussion programmes holding up a card saying 'Be more controversial'). TV meant putting on an act, with the danger that, in the end, the act became the reality. As time progressed it was noticeable, particularly to disciples like Christopher Booker, how Malcolm's articles and television appearances were rendered automatic and stylized. The same Muggeridgean clichés appeared over and over again: 'some future Gibbon' would chronicle the absurdities of the day, 'Blake's fear-ful symmetry' was to be discerned at work almost everywhere, and Malcolm saw himself invariably as 'a pianist in a brothel'.

Perhaps, all this aside, it was not so surprising that Malcolm had written himself out. For the last fifteen years he had been producing reams of journalism: columns in the *Daily Herald* and *Sunday Pictorial*, book reviews in the *Evening Standard*, the *Observer* and *Esquire*, regular articles and diaries for the *New Statesman* – all this in addition to his television work. There had to come a time when he had said all that he had to say and could only repeat himself.

In March 1973, he celebrated his seventieth birthday, though if anything he looked younger and healthier than he had done twenty years previously when he had seemed prematurely old, gaunt and white-haired. Now he was benign and rosy-cheeked. The 'simple life' which he had longed for intermittently over the years was benefiting him as he always knew it would. More important to his state of well-being had been his rediscovery of Kitty. Malcolm turned back to her not from any feelings of duty or remorse but from a deeply felt love which he had never wholly lost, even in his years of philandering. At the same time, in his more reflective moments, he felt overwhelmed with gratitude for the devotion of this exceptional wife who had remained true to him when any other woman would have long ago deserted him. More and more he came to rely on her support.

Kevin Billington noted how when filming away from home he would speak to her at length on the phone every day. If he went abroad he wrote her long letters. In one of these when making his BBC film in Lourdes he wrote:

> You're always so much in my mind when I'm away from you and I realize how infinitely dear you are to me, and how happy I am with you – life's a fearful struggle and as one gets old one gets tired and sometimes, alas, fretful. Please be what you've always been – my beloved companion. I know how often I say and do tiresome things and wear myself out over nothing; but darling, it is true that I love you dearly and long to see you – as I do at this moment with a great longing.

Kitty's view of her husband was more that of a mother than a wife. She treated him like a little boy, her main concern being to keep him occupied and stop him getting up to mischief. The only time she openly took charge was when Malcolm was driving their car in a town when he would become panicky and confused and she would quietly and firmly tell him which way to go. A picture of the two of them was provided by Eva Taylor, Alan's third wife, when she attended a Foyles Literary Lunch at the Dorchester hotel in December 1982. 'At the end of the lunch I saw the Muggeridges trying to find the way out – they had great difficulty finding it and it struck me that this is how they have tried to find their true faith, just one way, then another, always close together.'

Visitors to Robertsbridge, of whom there was an almost continuous stream, noticed some changes. Malcolm had built a little self-contained annexe at right-angles to the house which he called 'The Ark'. He spent more and more time there in order to avoid the telephone which was constantly ringing. At the bottom of the garden there was now a chicken run and, after breakfast, Malcolm would put on his wellingtons and go down to pick up eggs. The kitchen shelves were lined with apples from the orchard, kilner jars containing the plums that Kitty had bottled. In addition to giving up drink and cigarettes Malcolm had now given up meat and become a vegetarian. He told everyone that it was a decision taken as the result of a visit to an abattoir, but he had suffered all his life from gastric troubles caused by eating meat. Kitty loyally followed him in all these abstinences, though she found it hard to give up smoking initially and would whisper to Malcolm's brother Jack when Malcolm had retired to his study after breakfast, 'Give us a fag, Jack.'

Malcolm never imposed his eating and drinking habits on visitors and meat was always provided even if it was only a few slices of ham. After lunch, Kitty would read aloud to him from one of the classics – Dostoevsky was a favourite – with Malcolm invariably falling asleep in his chair, though he always woke up if she stopped reading. Then there would be the long walk and after tea Malcolm would sit by the fire with a little table over his knee endlessly playing patience.

Having at one time subscribed to all the newspapers, he gradually whittled them down to one – his old paper, the *Telegraph*. By the mid-Seventies he had given up the Sunday papers altogether. Eventually he got rid of his television set, proudly telling everyone that he had had his 'aerials removed'. But he continued to listen to the radio news which blared out over the breakfast table and he was for some reason especially keen on the BBC arts programme *Kaleidoscope* which in those days was broadcast at 9.30 p.m. – though this again, like Dostoevsky, would almost always send him to sleep over his tisane.

What eventually led to the removal of the television set was a BBC fly-on-the-wall series called *The Family*. The camera followed the members of an unappealing working-class family in Tilehurst, Reading who were supposed to be carrying on life as normal despite the presence of a TV crew. Even before that Malcolm had started to inveigh against the medium that had made him famous: television was 'the repository of our fraudulence', the camera 'the most sinister of all the inventions of our time'. He repeated endlessly how he never left a TV studio after doing a programme without a feeling of despair. Critics, by now familiar with Malcolm's habit of biting the hand that fed him, were not slow to point out that an attack on television from a television personality could never be wholly convincing. Others, more friendly, made the obvious point that no one had shown better than Malcolm how television could be used for people's good. After all, it was mainly as a result of his programme *Something Beautiful for God* that Mother Teresa's name was known throughout the world.

Malcolm was too clever a man not to see the anomalies of his position. It was, in a way, a repeat performance of his attitude towards sex when having, it seemed, taken his fill of the pleasures of the flesh, he turned around and denounced it all as a fantasy and a fraud.

Quite apart from the 'boredom factor', Malcolm had begun to feel increasingly jaundiced about the BBC. It was not merely a case of bitterness over the mocking coverage of the Festival of Light. In 1969 he had written to the producer of *Any Questions?* Michael Bowen, saying that he felt the programme had become too 'trendy' and asking to be excused in future. (In the event he was persuaded to soldier on.) Later he decided to give up his

Sunday evening television programme *The Question Why* despite the fact that it was still attracting very large audiences.

Although he still had the support of Paul Fox, the Controller of BBC1, Malcolm, like anyone who appears on television too often, was attracting criticism from within. Many of his friends had left the BBC and even in the Religious Department his uncompromising views were regarded in some quarters as unhelpful. Dr Colin Morris, who later became Head of Religious Broadcasting in 1978, wrote in the *Observer* (5 March 1972):

> BBC religious television also has Malcolm Muggeridge. To carry personal responsibility for keeping God alive in the modern world would be a grievous burden for anyone, even Muggeridge whose search for the Kingdom has been fascinating to observe, but who, since he found it, has been sadly in danger of becoming Christianity's most bizarre exhibitionist. Face contorted, hands clawing the air to pantomime his inner anguish, world-weary and longing for an apocalyptic end to a Naughty Age, Malcolm reviles the medium which feeds him and begs reassurance that he is still loved from the assorted personalities who gather about him like Plato's disciples. 'Why?' his strangulated cry goes up – tempting a heavenly retort 'Why indeed?'

The uncompromising evangelical tone of Malcolm's religious pronouncements did not endear him to British audiences, who tend, in any case, to be easily embarrassed by any form of religious enthusiasm. Although he was in constant demand as a speaker and preacher in various evangelical churches, Malcolm now found that his message was more appreciated on the other side of the Atlantic – in the USA and Canada – where, especially on television, evangelism is regarded as part of the everyday fare. Rejected by the BBC during the Seventies, Malcolm was taken up by assorted Americans and Canadians eager to spread the word. In July 1974 he addressed Billy Graham's Congress on World Evangelization in Lausanne. The same year he began a series of films for the Canadian Broadcasting Company on St Augustine, Pascal, Blake, Kierkegaard, Tolstoy and

Bonhoeffer, the scripts of which were later published under the title *The Third Testament*. He also made for CBC a film about Jean Vanier, founder of a community for the handicapped called 'L'Arche' (the ark) in the Forest of Compiegne in France. Vanier, a Catholic, appeared in the film along with his mother, the widow of a former Governor General of Canada who after her husband's death had joined him in what had once seemed to her an unappealing life. This moving film was never shown on British television, much to Malcolm's disappointment.

Malcolm had by now found a new fan in the American commentator William F. Buckley Jnr. A rich Catholic and right-winger, Buckley edited the *National Review* and also compered a talk show on American TV called *Firing Line* on which Malcolm appeared no less than seven times doing long interviews. Buckley was also instrumental in arranging Malcolm's meeting with the Pope in 1980 when the two flew out to Rome to film a discussion programme in the Sistine Chapel in the unlikely company of Grace Kelly, Charlton Heston and David Niven. However, when the Pope was finally introduced to Malcolm, he plainly had little idea who he (or for that matter, David Niven) was. 'Ah – you are radio,' was his greeting to Malcolm, while he appeared to think that Niven had been a great friend of his predecessor, Pope Paul VI. Malcolm, however, was delighted with the occasion and a photograph of himself shaking hands with the Pope was framed and put on show in the sitting room at Park Cottage.

Invitations from Canada were especially welcome as they gave Malcolm an opportunity to see his son John, now married with four children and lecturing in Ontario. In 1977 he accepted an invitation from Western University, Ontario to become a guest lecturer on journalism. At the same time Ian Hunter, a law professor at the University who had helped to fix up the appointment, exchanged houses with Malcolm so that he could write his biography. (This book was eventually published in 1980.) Though Kitty was initially homesick they eventually settled into a Canadian routine and could even be seen doggedly trudging through the streets of town with their walking sticks.

Another of Malcolm's new admirers was the young Canadian

tycoon Conrad Black (who later acquired the *Daily Telegraph* from the Berry family). Black, like Bill Buckley and others – all Christian conservatives – regarded Malcolm as a guru in much the same way as young satirists had done in the Sixties. Unlike the British public, these Canadians and Americans had the advantage of not having to reconcile the 'born again' Malcolm with their knowledge of him in his previous incarnations.

Not everyone, however, subjected him to uncritical veneration. It was interesting that while Pat Ferns, one of the two CBC producers who worked with him on his *Third Testament* programmes in the early Seventies, revered Malcolm and even named his son after him, his colleague Richard Nielsen tempered his admiration with a degree of acute observation. In an obituary published in the short-lived Canadian magazine *The Idler* (July–August 1991), he wrote:

On my first visit to Robertsbridge, he spent lunch attacking Ingmar Bergman, the great Swedish film director. Bergman's preoccupation with sex (sexx as Malcolm pronounced it) and psychology were enough to condemn him in his eyes, but he carried his criticisms further, to a denunciation of all sorts of tendencies in Bergman's films I must have missed.

After lunch, we put on our wellies and went for the mandatory Muggeridge walk; Pat Ferns, my partner, walked ahead with Malcolm, while Kitty and I brought up the rear. I confessed to her that the attack on Bergman had surprised me, since Bergman was undoubtedly the only significant film-maker who has taken religion seriously and explored great religious themes.

'Oh,' said Kitty cheerfully, 'I doubt that Malcolm has actually seen a Bergman film. In fact, I'm sure he hasn't.'

Later when they came to film the programme on Kierkegaard, Malcolm prevailed on Nielsen to prepare a 120-page précis on the life and work of the Danish philosopher. Nielsen, himself the son of Danish parents, was happy to oblige. But when he submitted his 120-page draft, Malcolm asked if he would be very kind and whittle it down to 50 pages. Three months later when they were about to begin filming Nielsen was surprised to find Malcolm in a desperate state leafing through the 50 pages. 'This is gibberish, absolute gibberish . . . Kierkegaard could not have said these things.' Nielsen, who now realized that this was the first time Malcolm had looked at the 50 pages – what's more that he had never looked at the original 120-page draft – tried to explain what he thought it meant and Malcolm in the meantime decided that the fault must lie with the translator, a Professor Hong of Minnesota, leaving Nielsen a little puzzled as to how Malcolm had come to include Kierkegaard as one of the foremost influences in his conversion to Christianity in his book *Jesus Redis-covered.*

Such reservations were a healthy antidote to some of the more extravagant claims made for Malcolm as an important Christian thinker by assorted American and Canadian admirers. Unlike, for example, C. S. Lewis (to whom he was sometimes com-pared), Malcolm was not a theologian and certainly not an intel-lectual. He was a journalist and television personality who had very publicly and courageously embraced the Christian faith. Given the paucity of such apologists, he was naturally welcomed with open arms by assorted religious crusaders, some of them linked to right-wing political movements, who valued the sup-port of someone who was not only a Christian but a lifelong opponent of communism. William F. Buckley, for example, described Malcolm as 'perhaps the most eloquent English-speaking lay apostle of Christianity'. But Malcolm's thoughts on Christianity were too idiosyncratic and too bound up with his personal obsessions to qualify him as a religious guru with a universal message. Unfortunately, by this stage in his life, Mal-colm was too taken up by his public persona to query the status which his new admirers had conferred on him, whilst the hun-dreds of letters he received from television viewers merely but-tressed his complacency. He had become in old age the sort of person that in his youth he would have mercilessly mocked.

In Britain there was renewed interest in Malcolm in 1980 when Professor Ian Hunter's biography was published. It was followed closely by a selection of his diaries edited by John Bright Holmes under the title *Like It Was* (1981). Malcolm had kept a diary intermittently since he went to India in 1925 until about 1960 and the complete manuscript ran to hundreds of thousands of words. Of this, only a small selection could be printed in one volume, which was unfortunate in view of the fact that it contained some of his best writing as well as giving an utterly different picture of Malcolm than the one the public was familiar with from television and his memoirs. Although Graham Greene had a personal grudge against Malcolm, there was a certain truth in some of the rude remarks he had scribbled in his two volumes of the *Chronicles of Wasted Time*: 'Waffle . . . more waffle . . . such woolliness he would mock in another writer . . . the tone of this book in spite of MM's comedy of mysticism and Christianity is one of ineffable superiority – the style – it would be an insult to such writers as Chesterton to call it journalistic – a melange of knowingness, melodrama and self-praise.'*

The diary had none of these faults, for, although at times it had the feel of a literary exercise, it revealed at last the true Malcolm, a man who for most of his life had been a restless and tormented figure, over-sexed, a prey to depression and insomnia – all made worse by his awareness of forces pulling him in another direction.

In a long review in the *Times Literary Supplement*, Christopher Booker noted first of all the extraordinary way that Malcolm in the course of his life had managed to bump into almost all the celebrated figures of the century – from a visit to the Bolshoi in 1932 when he was accompanied 'by a man called Macmillan . . . seemed pretty hopeless about British politics', to a chance encounter in a Hamburg rock-and-roll bar in 1961 when 'the band was English and recognized me. Long-haired; weird feminine faces; bashing their instruments and emitting nerveless sounds into microphones.'

It was, of course, the Beatles – at the time quite unknown. Malcolm, who spoke to them, found them 'rather touching in a way' – a typical comment in the diary, where, as Booker noted,

---

* 'And yet,' Graham Greene conceded, 'after reading this very honest, badly written volume, I still feel an affection for the clown Malcolm – his absurdity produces a sort of affection as one might have for an old dog.'

his impressions of people were more tentative and charitable than in the memoirs and even Monty was said to 'have a certain sweetness'. It was only regrettable that the final text of the diaries should be so short in comparison with the original which contained quite enough first-class material to make two, or even three volumes. It was also regrettable that Malcolm was allowed to doctor the manuscript prior to publication. Rude remarks about friends like Lord Longford were blue-pencilled, all references to Dorothy Kingsmill were omitted, as were the details of his various love affairs – including the very moving story of his Mozambique romance. Less excusable, perhaps, was his own blue-pencilling of any traces of anti-Semitism, of which there were many. Typical was the entry for 11 February 1948 describing a lunch with Tony Powell, Alan Pryce-Jones and Phillip Jordan, then Attlee's adviser on pubic relations. 'We discussed [Professor] Namier, ridiculous fat Jew I used to know in Manchester, who has now become a member of the Church of England.'

For a man of Malcolm's generation, such remarks were perhaps more excusable than they would be today. But it was not only Beatrice Webb who detected an anti-Semitic note to Malcolm's writings, particularly in his novel *Winter in Moscow* which, in her case, she seized upon as a sign of insanity. When in 1983 a publisher proposed to reissue the novel he invited the Russian historian Leonard Schapiro to write an introduction to the new edition. Professor Schapiro reluctantly declined, explaining his reasons in a letter to Malcolm:

> When Mr Zubal recently asked me to write an introduction to *Winter in Moscow*, I readily agreed. My recollection of the book, fifty years back, was that it was a rare example at that date of the work of an honest correspondent in Russia who was not bamboozled by Soviet lies, and a fruitless exposure of the dupes and fellow travellers of the day.
>
> Having obtained a copy with difficulty, my opinion of half a century ago is fully confirmed. Yet, to my regret, I find I cannot write an introduction to it. I had no recollection, when I agreed to do so, of the numerous references in the book to

unsavoury and unprepossessing Jewish characters. I assure you that I am not suggesting that this was prompted by anti-Semitism; no one who knows your work could suspect you of this. But the overall impression is inevitably, if unwittingly, created by the book that Communism was imposed on Russia by Jews thirsting for vengeance for the wrongs they had suffered under the old regime . . . There is one remark on page 234 when a particularly vile pronouncement of a Jewess has the effect that 'Wraithby understood pogroms' which, forgive me, is in particularly bad taste . . . You will, I feel sure, understand why I, as a Jew, find it impossible to write the kind of introduction which your brilliant book deserves.

Perhaps for the reasons given by Professor Schapiro, *Winter in Moscow* was never republished in the UK. However, *In a Valley of this Restless Mind* was reissued in 1978.

In February 1981, the BBC began a series of eight programmes in which Malcolm looked back over his various television appearances in the company of the interviewer and producer Jonathan Stedall (who was later to perform the same service for John Betjeman). It was some years since the public had seen anything of Malcolm on British television and the occasion was a reminder of just how good a broadcaster he had been. The *Telegraph* called the series 'vastly entertaining'; in the *Daily Express* Herbert Kretzmer wrote, 'British TV would be incomparably poorer without this splendid old man', and Sean Day Lewis called it a 'mellow, lucid, funny programme'. Even Malcolm's most vituperative critic, Clive James, was forced to concede that *Muggeridge Ancient and Modern* was the television equivalent of an unputdownable book. Particular praise was lavished on Kevin Billington's *Twilight of Empire*, Jack Gold's lecture tour film and Michael Tuchner's *Lourdes*.

A few months after the showing of *Muggeridge Ancient and Modern*, Malcolm was once again filming with Jonathan Stedall. Svetlana Stalin had defected to the USA in 1967 at the age of forty-one. While still in Russia she had become a Christian convert and first made contact with Malcolm in 1970 after reading his book *Jesus Rediscovered*. She was so impressed that she bought five copies and sent them to her friends. In 1980 they resumed their correspondence and Malcolm suggested that she might come to England and do a television interview with him. Initially she was very much against the idea but, in the end, so great was her desire to meet Malcolm that she agreed. By now, she was divorced from her French architect husband and living on her own in Princeton, USA. Jonathan Stedall went over to see her and make the necessary arrangements for the film.

Nothing in the course of Malcolm's life could have been more bizarre (to use his own favourite word) than the appearance at Park Cottage, Robertsbridge of the daughter of Stalin, the figure who had to so great an extent dominated his life since he went to Moscow in 1932. To make it more incongruous, Svetlana was anxious to discuss Christianity rather than politics and more than happy to be filmed driving off on a shopping trip to the village with Kitty or walking in the garden picking flowers. Even so, there were one or two awkward moments. Thinking that it would ease things to have a priest on hand, Malcolm had invited Alec Vidler to take part in the filming. But although he looked the part with his long white beard, Svetlana was profoundly irritated by his apparent frivolity and his overpowering reluctance to discuss religion. She also became incensed when Kitty, who had agreed to be filmed picking flowers together and was finding it hard to make conversation, said: 'Do you have pretty flowers in Siberia?' 'Do not speak to me of Siberia!' Svetlana snapped angrily.

In the end the programme (which was shown on BBC2 on 6 March 1982) was rather disappointing as Svetlana was so reluctant to talk about her father. The nature of her extraordinary childhood had to be inferred from stray remarks like her reference to 'two aunts coming back from six years of solitary confinement for nothing'. She did, however, tell the strange story of Stalin's death in 1953. He had been discovered by his maid unconscious from a stroke lying on the floor of his villa outside Moscow. But no one would take the responsibility of calling for a doctor. Instead, the maid called the Government. 'In bunches they used to come: Beria, Malenkov, Bulganin. The frightened

maid and the frightened guard led them, and in the procession
went. Beria looked at him and said, "He is sleeping, why do
you bother us?" And they walked away and left him.' It was,
Malcolm said, the perfect commentary on the nature of power,
that a man had become so powerful that no one dared to help
him unless ordered to do so.

Svetlana was delighted with the film. 'For me our conversations were most inspiring,' she wrote to Malcolm and Kitty.
'I enjoy every minute of that exchange of thoughts.'

Later, she wrote at length saying that she was thinking of
emigrating to England with her daughter Olga and asking advice
about schools. Malcolm advised her against this, whereupon
Svetlana, thinking that he was trying to put her off coming, let
fly in a manner rather reminiscent of her father:

'Dear' Malcolm,
    I curse the day when I wrote to you 3 years ago and *every*
    day I've *ever* had written to you before [sic]. You are one
    of those obsessed demoniac natures who ought to be avoided
    at all costs; they bring misfortune into the lives of others; they
    ruin the lives of others. The *real good* people *are* humble and
    silent (like your Kitty is). But beware, God sees all vanity and
    pride and you cannot fool him.
                    Svetlana

This unprovoked attack ended what had been a touching if
rather unlikely friendship. Later Svetlana turned against the producer Jonathan Stedall in a similarly vicious fashion.

Now aged seventy-nine, Malcolm had one further surprise up
his sleeve. On 27 November 1982, above an article by him, *The
Times* announced: 'This morning Malcolm and Kitty Muggeridge will be received into the Roman Catholic Church.' Apart
from a few friends like the Longfords and Alec Vidler, no one had
any inkling that such a move was imminent. Asked as recently as
April 1981 by John Mortimer in a *Sunday Times* interview
whether he would have liked to have been a Catholic, he gave
no indication at all that he was moving in that direction and
turned the discussion instead to Graham Greene. But although

the announcement in *The Times* came as a surprise, the conversion itself, to anyone who had followed Malcolm's career over the years, came as a logical conclusion.

Yet there had been many obstacles for him to overcome. He was particularly attracted to the Church and in particular to Pope John Paul for his firm stand on the issue of abortion and contraception. (Like his friend Orwell, Malcolm had a lifelong distaste for contraception which had nothing to do with religion.) Yet the outward and visible signs of Catholicism which meant so much to other converts – the Sacraments, the Rosary, the Blessed Virgin – had little or no meaning for him. Indeed, all the evidence suggests that for most of his life he found them acutely distasteful and even repugnant.

Two people influenced him profoundly in his slow progress towards Rome. The most important of the two was Mother Teresa. Since the showing of *Something Beautiful for God* they had kept in regular contact. Malcolm had actively campaigned for her to be given the Nobel Peace Prize (1979) and happily lent his name and support to her fund-raising. On her many visits to England they would meet. On one of these visits, soon after the Calcutta filming, they met in London and walked by the Serpentine. Mother Teresa, as usual, asked him why he didn't join the Church and Malcolm, as usual, parried with his criticism of its deficiencies: 'the crumbling barricades and woeful future prospects.' Afterwards, she sent him a little devotional book by a Jesuit, Father Paul de Jaegher, and wrote:

> I am leaving for Paris tomorrow and then for Venezuela on Sunday. I am sure you will pray for me. These days in England have been full with continual sacrifices, or rather the continuation of the Holy Mass. I think I understand you better now. I don't know why, but you to me are like Nicodemus, and I am sure the answer is the same – 'Unless you become like a little child'. I am sure you will understand beautifully everything if you would only 'become' a little child in God's hands. Your longing for God is so deep and yet he keeps himself away from you. He must be forcing himself to do so because he loves you so much – as to give Jesus to die for you and for

me. Christ is longing to be your Food. Surrounded with full-
ness of living food, you allow yourself to starve. The personal
love Christ has for you is infinite. Christ has created you
because he wanted you. I know what you feel – terrible longing
with dark emptiness. And yet he is the one in love with you.

The other important influence was that of Father Paul Bidone
(1914–86), an Italian priest who belonged to an order called the
Sons of Divine Providence founded by Don Orione to help the
handicapped. Father Bidone was ordained in 1937 and in 1949
was sent by Orione to Britain to establish the Order there. He
had only ten shillings and could speak no English, yet such was
his energy and dedication that within three years he had established a home for elderly men in Molesey to be followed by
many other centres for the handicapped.

Father Bidone first met Malcolm when celebrating Mass in
Hilaire Belloc's old home, Kings Land at Shipley near Horsham.
Later he enlisted Malcolm's help in fund-raising for his many
causes. He also took a group of theological students to Robertsbridge to be addressed by Malcolm and was very impressed by
his grasp of Christianity: 'He was better than anyone in the
Church.' In August 1979 Father Bidone was invited to say Mass
in the crypt of Salehurst Abbey, the remains of the Cistercian
foundation a mile or so from Park Cottage. Afterwards, he
noticed that Malcolm seemed especially happy and mentioned
to him that he ought to join the Church. Very typically, Malcolm
just said, 'You fix it'. Remembering an Italian proverb that
'Between the saying and the doing there is a sea', Father Bidone
decided to do nothing apart from pray. Then, exactly three years
later on 20 August 1982 he wrote:

My Dear Malcolm,
    On August 20th three years ago after I celebrated the First
Mass . . . in the Heath Abbey crypt, you seemed to be beaming
with joy more than usual – and in taking me to the station,
in answer to my invitation to join the flock you told me
'You arrange it for me.' Ever since I have asked Jesus in the
Blessed Sacrament to open the way and guide you and me.

The time seems ripe – and I must write to you. Somebody told me you are the apologist of the Church in this tormented period of history when another giant sits in the chair at St Peter's.

You are a pair! When recently you were telling our students the producing of Mother Teresa to the world, I could not silence in me an internal voice 'It is time, Malcolm is ready!' I will arrange it. I need only your hint. I will make it so easy for you that only the angels in heaven will notice it and glorify God the giver of eternal life. And Kitty will join in. Together we will sing Alleluia! Alleluia!

With much love, looking forward to your hint.

Affectionately,
Paul

If Father Bidone had been hoping that only the angels would notice Malcolm's conversion he was to be disillusioned. As a result of Malcolm's article appearing in *The Times* that morning, journalists and photographers descended on the Church of Our Lady of Help, Hurst Green, adjacent to the Longfords' house. The service, interrupted by the clicking of cameras, was conducted by the Bishop of Arundel, Rev. Cormac Murphy O'Connor assisted by Father Bidone, who had brought along some of his handicapped children from Teddington. They kept up a constant accompaniment of inarticulate noises. Members of the congregation, who included Alec Vidler and the Longfords, noticed that Kitty was obviously upset by the presence of the photographers and held up her order of service to stop them taking her picture. Afterwards there was a lunch at the Longfords' house.

Malcolm's only regret was that Mother Teresa would not be present at the Church. She wrote to them both:

Dear Malcolm and Kitty,

My heart is full of deep gratitude to God and his Blessed Mother for this tender love for you for giving you the joy of his coming in your hearts on 27th Nov. I wish I was with you that day but the good needs me at home in India therefore my prayer and sacrifice will be with you that you may grow in holiness and be more and more like Jesus. I also want to thank you for all you have done for Jesus through your writings. Still, I get letters and meet people who say that they have come closer to God through reading *Something Beautiful for God* . . . Keep the joy of loving Jesus in your heart and say often during the day and night 'Jesus in my heart I believe in your tender love for me. I love you.'

     God Bless you,
     Teresa

Malcolm and Kitty received about a thousand letters after their reception. In addition to Mother Teresa's, two gave particular pleasure, one from Graham Greene (whom Malcolm had told in advance of his decision) saying 'I hope that you make a better Catholic than I have done', and the other from Alec Guinness:

Dear Mr Muggeridge,
  The news in *The Times* this morning of your reconciliation with the Church made my day. Doubtless you will receive hundreds of letters of congratulations and perhaps a handful of spiteful ones from fanatics. This scribbled note is just to add to the number who rejoice – and there will be much rejoicing. I have often wondered if you would take the step and find it enormously encouraging that you have done so. May I wish you and your wife peace and happiness.

Nothing is more difficult than to describe precisely what religion means to someone. Malcolm's very public conversion – the article in *The Times* and the presence of photographers at the Mass, prompted charges that he was engaged in some kind of publicity stunt or simply trying to be controversial as with his attack on the Monarchy. Such charges of cynicism were quite unfair, yet it was true that his *Times* article contained little by way of personal apologia and much that was already familiar about the Church's stand on contraception and abortion, Malcolm's admiration of St Augustine, and the 'moral crisis' threatening Western societies.

It is unlikely that Malcolm subscribed to all the central teachings of the Catholic Church – purgatory, the intercession of

237

saints, the Devotion of Our Lady – but then the Church itself had become less demanding in this respect, no longer insisting that every convert should be 100% convinced about everything, so long as he or she accepted certain truths. The irony was that the liberalization which Malcolm had deplored in the modern Church was the very factor that enabled him to join without too many problems.

Nor did Malcolm have much time for confession. He had wanted originally to confess 'en bloc' and was rumoured to have answered Father Bidone, when he raised the issue of confession, 'Well, you've read my diaries' (forgetting perhaps how carefully he himself had censored them). He had no great love of the sacraments, the rosary or any of the comforts which meant so much to a Catholic like Graham Greene. Yet perhaps Greene's doubts and uncertainties, his hope that Malcolm would prove a better Catholic than he had been, were truer to the spirit of Christianity than Malcolm's sermonizing in *The Times*. 'Perhaps in paradise', Greene wrote ten days before his death, 'we are given the power to help the living. Sometimes I pray not for dead friends but *to* dead friends asking for their help. I picture paradise as a place of activity.' Such thoughts would have meant little or nothing to Malcolm.

Curiously, it was as his mind deteriorated towards the end that Malcolm showed signs that his faith did mean something more than a mere public stance. When his son John visited him in hospital just before he died, he observed how his father, by then completely senile, adamantly refused a pill that a succession of nurses tried to get him to swallow. Yet when shortly afterwards a priest appeared and offered him the consecrated host, he took it at once without a murmur.

to make your plans and collect your thoughts without the intrusion of press and media scavenger birds? It was just a thought.'

The interview was finally arranged in May 1983 when Solzhenitsyn came to London to receive the Templeton Prize. Jonathan Stedall was once again the producer. The presence of a stout lady interpreter sitting at Solzhenitsyn's side slowed things down considerably but at the same time lent the proceedings an old-fashioned and agreeably comic air. Solzhenitsyn, who seemed much mellower than he had done in the past, refused to share Malcolm's pessimistic forecasts regarding the inevitable catastrophe. He said he was convinced that there would not be a nuclear war and that what seemed like the triumph of communism was only a temporary eclipse. When, towards the end, Malcolm asked him if he expected ever to go back to Russia, he replied: 'In a strange way, I not only hope, I'm inwardly absolutely convinced that I shall go back. I live with this conviction: I shall go back. Now, that contradicts my rational assumption; I'm not so young, and I can't point to any actual facts which make me say this. History is so full of unexpected things that some of the simplest facts in our lives we cannot foretell . . .'

Two years later Mikhail Gorbachev became the head of the Communist Party and instituted the policy of Glasnost which precipitated the eventual collapse of communism. (Solzhenitsyn returned to Russia in 1994.) The tragedy was that by this stage Malcolm was in no state to fully comprehend what was going on in Russia. His Solzhenitsyn interview, as it turned out, was to be his final appearance on BBC television. Old age was starting to catch up with him. He had been forced to give up driving in December 1982 after a minor accident. By September 1984 when he was installed as President of the Johnson Society in Lichfield it was noticeable how his speech at the dinner lacked his usual wit and sparkle. He found it an effort to compose and during the course of delivery was obviously troubled by his failing eyesight. He still insisted to interviewers that he was working busily on the third volume of his memoirs, whereas the reality was that he had never made any progress on the book. Eventually he agreed to write a book on conversion for Collins and though this was in the end completed and published in 1988 it was done only with enormous effort and consisted, in the main, of extracts from his previous writings padded out with long quotations from favourite religious writers of the past. He had been commissioned by the *Dictionary of National Biography* to supply an entry for Claud Cockburn, but though he read through Claud's books, he found himself unable to fulfil the commission.

A few years earlier when he first became aware of the onset of old age he had written:

Being then, well past my allotted span of three score years and ten, as the old do, I often wake up in the night and feel myself in some curious way, half in and half out of my body, so that I seem to be hovering between the battered old carcass that I can see between the sheets and seeing in the darkness and in the distance a glow in the sky, the lights of Augustine's City of God. In that condition, when it seems just a toss-up whether I return into my body to live out another day, or make off, there are two particular conclusions, two extraordinarily sharp impressions that come to me. The first is of the incredible beauty of our earth – its colours and shapes, its smells and its features; of the enchantment of human love and companion-ship, and of the blessed fulfilment provided by human work and human procreation. And the second, a certainty surpassing all words and thoughts, that as an infinitesimal particle of God's creation, I am a participant in his purposes, which are loving and not malign, creative and not destructive, orderly and not chaotic, universal and not particular. And in that cer-tainty, a great peace and a great joy.

Alas, as he grew older serenity was replaced more and more by feelings of frustration. It is the common lot of the television personality that if he fails to appear on the screen for only a short time the public will soon forget about him. This was to be Malcolm's fate. Little by little, the tide of visitors to Roberts-bridge began to recede. Journalists no longer called him up seek-ing his opinion on every subject under the sun. After over thirty years in the limelight his vanity was such that he could not readily adjust to the new situation in which the world had begun to ignore him. Volume three of his memoirs became something of an obsession, as though he needed it to reassert himself in the public eye.

He was briefly consoled when in 1987 his banned *Guardian* novel *Picture Palace* was republished by Weidenfeld & Nicolson. To all intents and purposes it was a first edition – although Anthony Howard had printed long extracts in the *New Statesman* some years previously. Malcolm had agreed originally to write an introduction but, once again, found it an impossible task. The book was widely and favourably reviewed. Yet the irony was in the uncanny similarity of the portrait of C. P. Scott, the eighty-year-old editor of the *Guardian*, with Malcolm himself – both of them old men, seeking to reassure themselves of their indestructibility: 'The press cuttings were a solace to him. As the future dwindled they became more precious . . . Bending closely over his press cuttings he read them through yet once more, turning each word over and over in his mind to enjoy its full flavour . . . British journalism owes much to him. His name will live. His name would live! The old man rubbed his hands gently together. If his name lived then death lost much of its terror.'

The combination of vanity and the slow deterioration of his mind meant that Malcolm could not adjust to his new situation. He had often said that at a certain stage, when they became too old for Park Cottage, he and Kitty would move into their newly built annexe 'the Ark', a bungalow ideally suited to the needs of an elderly couple. But when the time came he seemed unwilling to make the move. In the same way he resisted all pressure to get a hearing aid and when his eyesight became seriously affected by cataracts he refused to have anything done about them. When an item on the subject appeared in the Peterborough column of the *Daily Telegraph* several people wrote to him urging him to have the simple operation, but Malcolm replied with a confused letter to the editor: 'My reply to these well-wishers is that I have seen enough of time and the Creatures (Blake) with my eye and prefer to see through my mind's eye Eternity and God's love.'

Such obstinacy put more of a strain on Kitty, who now had to read even the newspapers aloud to him. However, she did finally persuade him to have a hearing aid fitted. Luckily for him, though she was only a year younger, her mental faculties were in better shape. She did her best to keep Malcolm from sinking into apathy, but it became more and more of an uphill task. He had lost all interest in his collection of gramophone records which had once meant so much to him. His brother Jack bought him a cassette recorder and tapes of some of his favourite music, but neither Kitty nor Malcolm could operate the simple mechanism. Faithful friends like Andrew Boyle continued to call and they kept up their regular visits to the Longfords and Alec Vidler, now living in a home for the elderly on the outskirts of Rye. Yet their new-found faith seemed to offer little comfort. Although to begin with they had regularly attended Mass in the church at Hurst Green, they neither of them particularly enjoyed the services. (They had, in fact, previously received an assurance from Father Bidone that it would be permissible to go on reading the Book of Common Prayer first thing in the morning as was their custom.) Eventually Malcolm converted a garden shed into a tiny chapel where a visiting priest, Father Wilson, occasionally said Mass for them.

Malcolm's grasp of reality had begun to slip away. In May 1987 he appeared with his old *Telegraph* colleague Bill Deedes in an ITV film about the Romney Marsh churches. It was to be his last appearance on television, which was as well, considering that his proposed solution to the problem of how to save the remote churches from decay was to remove them, stone by stone, to a more populated part of the country. At about the same time he gave an interview to Stanley Reynolds of the *Guardian* in which he referred to the decline of *Private Eye* under its 'new Jewish editor Ian Hislop', adding insult to injury when he later wrote a letter of apology addressing it to Leon Hislop. He also wrote to Mrs Thatcher advising her to bring Mrs Whitehouse into the Cabinet to deal with the AIDS epidemic. More worrying for Kitty were the growing signs of paranoia. He complained that his children didn't want to know him and falsely accused Andrew Lambirth, a young researcher cataloguing his papers for the purchasers (Wheaton College, Illinois) of stealing a letter addressed to him by Gandhi. When his son John came over from Canada, he was so unpleasant to him that he had to move out and stay in a hotel.

To those who knew him well, these signs of senility, in someone who had always been so full of vitality and so generous and forgiving, were infinitely sad. It was also sad that the break-up of communism which began under Mikhail Gorbachev came too late for him to grasp what was happening. The news bulletins blared out, ever louder, over the breakfast table but Malcolm finally lost all grasp of what was going on in the outside world. But people, even in the media, were slow to acknowledge the fact – not surprising, perhaps, when photographs showed him apparently in robust good health, with rosy cheeks and twinkling eyes. When he was nearly eighty-five the television programme *This is Your Life* sent a representative to Robertsbridge to persuade Kitty to co-operate in a programme about Malcolm. Luckily his brother Jack happened to arrive when they were there and eventually persuaded them that it would be a pointless exercise.

Such misunderstandings were partly Kitty's fault. Believing that it was good for Malcolm to be stimulated, she never did anything to discourage interviewers by suggesting that her husband was no longer up to it. The result was that, even in the media, many people remained unaware of the sharp deterioration in Malcolm's condition. As late as May 1990, only a few weeks before his death, Conrad Black (by now the owner of the *Daily Telegraph*) was writing under the impression that he was planning a trip to the Middle East and suggesting that he might contribute something about it to the *Telegraph*.

In the same way, in 1987, a book, *My Life in Pictures*, was published by the Herbert Press. This photographic record of Malcolm's career did little to suggest any deterioration and contained several carefully posed pictures of such unlikely scenes as Malcolm playing chess with Kitty, mowing the lawn and even wheeling a trolley through the Robertsbridge supermarket. However, when Christina Foyle arranged one of her famous Literary Lunches to celebrate the book's publication, both Malcolm and Kitty forgot all about it. When the car called to take them to London and the Dorchester Hotel, there was no time for them to change and Malcolm delivered an incoherent speech to the Foyle's lunchers, still dressed in his scruffy gardening clothes.

As Kitty herself became more absent-minded and frail, the family grew justifiably anxious about what might happen if either of them became ill or suffered an accident in such a remote cottage. Leonard had recently become a widower and was finding it hard to leave his own children and with both Val and John living abroad, a heavy responsibility fell on Malcolm's brother Jack. He did his best by making regular visits, cutting the lawn and ensuring that they had enough firewood but felt, along with the children, that Kitty and Malcolm would be better off in a home. Kitty was in two minds – not wanting to leave Park Cottage but at the same time worried by the possibility of not being able to look after Malcolm as his behaviour became more and more unpredictable. In the summer of 1990, Val and her husband Gerrit Jan stayed some weeks at Park Cottage and persuaded them that as Kitty was due to go into hospital to have her cataracts operated on they should both move temporarily to Loose Farm Rest House near Battle – the hope being they would, in fact, stay there. After a week or so, Kitty seemed resigned to life in the home, but Malcolm became very restless and took to wandering about the house during the night and on one occasion set all the alarm bells ringing. Mrs Curtis, the proprietress of the home, was not even sure that she could go on looking after him.

Shortly after moving to Loose Farm, Malcolm had a minor stroke and was admitted to the intensive care unit at St Helen's Hospital in Hastings. A few weeks later both Kitty and Malcolm had falls and were taken to the Royal East Sussex Hospital where it was decided that they should both be given hip-replacements. Although Kitty recovered quickly and was soon up and about with the help of a stick, Malcolm's operation was delayed because of a chest infection. After his operation he was sent to a rehabilitation centre at Bexhill but proved incapable of co-ordinating his movements because of the deterioration of his brain.

Neither the Battle rest home nor the hospital could cope with him now, but Jack was able to get him into Ledsham Nursing

Home, Cambridge Road, Hastings which had all the necessary facilities. Both Kitty and Malcolm moved in on 15 October and thereafter Malcolm's condition deteriorated rapidly. He received the last rites and died on 14 November 1990. For someone who had spoken so often of his wish to die and even romanticized about the beauty of dying, his end, preceded by the slow breakdown of his mind, had been tragic and, for Kitty and his family, a painful ordeal.

The funeral, conducted by Bishop Cormac O'Connor took place at Salehurst Church on 19 November. Frank Longford gave the address and Malcolm was buried in Whatlington churchyard near to his father. A Requiem Mass was held in Westminster Cathedral on 26 February 1991, the Principal Celebrant being Cardinal Hume and the speaker, in the absence of Alan Taylor, Bill Deedes. At the end of a brief and moving address, Deedes referred to the slightly patronizing tone in which some colleagues and commentators had viewed Malcolm's conversion, gleefully, in some cases, retailing stories of his past misdemeanours: 'Reflecting on it, though, I have come to the conclusion that herein perhaps lies Malcolm's most valuable bequest to us. For, it seems to me, we are offered a welcome reminder that Christ came to call not the righteous but sinners to repentance. The life of our friend Malcolm was surely not all that far removed from something at the centre of our beliefs.'

Following Malcolm's death, Kitty went to stay with her son John and daughter-in-law Anne in Canada. She was very frail and was eventually admitted to a nursing home. She died in June 1994 at the age of ninety and her body was brought back to England to be buried alongside Malcolm in the churchyard at Whatlington.

EPILOGUE

MALCOLM'S DEATH WAS reported throughout the world and
there were lengthy obituaries in all the British and most of the
major American newspapers. They ranged from the affectionate
memoirs of his many journalistic friends to the pious platitudes
of the Catholic Press. The word 'irreverent' was in constant use.
The *New York Times* paid tribute to his 'impeccable prose style',
a writer in the *Guardian* called him 'the most gracefully tongued
and limelight-drenched cynic since Diogenes'.

Some years previously Malcolm had asked his old friend
A. J. P. Taylor to deliver his funeral address, but it was not to be,
as Taylor pre-deceased him. Proving, however, that Malcolm's
hunch had been right, Taylor had previously written (while
Malcolm was still alive) an obituary for the *Guardian* which somehow managed to catch the real Muggeridge better than any of
Malcolm's co-religionists.

Answering the charge that Malcolm had been, for much of
his life an embittered cynic, Taylor replied: 'Malcolm was a cynic
who got great fun out of it.' To Taylor, the title of Malcolm's
early novel *In a Valley of this Restless Mind* summed him up: 'I
have never known a man so restless', he wrote, 'physically and
in his thinking. He could not write a leader or a chapter in a
book without jumping up half a dozen times to pace around the
room or rush out for a walk along the bank of the Mersey . . .

'The greatest change in him was his discovery of God and
Jesus Christ. All religion is to me a buzzing in the ears, and I
cannot explain or even describe what happened to Malcolm. All
I know is that he was utterly sincere.'

The subject of obituaries had always been a favourite one with
Malcolm, who had spent so much of his life in and out of newspaper offices. 'Newspapers', he wrote in *The Thirties*, 'have their

obituaries ready filed. We regret or, in the case of important persons, deeply regret to announce the death of so and so, still breathing, ambitious, with money and passion left to expend. These obituaries require periodical revision, he who once deserved a column and a half later only deserving perhaps three-quarters of a column . . . in ten years reputations greatly fluctuate, and much obituary revision is necessary, apart from the inevitable weeding out – "died on such a date", scrawled across used obituaries, yet these also kept on a little while in the unlikely event of curiosity about the already dead and buried requiring to be satisfied.' He returned to the theme in his last novel *Affairs of the Heart*: 'Obituaries of the great, indeed, are usually highly composite, several hands participating in the work of preparing them; bits pasted on, cancelled out, pinned together. Like geological strata, they reflect the careers they chronicle – the adulatory age, the period of obscurity, the beginning when a career is young and in the spring, its heyday of all the talents, and its twilight or perhaps Indian summer, or perhaps almost total night.'

In Malcolm's own case any assessment of his reputation was complicated by the enormous fame he had gained late in life and then almost accidentally from appearing on television. For the public, the television personality exists only on television and only at the present time. His past, his future, his achievements outside the studio, are of little concern. Again, it is the nature of television to be ephemeral and very limited in its impact. A programme, even a good one, is largely forgotten by the following morning and once someone ceases to appear on the screen their memory quickly fades away, sometimes in only a matter of months.

Malcolm was no exception to these rules. The viewers, many of whom had little or no knowledge of him as anything other than a TV pundit, quickly forgot about him with the result that even by the time of his death his memory had already begun to fade. To a younger generation growing up in a world which had less and less interest in the past, his name meant nothing.

Obituarists, like biographers, feel a need to sum up, to find a theme running through all the tangled episode of a life, but in

Malcolm's case such a task was made difficult by his constant change of tack – from one job, one set of beliefs to another. In his latest manifestation, the one that was freshest in the public's mind, he had been an evangelist nicknamed affectionately St Mugg, a Christian apologist marching side by side with Mrs Whitehouse on anti-abortion demonstrations, denouncing the sex obsessions of the media and very publicly joining the Catholic Church, partly from a wish to ally himself with Pope John Paul II. Was this the real Malcolm Muggeridge, or was it the anarchic figure of the Fifties and Sixties – the Muggeridge of *Punch* and *Tread Softly*? Or, going back still further, the youthful Fabian idealist or the man who went to Moscow in search of a heaven on earth?

Malcolm would have replied that it was all of a piece and that his religion had been a constant preoccupation throughout his life. This was true – even if Malcolm was unwilling to recognize the way in which he had deliberately turned his back on it so long as it had suited him to do so and until, in early old age, the strain and unhappiness of a life of hedonism became too great to bear.

If it was true that he had always been in some sense religious, it was equally true that he had always – or at any rate since he heard the call from Arthur Ransome in Cairo – been a journalist. He had had his dreams from boyhood of writing novels, plays and poems, but in the end he had found his vocation in the offices of the *Guardian* in Manchester and though he may have changed papers, or oscillated between contract and freelance status, he remained for nearly all his life a man with a typewriter pounding out words to meet a deadline in what seemed at times a ceaseless flow. Journalism is a dirty word to some and the journalist is considered an inferior species compared, say, to the writer of novels or history. Yet there is a respected tradition of writers, much of whose work has been done for newspapers and magazines – Hazlitt, Cobbett, Chesterton, Orwell – and it is in this company that Malcolm belongs (though it is too early to say if his writing will survive as theirs has done).

But it would be wrong to regard Malcolm merely as a gifted journalist. In his life, his restlessness, his inconsistency, his

249

obsessions (whether with Marxism or sex) he seems at times like a symbol of twentieth-century man. It is no accident that in his capacity as journalist he should have reported so much of this century, from his early encounter with Gandhi, from the famine in the Ukraine, along the way bumping into – never seeking them out – nearly all the great figures of his time, until in the end he becomes (again by accident) the man who introduces to the world via his despised medium of television an obscure Albanian nun working in the slums of Calcutta.

My personal and strongest impression, whether reading him or listening to him face to face, was of a man who told the truth – not as a result of any special scruples or sense of religious obligation, but because he was blessed with natural powers of insight and occasionally of prophecy which enabled him intuitively to see events and people for what they were. Being himself without worldly ambitions, he exercised this gift indiscriminately, thus getting himself over and over again into hot water, especially when he went in pursuit of sacred cows. 'Nothing enrages people more', he once said, 'than to think they have engaged in unprofitable adulation.'

In the end, for me and for all those who were lucky enough to know him, the memory will remain of his endlessly stimulating friendship, the laughter, the gossip and his unfailing kindness and generosity. It is to try to repay what I owe to him that I have written this book. RIP.

BIBLIOGRAPHY

BOOKS BY MALCOLM MUGGERIDGE

Three Flats, (Play) Putnam, 1931
Autumnal Face, Putnam, 1931
Winter In Moscow, Eyre & Spottiswoode, 1934
Picture Palace, Eyre & Spottiswoode, 1934 (withdrawn, re-published
    Weidenfeld and Nicolson, 1987)
In a Valley of this Restless Mind, Routledge, 1938, re-published
    Collins, 1978
The Thirties, Hamish Hamilton, 1940. Reissued Collins, 1967
Affairs of the Heart, Hamish Hamilton, 1949
Tread Softly for you Tread on my Jokes, Collins, 1966
Muggeridge Through the Microphone, BBC, 1969. Re-published with
    additions as *Muggeridge Ancient and Modern*, 1981
Jesus Rediscovered, Fontana, 1969
Something Beautiful for God, Collins, 1971
Chronicles of Wasted Time, Vol I *The Green Stick*, Collins, 1972. Vol
    II *The Infernal Grove*, Collins, 1973
Jesus the Man who Lives, Collins, 1975
A Third Testament, Little Brown, 1976
Christ and the Media, Hodder & Stoughton, 1976
Things Past, Collins, 1978
Like It Was (Diaries), Collins, 1981
Some Answers, Methuen, 1982
Conversion, Collins, 1988
My Life in Pictures, The Herbert Press, 1987

WITH HUGH KINGSMILL

Brave Old World, Eyre and Spottiswoode, 1936
Next Year's News, Eyre and Spottiswoode, 1938

WITH HESKETH PEARSON

About Kingsmill, Methuen, 1951

WITH PAUL HOGARTH

London à la Mode, Studio Vista, 1966

WITH ALEC VIDLER

Paul: Envoy Extraordinary, Collins, 1972

BOOKS CONSULTED

Guardian: Biography of a Newspaper by David Ayerst, Collins, 1971
Behind the Screen by Michael Barsley, Deutsch, 1957
A Game of Moles: The Deceptions of an MI6 Officer by Desmond Bristow, Little Brown, 1993
Destined to be Wives (The Sisters of Beatrice Webb) by Barbara Caine, OUP, 1986
Russia's Iron Age by W. H. Chamberlin, Duckworth, 1935
I, Claud by Claud Cockburn, Penguin, 1967
The House the Berrys Built by Duff Hart Davis, Hodder & Stoughton, 1990
The Knox Brothers by Penelope Fitzgerald, Macmillan, 1977
William Camrose, Giant of Fleet Street by Lord Hartwell, Weidenfeld, 1992
British Intelligence in the Second World War by F. H. Hinsley, HMSO, 1993
Political Pilgrims by Paul Hollander, OUP, 1981
Hugh Kingsmill by Michael Holroyd, Unicorn Press, 1964
Malcolm Muggeridge, A Life by Ian Hunter, Thomas Nelson, 1980
Assignment in Utopia by Eugene Lyons, Harcourt Brace, 1937
Father Figures by Kingsley Martin, Hutchinson, 1966
To Keep the Ball Rolling (Abridged one-volume edition) by Anthony Powell, Penguin, 1983
A History of Punch by R. G. G. Price, Collins, 1957
A Personal History by A. J. P. Taylor, Hamish Hamilton, 1983
Stalin's Apologist by S. J. Taylor, OUP, 1990
Scenes from a Clerical Life by Alec Vidler, Collins, 1977
The Diary of Beatrice Webb edited by Norman and Jeanne Mackenzie, London and Cambridge Mass. 4 Volumes, 1982–5

INDEX

Nietzsche, Frederick 120
Night and Day magazine 107
Niven, David 226
Norman, Montague 46
Not So Much A Programme (TV) 203
Nova Scotia sinking (1942) 128

O'Brien, E. D. 'Tubby' 151–2
Observer 210, 225
O'Connor, Bishop Cormac 236, 246
Oratory House, Cambridge 15–16
Orwell, George xii, 117, 149, 180,
    203, 234, 249
Oumansky, Constantine 69

Pakenham, Frank and Elizabeth *see*
    Longford
Pakenham, Rachel 205
Panorama (TV) 173–8, 182, 183
Paris: MM's wartime posting 136–8
Passfield, Lord *see* Webb
Paul VI, Pope 226
Pauli, Charles 112
Peacock, Michael 143, 176
Pearson, Gladys 141
Pearson, Henry 141
Pearson, Hesketh
    friendship with MM and Kingsmill
        101, 106–7, 111–12, 121, 134,
        153–4, 220
    literary work 106, 150, 153, 154
    affair with Kitty 141–3
The People 183, 186
Philby, Sir John 123
Philby, Kim 123
Phillips, C. W. 11
Picture Palace (MM) 43, 58–61, 81–3,
    133, 242
Picture Post 154
Pitman, Dora 10, 11, 18, 38
Pitman, Effie 38
Porcupine magazine 107
Potter, Beatrice *see* Webb
Potter, Kate *see* Courtney, Lady
Potter, Mary 29
Potter, Richard and Laurencina 28–9
Potter, Rosie *see* Dobbs
Powell, Anthony
    literary work and friendship with

    MM 103, 148–9, 152, 164, 169,
        230
    Pamela Berry affair 172
    rift with MM 197–9, 221
    on MM 77–8, 216
Powell, Enoch 120
Powell, Violet 148, 196
Pratt, Lady 170
Price, R. G. G. 163
Priestley, J. B. 169
Private Eye xi, 181, 190, 208, 243
Pryce-Jones, Alan 230
Punch xi, 150, 161–9, 178–81, 189

The Quare Fellow (Behan) 176–7
The Question Why (TV) 200, 210–11

Ransome, Arthur 41–2, 45, 50,
    81–2, 249
Ransome, Genia 41, 45
Ratcliffe, George 8
Reynolds, Stanley 243
Richard, Cliff 217
Richardson, Maurice 210
Robertsbridge 104, 194–6, 223, 232,
    235, 242–3
Robertson, Fyfe 204
Robertson, Max 175, 182
Robinson, Bishop John 214
Roche (*later* Muggeridge), Anne 195
Roosevelt, Eleanor 176
Roosevelt, President F. D. 56, 69,
    144
Roquebrune 158
Rosen, Dr (American emigré) 63
Ross, J. Maclaren 169
Ross-Atkinson, Colonel 120
Rothenstein, John (Tusky) 32
Rothenstein, William 32
Rothermere, Lord and Lady Anne
    161
Rothschild, Lord Victor and Lady
    Tessa 122, 136
Russell, Lord Bertrand 56, 174, 200
Russia's Iron Age (Chamberlin) 56

Sankey, Lord 46
Saturday Evening Post 181–3, 197
Sayers, Dorothy 170